Daniel Jeffreys grew up in Bristol but has spent the last ten years travelling in America as a New York Correspondent for BBC Television and now as a regular contributor to *The Daily Mail*, *The Times* and U.S. *Marie Claire*. The father of triplets, he lives in New York City with his wife Debbie and is co-producing three feature films based on his stories. He is also working on his next book *New York Dreams*.

America's Back Porch

DANIEL JEFFREYS

QUARTET BOOKS

First published by Quartet Books in 1998
A member of the Namara Group
27 Goodge Street
London W1P 2LD

Reprinted in 1999

This edition published by Quartet Books Limited in 1999

A catalogue record for this book is available from the British Library.

ISBN 0 7043 8122 2

Phototypeset by F.S.H, London
Printed and bound in Great Britain by Cox & Wyman

Acknowledgements

I owe a debt of gratitude to almost everybody I have met in America. Special thanks are due to my agents, Mike Lubin and Matthew Bialer at William Morris for their wisdom; my friends Damian Fowler and Addison Armstrong for their support; Veronica Wadley and Lorraine Butler for making sure my writing rose to their standards, which are so much higher than my own; Graham Jones, who sent me on my first trip to New York, and Lori Dusena, who Charlie Horse says is doing well in heaven. Above all I thank Stella Kane, my publisher, for her patience, and Helen Birch, who asked me to write my first feature story and encouraged me to step deeper into the great American night. They gave me a chance and that's an invaluable gift.

To Debbie, Matthew, Max and Isabella.
Sun, Moon, Stars and Air

Contents

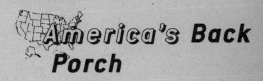

America's Back
Porch

Introduction

'The only people for me are the mad ones, the ones who are mad to live, mad to talk, desirous of everything at the same time.'

Jack Kerouac, *On the Road*

In the middle of Kansas there's a highway that runs straight across the flat plains for over four hundred miles. It is possible to travel this stretch of blacktop for a whole day and never see another car. The only evidence that people live here is the road itself, a few rotting tractors and an occasional column of smoke from a farmhouse far away. McDonald's might never have been invented. It's a road where a man was once murdered in his own car and his body lay undiscovered for eight days.

The existentialists wrote about man's loneliness but they never visited Kansas Route 17. Jean-Paul Sartre could play games with being and nothingness but he always had good food or coffee on hand. Travelling the road to Shut Creek, Kansas, he could have experienced the kind of isolation which shrivels a man's soul and makes him long for a tacky fried-chicken joint packed with folks wearing polyester.

When pioneer cowboys sat beside a camp fire and ate beans they were closer to the mysteries of Sisyphus than Sartre could have ever imagined. Each morning they woke to the big sky of the Americas, a canvas so large that it creates an impossible sense of vertigo. They kept their heads down and saddled up, hiding from the sky behind dust created by the cattle trails.

At night the American prairie sky fills with a trillion stars, the punctuation marks of faraway civilizations, all of which may be more advanced than ours. Or worse, they may be stars long dead, a reminder that we are all alone. This is why America invented shopping malls. Earth-bound strips of light which are places to hide when the sky gets too big.

The American Indians could cope with the space above the plains. It was part of their religion, a tribute to elders who departed for the happy hunting grounds. The big sky made them feel good because it gave their souls room to expand. For these complex people the enemy came from the ground, rapacious settlers intent on domination.

A withered old man outside a trailer on a Crow Indian reservation once told me a story. 'A long time ago,' he began, as hungry dogs chewed scraps at our feet, 'the tribes of America met on a plain beside a stream. They were battle-weary. Sixty years of fighting had reduced their numbers and they faced overwhelming odds. The pale-faced enemy was numerous and well armed, with little regard for the Indian way of life.

'The wind howled that night, whipping their fires into bright red embers. The elders would look at the points of light, seeing in each one the soul of a warrior slain in battle. The Sioux were present, also the Cree and the Cherokee. The Pequot and Mohegan tribes had travelled from the north with stories of new weapons in the hands of the enemy, sticks that belched flame and death from many paces away.

'As dawn broke, the chief of each tribe made his way to a

sacred circle laid out in the sand, defined by skulls of wise men after a thousand years spent in harmony with this great land. A six-foot-tall warrior with clear eyes and a muscled back stood in the centre. "Let all the gods be witness," he called, and the tribal chiefs fell silent. The warrior took a sharp knife from his pocket and laid it against his throat. "With my blood and my spirit I lay a curse in the soil. As the white man eats so let the white man go mad. Let his mind be besieged with panic and confusion."

'With that the warrior passed the blade across his jugular and began to rotate in an ancient dance of death. The blood from his wound spun to all parts of the sacred circle, leaving the entire area stained red. The warrior remained standing until the last drop of blood had drained from his body. Only then did he fall to the ground. Seconds later all that remained was his crumpled clothes.'

The old Indian paused to cough loudly. His body shook and rattled a string of steel wheel-rims hanging off the back of his chair. The dogs began to howl as a ball of phlegm rose in his throat. He sent the green spittle flying at the nearest mongrel, then continued. 'That night by the light of a desert-dry electric storm, the chiefs gathered the bloodstained sand and measured it carefully into leather sacks. Each tribe was allocated a portion of the cursed grains, depending on their numbers at the time of the sacrifice. They each took their sacks back to their homelands, and on nights when there was no moon they sprinkled it wherever there was fertile soil.

'Since that day, food grown on soil that once belonged to the Indians has slowly been driving Americans mad. It's an unusual kind of madness. The victims do not go completely insane. There wasn't enough sand to do that. Sufferers just develop a skewed way of looking at the universe and the folk around them. They still have contact with reality but each time they try to get a real grip it dances just out of sight. When they eat, another tiny part of the curse enters their soul. The areas of the country where there were most Indians – Texas, Montana, Alabama, Arizona, Utah – got the most sand.'

I thought about what the Indian had told me, driving towards sunset on Rural Route 3, a dog-leg off Route 17. Maybe it's a coincidence, but the areas where the Indians left their cursed sand are also where we find the most bizarre Americans, the inhabitants of America's Back Porch – which is a place but also a state of mind.

The site of the original sand ceremony is now occupied by a Big Hat Gunstore and a delicatessen. It sells po-boys. Sausage, double-sausage, meatball, double meatball, double meatball with cheese. A po-boy is a kind of sandwich. In some parts of the US it's known as a submarine, whilst in other areas they call it a hoagie, but in Fort Worth, Texas, it's a po-boy. Darryl and Vicky love po-boy sandwiches. It's their favourite kind of food.

1. 'Dead Serious'

'This is not for the faint-hearted,' said Darryl Frank. 'This is not for those who still have faith in the criminal justice system.' Darryl was relaxing with his wife Vicky at their modest home in a lower-middle-class section of Fort Worth, Texas. Darryl is the founding father of Dead Serious Inc., America's answer to small-time crime. As the twentieth century comes to a close, suburban Americans no longer trust their government, their police force, their President and they damn well don't trust their neighbours. They do trust guns and vigilante groups made up of friends with similar delusions. Like Vicky and Darryl.

The couple are dressed in black jeans and black T-shirts. They look like heavy-metal fans and on first sight you notice Darryl has a weak chin and Vicky has been eating too many fries.

'The idea is very simple,' said Darryl. He had grabbed my arm buddy-style for the fifth time in five minutes. 'If you are a member, Dead Serious will pay five thousand dollars if you kill someone in accordance with the law. That is whilst they are in the process of committing a crime against you, your family or your property.' The money will not be forthcoming if the criminal survives.

'If you just wound somebody that same criminal could sue you,' said Vicky. 'He could come back and kill you or commit other crimes which would cost the taxpayer money.'

Vicky is fully prepared to avoid mistakes. She was carrying a 9mm pistol in her handbag. It was fully loaded with Federal Hi-Shot ammunition, bullets that can punch a grapefruit-sized hole in a man's chest. 'If some son of a bitch is trying to rape me I'm not gonna lie back and be the little lady. I'm gonna blow his goddamn head off, with interest.'

She produced the weapon for my inspection. It was beautifully engineered by Colt, America's oldest gunmaker. The design and construction are like the American automobiles of the 1950s, with just a little more chrome than is absolutely necessary for something made to maim or kill. Darryl gave it to Vicky for their third wedding anniversary. It sat in her slightly pudgy palm with an air of ease, like she was born to pack heat. The black detailing along the barrel went well with her bright red nail polish. In Vicky's handbag, bullets and nail-polish remover sat side by side. When she's dressed to kill, she's dressed to kill.

Darryl said he was thirty-five years old; Vicky thirty-three. They'd been married for four years. They had no children yet, just a couple of cats. Their small apartment was neat and tidy. Darryl and Vicky might get called rednecks but they are far from white trash. Darryl works as a technician for a company that builds minivans for the handicapped. Vicky is an accountant at the local country club. In 1998 they will take home about $30,000, before tax – the kind of money a Wall Street big shot would regard as insulting if it were offered as one month's bonus.

The friends who gathered at the Dead Serious Friday committee meeting were similar: Brad's a car mechanic, Paul works at the local supermarket. Like Darryl and Vicky, they're losing the battle to be middle class.

The Franks live in an apartment complex called The Bennington. It sounded posh but it was not, although all the units looked well maintained. There was a strange smell hanging over the place. It might be the local stockyards where they slaughter pigs; it might be fear. The landlord built a fence around the two-acre complex after a spate of burglaries, making The Bennington resemble a low-security prison. Some residents said they felt besieged by crime. That's one reason Darryl and Vicky turned their spare bedroom into the head-quarters of Dead Serious, where computers and fax machines take up space alongside cute photographs of cats and friends.

Next door their bedroom houses a huge oak bed, a four poster with a 27″ television slung from the cross-beam. Darryl and Vicky kick back there, lying on their overstuffed cushions, watching the local news with its parade of bloody crime. 'We were just an ordinary couple,' said Vicky, adjusting a pink and blue pillow in the shape of a puppy dog, 'until we got pissed off.'

Dead Serious had almost five thousand members in February 1998 and there were chapters in eight different states. It opened for business in 1994. Membership costs $10 a year and members are registered for a $5000 payout should their big day arrive. To make sure they shoot straight, Dead Serious people are given free hand-gun training. 'A gun is an essential part of being American. Gun ownership is our most fundamental right. It's the basis of the constitution.' That is actually bullshit. Contrary to Charlton Heston and his National Rifle Association, it is one of the great myths of the US constitution that it guarantees the individual right to bear arms. It simply does not. When I mention this to the Franks, they look at me as if I had spoken in tongues whilst spewing green vomit. Darryl shrugged me off and pulled back a slug of beer from a long-necked Budweiser. 'Y'know, I reckon history would have been different if the Indian had had guns – just imagine, if the Cherokee could've defended themselves with a few Magnum .357s'. The idea sent Darryl into peals of laughter and he spilled a puddle of beer on the floor. 'Whoops, hey, Wayne,' he said, calling the cat. 'Come get it, buddy.' The cat came by and took a lick, then looked up at Darryl with disdain. It seemed that, like any sophisticated creature, the cat did not like America's favourite beer.

Vicky came by to show me the two Dead Serious stickers they send to new members, one for their car and one for the home. 'These stickers send a clear message to the criminal,' said Vicky, picking up the cat and dabbing Bud between its ears. 'Mess with my car or my house and I'm going to pop you.' She held out one hand and made the shape of a gun with her fingers. 'Boom,' she said and laughed until the button on her trousers burst.

In the next room, a friend turned up the volume on the stereo. It was a country and western song with a pleasant tune but unusual lyrics: 'I'm warning you, Jack, I'm gonna shoot back/You better just let me be.'

Vicky giggled. 'This is our theme song. Listen.' The song swelled into a chorus. 'I'm serious, dead serious/You'll be laid out at my feet/I'm serious, dead serious/And you're gonna be dead meat.' The song was nicely sung with a professional mix and made Darryl swell with pride. 'A member sent us that, wrote it himself. He said he wanted to give something more than his ten dollar fee.'

Dead Serious reaped a fat harvest of publicity after Darryl went on national radio for the first time. American tabloid TV loves Darryl and his chums. The brand leader, *A Current Affair*, on Fox TV gave them a whole seven minutes. Vicky and Darryl often lie in bed at night watching the segment over and over again. In the twenty-four hours after the show aired they had over 700 requests for membership details. We all stopped preparing barbecue meats and went to the Franks' bedroom so we too could watch the video of Darryl's appearances on the big screen teeee-veeee, as they pronounce it in this part of

Texas. Crowded on to the big four-poster bed, the members of Dead Serious became just that as the screen flickered to life. And when Darryl appeared, slouching his way through a neighbourhood park accompanied by a 'blonde' woman wearing too much hairspray, his 'buds' set off a round of high fives that sent the cats running for cover. 'Way toooo00 go Darr-yll,' they shout, as if hoping that the blonde interviewer might become a target for some good old Dead Serious marksmanship. The irony is that Darryl Frank couldn't fire a weapon at anybody unless he were willing to break the law.

Mr Frank is in an odd position. He's a convicted felon and that disqualifies him from membership of Dead Serious. He can't join his own vigilante group and he certainly cannot own or carry a firearm. In 1977 the Texan crime fighter spent nine months in prison on a burglary charge. 'It's quite possible if something like this had been in effect fifteen years ago he would be dead right now,' said Vicky, her Texan accent thicker than the late summer air. 'He was in his teens when this happened, but if he were to break into a member's house today he could easily get killed.' Dead. At fourteen, for trying to steal a VCR.

'Don't let these kids fool you,' said Darryl, seeing me recoil in horror. 'They will cut you up just for kicks.'

The phone rang as Vicky stuffed more envelopes with membership forms. It had been ringing once every few seconds for the last two hours. Darryl leapt for the receiver and put it on speakerphone. It was a police officer from Arizona. Darryl explained that police officers were not allowed to join, something about a conflict of interest. 'I know that,' said Sergeant Adine. 'I want to join up all the members of my family, is that OK?' Darryl gave his assent. 'I just admire what your group is doing,' said the sergeant with a hard country accent that mangled all the vowels. 'Our hands are tied. I love the way you say the criminal must be killed. We are told to only aim for the legs and arms. That's crap. At mid-range, you should aim for the chest. Close-up, go for the head.'

Darryl was ecstatic. 'Yeah, man, we're tired of being afraid, we're going to take back the streets.' He embarked on a long debate about which firearms can do the most damage at short and medium range. The products of Mr Colt were mentioned often, with an air of reverence. Heaven for Mr Frank would be the Colt factory with him inside, a bottle of Bud in one hand, a can of gun oil in the other. He'd be so happy he would probably drink both.

Putting the phone down, Darryl turned to Vicky. 'The gun I bought you, the sergeant says it is *the best*.'

Vicky gave her man a look of adoration, normally reserved for guys who bought the ring from Tiffany's. 'Oh, Darryl,' she said. 'You're so sweet, honey. I know you always do right by me.'

The official reaction to Dead Serious has been more critical. Although Darryl claims that police officers on the street back his cause, that he's visited every local police station and found support in them all, prosecutors are less enthusiastic. 'If I had to shoot somebody in self-defence and it turned out to be a close call, I'd probably be glad I had not joined Dead Serious,' said John Holmes, a Texas District Attorney. 'Grand juries might cite the added incentive of a financial reward as a reason to indict someone for murder.'

The Fort Worth police department said Mr Frank may soon become irrelevant. 'Crime figures are way down,' says Deputy Police Chief Sam Hill. 'Crime fell by 23% in 1996 and by 24% in 1997. So far in 1998 the figures are down by another 11%.'

Patrol officer Sergeant McGuirk gave those numbers a different spin. As we rode in his squad car he laid out the familiar geography of America's big cities. 'The west of the city is white and affluent. The north is black and poor. The east is Hispanic and poor. The south is mixed race and struggling. Crime figures are not falling in the north, south or east of Fort Worth.' The police radio crackled to life: 'Alliance base, Hap Worsham has signed on.' McGuirk smiles. 'Worsham is a Citizen on Patrol (COP). It's a new programme, they've become our eyes and ears.' COPs travel in their own cars marked with police insignia. They patrol neighbourhoods at night. They're volunteers and mostly pensioners. 'They want to give something back,' said McGuirk. 'Plus, they love the police radios and the official badges.'

They certainly do, along with polyester pants and monogrammed pullovers. We met up with some COPs in the parking lot of a shopping mall. They were driving the kind of big Chevrolet that nobody wants to buy any more. Sal Patterson used to be a mechanic and his wife Judy was an insurance agent. 'Gotta do something. To control crime. It's only right. Can't stand by.' Sal's clipped sentences seemed unusual, as though he was playing a game where you could only use so many words each day. Then Judy spoke and she was conserving words too. 'Crime is bad. Real bad. Can't give up. We built the neighbourhood. Shame to let go.' They both have a strong Texan accent but it's not the same one as the Franks use. The Pattersons speak the abbreviated patois of a petrified America that's growing in size. White retirees with too little cash for really good health insurance and no hope of buying that retirement home in Florida. Instead, they were out playing cops and robbers in an area where Sal once played little league baseball on fields long gone – replaced by public housing projects with basketball courts.

'Too bad what's happened to America. Gone bad. Too many immigrants. Don't mind them. Just too many.' Judy nodded in agreement. 'Got to go,' said Sal. 'Patrol up west. Had some joyriders.' The Pattersons pulled away. They probably know their lifestyle has as much mileage left as their mammoth automobile, but they won't give in. Couldn't do that. Wouldn't be prudent.

The COPs programme had some success in reducing crime in the west of the city but again the figures need interpretation. 'Most crime is an act of opportunity,' said McGuirk. 'If there are lots of eyes watching the criminals won't strike. They will move somewhere else.' From the affluent to the less so, from the west to the south. Where Darryl Frank lives with his pals.

'Most of the victims of crime are poor people,' said Scott Blue, the firearms instructor for Dead Serious. 'I want my family armed and I want them to shoot straight and I want the criminal to know that. Hopefully our members will display their bumper stickers and criminals will figure we're gun-happy lunatics and go somewhere else.'

District attorneys may be wary of Dead Serious but Texas politicians can smell a good populist movement and they are edging closer. Dead Serious urges all its members to get on the electoral roll. These crime fighters have guns and votes. The impact has been immediate. Texas passed a law in May 1997 that allows anybody with a gun permit to carry a concealed weapon. That's how Vicky got to carry a gun in her purse, a fully loaded firearm that would look fine in the hands of James Bond.

Until January 1995 state law said a citizen must first try to retreat from a criminal before using deadly force. In 1998 the Texas legislature removed that un-American condition as a New Year present to every gun-toting Texan. Now they can fire first and ask questions later.

'In effect, Texas has its own vigilantes' charter,' said Carl Senna, a law professor at the University of Massachusetts. 'Legislation like this encourages people to take violent action when they could be in error.' For example, the Japanese exchange student who was killed in Louisiana in 1993. He got lost at night and knocked on a stranger's door for directions. When nobody answered he began to leave. The homeowner appeared and shouted, 'Freeze.' The student was unfamiliar with the English idiom; minutes later he was dead. The killer was not charged. He was, in the words of the judge, defending his home and family in an urban battlefield. The student was an 'unfortunate casualty'. Louisiana was the second state in the US to open a local branch of Dead Serious.

'Nothing's perfect,' said Darryl Frank. 'Far more innocent people die because they don't open fire.'

'There is enormous frustration,' said Professor Senna. 'Big cities like New York have seen an unprecedented drop in crime but the medium-sized towns have seen the reverse and they never have enough police around to enforce laws. Saturation policing never lasts because the money runs out. When people are arrested they spend hardly any time in jail. In 1995, over 80% of all criminal cases did not go to trial because defendants plea-bargained. Less than one-third of convicted criminals were actually incarcerated.' For all that, more than 60% of gun deaths in the home involve one family member shooting another – in a domestic argument, whilst cleaning a weapon, when somebody comes home late without their key and climbs through a window. Pow. End of story. All that's left is a corpse with a damaged face that no longer matches the graduation photo or the pictures in the wedding album.

'The system is broken,' said Darryl, leaning against his pick-up truck. His male buddies, all dressed in black XL T-shirts, nodded happily. 'It's broke,' said Brad. 'Can't fix it wid money,' said Paul. 'Look at the O.J. Simpson trial, it's made a mockery of American justice. If O.J.'s lawyers believe he's innocent they're either crooked or stupid. If only Nicole Brown-Simpson had been with us, California could have saved all these wasted O.J. dollars.' He's not joking and he has an example as proof.

'We have a new member in Iowa. She was being pestered by her husband, they were separated but he liked to beat her up on Friday nights. She called the police lots of times, they did nothing. So she hears about us. In Iowa they have the same deadly force law as Texas. You can use a weapon to defend yourself, your family or your property. After she joins we sent a copy of her Dead Serious membership form to the husband, along with a copy of the Iowa penal code. He doesn't come by any more. It's a legal way of saying, "Come near me again and I'll blow your head off." If only Nicole Brown could have got the same protection.'

Across America there are thousands of Darryl Franks leaning on their pick-up trucks, drinking cheap beer and talking tough about crime. Darryl says he will soon have millions of members, with some in every state of the union. He's already close to the second ambition. The Dead Serious theme song is back on the stereo, its tune carried far on the hot Texan air. 'So if you fool with me, or my family/You'll be the victim instead/This ain't no bluff, ain't just talkin' tough/You'll be laying there dead.' The phone rang again. 'You know, this is just like the Alamo,' said Darryl. 'We are defending a way of life against invaders. When we start killing some suckers our membership list will go ballistic. Everybody who cares anything for their family is gonna want one of our stickers.'

He's not wrong. The gunslinger state is more likely to be copied within America than reviled. It's an easy solution; pack some heat, kill some sucker, warning sent. Plus, Darryl has academia on his side. A June 1996 study from the University of Chicago looked at all five states where it is legal for people with gun permits to carry a concealed weapon. Each state has seen a sharp decline in all categories of crime since people started strapping semi-automatics under their sports coats. Maybe the federal government should disband the police force and issue a firearm to every citizen. Imagine, a gun in every American waistband and plenty of ammunition on sale at Wal-Mart. That plus free po-boys and Darryl might finally be happy.

2. Conspiracies in the Air

American airports are the country's cultural mixing pot. The whole nation passes through them, ever since Ronald Reagan introduced new laws cutting air fares and drove half the industry to the verge of bankruptcy. There is nothing grand about this kind of air travel nor should there be. Cheap travel is an American birthright, a pillar of democracy. In past generations it was the Greyhound bus, now it's ValuJet or AirTrain. Travel on an American domestic flight and you could sit next to a politician, a chief executive, a model or a fugitive from justice.

Leaving Dallas from Fort Worth Airport, I made the journey to Birmingham, Alabama. It was a typical flight. Every seat was full and the air stewards were way beyond being just miserable. It was easy to understand why these poor men and women appeared suicidal. Bulky garment bags, far larger than the overhead lockers where they had been jammed, fell on them at regular intervals. There would follow a fight with some irascible businessman who had been trying to keep his polyester suit jacket neat, as if it were this season's Armani. A decade ago, these portly masters of commerce would have been in first class, with few worries about how to stow luggage. Champagne at their elbow, they would have been served by pretty young stewardesses who would not object to a pat on the butt because the covert commies in Congress had not yet passed damn fool laws against sexual harassment. Nobody would have expected them to lug out a laptop and spend the whole flight working. How things change. These days, in every American boardroom, executives begin their day with a period of meditation. After a few seconds their muttered incantations become louder. 'Downsizing', they chant, with a gleam of fanaticism in their hooded eyes, 'downsizing'.

Once a US executive proved his manhood by the size of his expense account. Now the test is how many people you can fire. Women do the same thing with even more zeal, proving their gender invented machismo and just lent it to men on a temporary basis.

In an airplane, you can tell each businessman truly resents this new era and blames anybody they can think of – the Japanese, Germans, Bill Gates, women, gays. They talk bravely about the pleasures of cheap hotels and cut-price meals, as though the cash they save went into their pockets and not to some retired shareholder playing the slot machines in Reno. Yet beneath this shrink-wrap of optimism festers an anger, one that inspires these corporate pawns with dreams of conspiracies: somebody must be masterminding the way the American dream is becoming one long sleepless night. That person or group is acting in concert with other powerful forces, maybe Jewish or black, and he's subverted the federal government which has become the enemy of all Americans who fear personal bankruptcy, and, believe me, that's most of them.

Flight 4566 was ten minutes shy of departure when Andrew Pennington took his seat beside me. He looked fifty-six and beat. The dust of a hundred thousand sales meetings littered the crevices on his cheek. The lines beneath his eyes were more numerous than his monthly count of frequent flier miles. On his left hand was a wedding ring that may have been loose 50lbs and one thousand hamburgers ago. His right pinky finger had a class graduation ring with a fat ruby that stood out like a gold-plated blood bruise. He looked like shit but smelt great, like he'd just been for a herbal wrap, then shampooed in exotic perfumes.

This was not good. The flight was full and I had been given the middle seat in a row of three chairs that would fit easily into a dolls' house. Anticipating that the aisle seat would be taken by another behemoth of American corporate culture, I practised being in pain, knowing this would be my condition for the next ninety minutes. I tried to look like a madman with a hijacking in mind who would kill hostages, especially the person sitting next to me. As it happened, another Andrew Pennington would have been so much better than Carrie Platt.

She bustled down the aisle carrying enough bags to equip a scout expedition, oblivious of signs in the departure lounge which advised that anything larger than a sandwich box was not to be carried on board. Carrie took no heed. She was an anarchist of the soul. As it turned out, she was a woman with a mission to liberate America and Pennington was soon to reveal himself as a fellow traveller of a different sort.

As we taxied for departure I noticed that Mr P had settled down for a good read. The gaudy coloured paperbacks that decorated the shopping mall recently installed at Fort Worth airport had not caught his eye. The man was opening a thick black book bound in cloth that carried a title which probably wouldn't appeal to the average fan of Jeffrey Archer: *The Federal Reserve, the Masons and America's Imminent Decline.*

Instantly the demure Ms Platt was galvanized. She reached across and pressed a thick finger into Pennington's dumpling of a shoulder. Expecting her to claim they'd met before, I was surprised when she squealed in unmistakable mid-western tones: 'Awww, ain't that book the greatest?' Imagining she must be mistaken, I waited for Pennington to remark that he was not reading John Grisham. Instead he smiled and asked what she thought about the book's analysis of the dollar bill.

Sensing that I might be in their way, I offered them both a seat change; I could move to the aisle or the window. Neither wanted to budge. I was trapped.

Platt kicked off: 'I think the best bit is the stuff about the Great Seal. I have no doubt that's true,' she said. 'A lot can be blamed on that.' She was referring to the pyramid within a circle that sits to the left of the 'one' on the one-dollar bill.

Pennington picked up the ball and ran. 'Yes! Yes!' he said, propelling well-masticated salted nuts into my ear, where they stuck like plaster. 'They have been using the seal to control our minds. It's masonic in origin and every time we look at it, the force exerts an influence.' Although Pennington was obviously mad, he could not be called insane. He was holding down a good job with a soap and perfume distributor. That must mean something. 'You know,' he continued, 'the masons use the pyramid as their most powerful symbol and the eye that sits on top is a sign of potent evil.'

I was forced to go to the lavatory. With the door closed I took a dollar from my wallet. There on the back is a curious sight. A pyramid does sit to the left, but the top has been removed and it hovers mysteriously above, surrounded by celestial light. Inside this top section is a rather lascivious-looking eye that appears as though it might be trying to stare down someone's cleavage, probably the ample-bosomed Ms Platt. And, according to Pennington and Platt, this eye was the source of some great evil. I hurried back to my seat to hear more – I didn't want to be alone in the toilet with Dollar Bill's eye any longer than necessary.

Pennington by now had pulled out a sheaf of papers. 'These were published on the Internet,' he said. 'They show that the Federal Reserve has conspired with masons and the Jews to control Wall Street. Why do you think we have to pay commission when we trade shares?'

Panting with interest, which gave my other ear a coating of damp peanut, Platt asked Pennington if he thought people should be able to print their own money. She was not alone in this question. The Federal Bureau of Investigation believes there are more than one million members of various militia groups in the US, all of whom think the Federal government should be abolished and US currency replaced with notes issued by individual states.

'The dollar bill is a magician's device,' said Pennington. 'It's a sorcerer's trick. Every American who carries one is subjected to daily mind control.' Rather than pressing her crew call button to summon assistance, Pratt leapt into a story about a friend at work who had committed suicide after she was moved into the cashier's department where she had to count money. 'I think looking at those symbols all day, every day must have fused her brain. It could happen to anybody.'

In the past, Pennington and Pratt may have kept their theories to themselves, scared of being forced to have lobotomies. Not now. The presence of political extremists on the Internet has given the ideologically insane a sense of community. Now they have the courage to stand up and have their multiple personalities counted. Hard numbers are difficult to come by, but it is safe to say a third of the US population believes in at least one conspiracy theory.

Flight 4566 had been cleared for its final descent into Birmingham, Alabama. Andy and Carrie, now on first-name terms, were swapping Internet addresses. On some cold windy night in the future they would probably sneak off together into an electronic private room where they would fuck each other's brains out at 9,600bps. For now, they were making plans to swap literature. But soon it would be bondage catalogues, and when they were caught by their spouses they would blame the evil eye of Dollar Bill.

'There's a document I have about how the Federal Reserve controls the White House and the Pentagon,' said Carrie, giving America's central bank credit for far more sense of direction than it deserves. 'That's part of a masonic conspiracy to defuse all our missiles, leaving us defenceless against attack.'

The plane docked with its walkway and we all rose to stand for ten minutes whilst they opened the doors. As we hurried through the airport I turned and glimpsed Pratt walking alone about twenty paces ahead of Pennington. They both looked like everybody else, middle-rank executives with too much on their mind. If you saw them passing, you'd never imagine the stories they'd could tell you.

3. Alabama in Chains

The crickets wake up the sun in Capshaw, Alabama. All through the steamy night their voices unite and screech for sunrise. As dawn breaks the crickets grow still, but the heat intensifies until midday when the temperature hits 100°. Whilst the crickets were still singing loud, I watched as almost four hundred men were forced awake. Soaked in sweat after a restless sleep in the humid air, they all stretched like older men, muscles cramped from tossing around in their narrow metal cribs.

'They call us around 4 a.m.,' says Marcell Harpin, an inmate at Alabama's Limestone Correctional Facility. 'The rest of the prison is still asleep but we're the chain gang, so it's all part of the drill.'

Like many Limestone inmates, Harpin has never been in prison before. Alabama says they want to focus on first offenders so they learn their lesson fast. Unlike anybody else at Limestone, Harpin is British. He was born in London and came to the US twelve years ago. In 1993 he took cheques from his landlord and used them to steal $3000. 'We're kinda proud of Harpin,' said Limestone's Deputy Warden, Tom Davis. 'It sends a message that Alabama is different. We don't care who you are, we won't take any of your nonsense. No fuckshit snobby Brit is gonna come here and rip off our olden folk.'

Limestone's chain gangs come courtesy of Ron Jones, Alabama's Commissioner of Corrections. That's what they call prisons in the US – correction facilities. They truly expect their inmates to change, a philosophy that is an immutable part of America's trademark optimism, which is really just a substitute for serious political thought – far too dangerous in America because it would mean engaging the commercial interests who really run the country. In case the chain gangs aren't enough, Jones is talking to Alabama governor Fob James about some other innovations. 'I'd like to have some real electric fence around the facilities,' he said with a rasping southern drawl. 'We need around 5000 volts. That's what you'd call extremely lethal. I think we should think about caning as well; some of our inmates come here with very fixed attitudes. I also want all the inmates in pink underwear, add an air of humiliation to their stay here.'

Jones has been quick to exploit the rightward shift in the US supreme court, which in 1998 had been running for over a decade. In 1995 the top federal judges ruled that inmates could be kept in open dormitories. Jones immediately opened Dorm 16 at Limestone for the chain-gang men, a spartan room with over one hundred and fifty three-tier bunk beds. 'There's just no privacy,' said Marcell Harpin. 'You can never escape the noise or the smell of other prisoners. I must hear and smell a thousand farts every night and that is not the worst thing about it.'

Commissioner Jones has no sympathy. 'We have created a class of parasites for whom prison has become an entitlement programme.' He paused, to let this immutable truth sink in. 'The chain gang is designed to erode the entitlement of prison.' In one sense, Alabama's move is a desperate response. For decades their prisons have been so overcrowded that state courts set limits on how many new inmates each jail can take. The overcrowding means a life sentence is never more than seven years. Jones hopes the chain gangs will persuade the next generation of Alabama criminals to look for other occupations.

The sun and the moon were both in the sky when the inmates began heading for the prison gates. It was a surreal moment. It seemed somebody should shout 'Cut' to confirm we're on a movie set, not in the US of A in the late twentieth century – but this is Alabama and the state has always done things its own way, lynching 'negroes' long after everyone else in America realized that wasn't nice or just. The guards broke the prisoners into six groups, but all eyes were turned to the inmates in the middle. Against the light a prison warden stood with a loaded shotgun on his shoulder. He spat tobacco in a dark brown stream and adjusted his trousers under the lee of his fat belly.

Two of the warden's colleagues led out a prisoner from the centre group and brought him forward. Inmate Freddy Gooden meet warden Sergeant Mark Pelzer, your host for today's correctional entertainment. Pelzer is in command of the chain and yesterday Gooden refused to join other inmates on the gang. As punishment he spent the day chained to a hitching rail usually used for horses. The rail had no shade and by midday the temperature and humidity made the air feel like 105° Fahrenheit. Gooden was serving a twenty-six-year sentence for burglary and Pelzer treated him with contempt. 'Kneel down,' he screamed, exchanging his shotgun for a truncheon. Gooden sagged to the floor and knelt in the red clay. Pelzer let loose another stream of tobacco juice and slapped the truncheon against his palm. 'You know you're going to have to act right now or I'll put this stick on you.' Gooden offered no resistance, all his stuffing seemed to have drained out during his day beneath the hitching rail. Nearby one of Pelzer's colleagues chambered a round in his shotgun and shouted a warning to the other inmates. 'Y'all know this bullet ain't got no kinda name on it, 'cept for the first one a y'all steps outta line.'

Since Alabama re-introduced chain gangs in 1996, forty-eight Limestone inmates have spent the day on the hitching post. 'Most don't last until midday,' said Tom Davis. 'We've had three last through a whole day but nobody has refused to work two days in a row. I think it shows the system is working real well. We need the hitching rail to overcome resistance.'

Like most of the staff, Davis does not see the chain gang as a process of degradation and torture. He sees it as a labour-saving device which gets more prisoners out in the open air. 'With the gangs we can put forty inmates with one guard, that's three times what we could do without the chains. I think the inmates are now taking a liking to it. They accept the price as a way of spending more time in the fresh air.' What if a prisoner tries to escape? 'The guard will shout a warning, then he'll fire a warning shot. After that he'll shoot the prisoner.'

Some inmates doubt they would get much of a warning. 'The first day I was on the gang I thought I'd be shot,' said Marcell Harpin. 'The guy next to me had annoyed a prison officer. The warder suddenly swung around and put two shells in his shotgun and took aim. Then he dropped the gun and it went off. We were lucky not to get hit.'

Outside Limestone's gates a pile of large rocks had been assembled. Some of the inmates would spend the day turning them into small stones. But first came the chains. The prisoners knelt in lines so their ankles could be linked with eight feet of chain. There were eight men in each gang, tethered together by metal that was less than half an inch thick. By now the crickets were quiet. The air filled instead with sharp commands and rattled steel.

Once they were hitched the prisoners tied the shoe-strings from their boots around the chains, so the metal wouldn't rub their ankles. 'It's rough work,' said William Crook, who was starting his second stint on the chain gang. 'They say this is supposed to be a learning experience. What are we supposed to learn?' Commissioner Jones would say not to sell drugs, the source of Crook's eight-year sentence, and maybe Jones is right. 'Before I come back on the chain gang I'd run, I'd get on the "Most Wanted" list. This is the hardest time I've ever done. Every morning I dread coming out here. The steel gets hot by midday and it burns your ankles raw.'

Marcell Harpin agreed; Limestone seemed a long way from his native Golders Green. 'The work is not so appalling. It's the humiliation out there in the hot sun, just knowing you're chained like an animal. The first gang I was on, there were all these rednecks and they would throw stuff at me and use lots of colourful language. The guards would just laugh.'

On one occasion a guard mislaid his keys and feared they had been taken by an inmate. 'We were on Interstate 65,' said Harpin. 'They did a strip search right there on the highway. We were chained and naked with all these cars zipping by. I think that extreme reaction shows the guards are afraid. I think they're scared the chain gangs increase the risk of a riot.'

The inmates spend ten hours in the scorching sun with a water break every thirty minutes. By 4 p.m. the air was thick and soupy. On the day Limestone first made the chain gangs start breaking rocks, Deputy Warden Ralph Hooks was ecstatic. 'Some of them will be too sore to get out of bed tomorrow but they will,' he said. 'They'll get up and work their soreness out ten hours a day, five days a week.' As the inmates were led back to their buses they looked exhausted and a long way from rebellion, but others aren't so sure.

Marcell Harpin says he thinks inmates are hoarding home-made weapons and he has seen their mood grow sour. 'The dormitory is only meant for two hundred and we have four hundred in there. The gangs don't go out at the weekends. By Sunday afternoon the atmosphere gets really explosive.'

Alabama is one of America's most conservative states, but there are pockets of resistance to the chains. In 1957, Alabama pastor Martin Luther King founded the Southern Christian Leadership Conference with the Reverend Joseph Lowery, who expressed concern about the potential racism of the gangs. The majority of inmates in Alabama are black, and that is reflected in the composition of the chain gangs, despite efforts to ensure each gang has at least two white inmates. 'The chain gangs are a form of crucifixion,' said Lowery. 'I got no problem with the state working a man, but I think they should be left with some dignity.'

Doubts about Albama's penal code was also found in more conservative quarters. 'I don't think it can work,' said Ed Meeks, the executive director of the National Sheriffs Association. 'Sitting in a cell is hard. It's hard on the mind, the body, the spirit. But a chain is degrading. When they get out, these guys will hit the street angry.'

The Limestone inmates returned to their dorm an hour before sunset. At that time the guards could be found sprawled in their office. A bare room with two metal desks, the door propped open with an American Heritage dictionary to help cool the stifling room. The impromptu doorstop was one of the few books in evidence. The prison beagles barked somewhere nearby. 'I don't care what you hear in Washington,' said Sergeant Pelzer, two thin streaks of tobacco juice lining his jaw. 'People all over this country want chain gangs.' He let loose a stream of tobacco juice that hit the spittoon dead centre. 'You only have to be chained up if you commit a crime. I say if you don't want no humiliation, don't become a felon.'

The sun set behind Limestone and the crickets began their racket again. The heat had settled down to become a dark presence outside the prison walls. Inside, Marcell Harpin had just finished working in the kitchens, where he spends the evenings. 'The first day I was in here they told me to unload this truck. It was full of fish marked "Unfit for Human Consumption". I complained to a guard. He laughed and said, "You want to spend your whole sentence on the chain gang?" So what could I do, I unloaded the fish.'

Headlamps threw yellow light against the barbed wire fence as Sergeant Mark Pelzer gunned his pick-up truck engine, and drove me away from Limestone. 'You want to get something to eat?' he asked, accelerating through the prison gates. 'There's a real nice place for ribs just by the interstate.' He wound down his window to eject a stream of tobacco juice. Some was caught by the wind which splashed it back down on the windshield, already heavily streaked with sticky brown lines.

Hanging from the rear-view mirror, where some people keep miniature football boots, Pelzer had a scaled-down pair of handcuffs. 'Tonight will be really fine at Crabbe's, they have barbeque pit beef on Wednesdays. We have our meetings there – for the Alabama Bear Fighters.' He chuckled merrily as he swung across two lines of traffic, leaving a chorus of squealing tires and horns in his wake.

Three years ago Pelzer and some friends went to Montana on a hunting trip. That's where they met George Cahew, who travels America's backwaters with a troupe of black bears. The creatures have been de-clawed and their teeth have been filed blunt. The animals are harmless, unless they sit on somebody. In bars throughout the west and south, Cahew pits his bears against drunks who pay $10 for five minutes in a makeshift ring of chairs and screaming punters. The bears are eight feet tall and most fighters can barely reach high enough to land a blow on their blunt snouts. Pelzer lasted fifteen minutes with one of Cahew's toothless monsters on his first try, and ever since bear fighting has been his recreation of choice. Like some neanderthal in Levi's, Pelzer believes the rush he gets as the bear tries to apply a bone-crunching hug is without parallel.

The pick-up bumped off the road on to a gravel parking lot where a line of similar vehicles was already assembled. Their windshields were all streaked with brown lines, just like those on Pelzer's truck. Each one had a gun rack and several carried a small reproduction of the confederate flag on their fenders. The lot had an air of menace. It said: black men, liberals and young blondes would all be advised to steer clear at closing time. We had arrived at the home turf of intolerance. An imagined flash of white sheets and dancing flames married curiosity to apprehension as Pelzer barged through Crabbe's front door. Still in his prison uniform, gun hooked close to his ample hip, Pelzer lurched to the bar, slapping big men on their backs.

No words were necessary for Pelzer to get a drink. The barman had a can of National on the counter before the chain-gang master had reached a stool. Inside Crabbe's the smell of the deep south hung heavy in what was left of the air. Cigarette smoke, barbeque sauce, sweat, stale beer and testosterone were the prevailing odours but there was something else. A dank scent, something between fear and anger. 'This here is my brother Cabe,' said Pelzer, introducing a man trying to find room on six feet of bone for 350lb of flesh. He stood to shake hands and subcutaneous layers of fat rollercoasted around inside his XXXL T-shirt. 'Yup,' he said. 'You git?' Before this could be deciphered Cabe had turned to order a bevy of beers, which it became obvious were on my tab and I understood what Cabe had been saying.

By this time, back at Limestone Correctional the inmates would be grunting in the dark, trying to snatch sleep before the chains came out again the next day. At Crabbe's it was time for the Alabama Bear Club to get drunk.

'Show him the album,' said Pelzer, pointing to a thick book behind the bar. 'Let's look at those pictures from the fourth of July.' The plastic-covered photo-book was hoisted on to the counter and Pelzer yelped with glee as the first page flipped open. There he was, hanging from the thick arm of a big bear. He seemed to be trying to swing a punch at the bear's head. 'You ain't allowed to punch,' Cabe bellowed. 'That's a foul stroke.' An intense debate ensued on the ethics of punching bears. It became clear that the rules were on Cabe's side. The informal laws of bear wrestling stipulate that it's not boxing. The permitted moves are grabs and pulls. A little judo mixed with a karate jab might pass muster, but punching would not. 'Cahew got real mad at you, when you tried that punch,' said Cabe, narrowing his eyes and shortening each syllable to half its natural length. The result sounded like an asthmatic donkey, but nobody else around had any trouble understanding every word.

Pelzer ignored his critics. 'Without me, there'd be no bear wrestling in Alabama,' he said, accurately. It was Pelzer who persuaded Cahew to bring his bears south and got a local law changed so that the sport could be legalized. 'I got a right to bend a rule or two.'

The six men around Pelzer seemed to agree. The topic was closed in favour of discussing the next time Cahew's bears would visit Capshaw. It seemed they now come five times a year. Weather permitting, the parking lot was cleared to the side of the bar and a circular arena built. In six hours five bears were available. 'I make a point of fighting each one,' said Pelzer, downing his sixth can of National, a pale beer with a less enjoyable taste than yesterday's bath water. 'If I can get them back on the ropes I count that as a victory.'

Alabama's bear fighters ordered their ribs, a dozen apiece, extra sauce on the side, with onion rings, well-done, swimming in thick rivulets of grease that was soon flowing down every man's chin. After a while, and a few more cans of National in the darkened bar, Pelzer and his buddies began to look and sound like bears themselves, heaving their big slack bodies from bar to seat and back, their language skills veering unsteadily towards the zerosyllabic. Outside, the crickets had reached a peak of frenzy. The weather had turned a little less humid. My motel was a few blocks away. As I walked past a small stream the road was suddenly full of frogs. Thousands hopped and squirmed, driven to travel by a compulsive need. Beyond the highway was a swampy wood and an army of choir-boy crickets. Dinner. A frog banquet, cricket barbeque and a noggin of rancid swamp water. Crabbe's for amphibians, and who could really tell the difference.

4. Love and Sidewalk Candy

Back in Manhattan and in search of love. New York – that has to be a sexy city, huh? Right. So you want to know the hot date spots? Try the corner of Broadway and 86th Street. That would be the Zoo Club, wouldn't it? Wrong. That's Barnes and Noble, a bookstore with tables and coffee. It's the new romance. Professional, no alcohol or loud music. Just polite conversation and courteous inquiry. No risks, no sex for weeks. Leave that to folks in the mid-west, hotbeds of lust like Iowa. It's awful.

New York in the nineties seems to be hiding from the madness outside, the hunger that stalks the suburbs. Copulation has become far too unrefined for New Yorkers. Sure, a few frat boys and girls may fuck on the first night during their first month in New York, but then they learn. Sex in places like Montana is still fast and raw, an open space of lust which reminds urbanites that love is emotional Formica. Beneath the tacky exterior is something raw that once lived somewhere wild. In New York love is the thing they crave, because it is quantifiable, a return on an investment made.

The Manhattan dating game has changed to reflect America's lost optimism. Both men and women now have different roles and that makes the dialogue of dating very difficult. With the risk of AIDS and the fear of commitment, New Yorkers are getting to know each other in different ways, with sex on a back burner that has gone cold. 'New York couples are courting again and finding each other through conversation,' a leading psychologist says. Hiding from sex, more like. Or at least making its noisy demands quieter when polite company is around.

'Do you come here often?' That's the line I decided against as I walked into a singles night at the York Theatre. It seemed too literal, not Shakespearean enough. I was amongst lots of suits and silk at the York's first singles night of the new theatre season. The event was sponsored by – you guessed – Barnes and Noble. The York sits in mid-town at the base of the large tower occupied by a monolithic bank, which squats on top of a catholic church where Jesus would have more than money lender's tables to overturn. Try sixty storeys of steel and glass. It is perfectly placed for a singles event featuring aspiring professionals. There are so many stockbrokers within spitting distance that three millionaires were killed when an air-conditioning unit fell from a skyscraper during rush-hour.

Nobody at the York Theatre had any obvious body piercing. We were there to unite our fabulous professional futures with somebody cute and compatibly successful. I was a long way from Sergeant Pelzer's Alabama and it had all the sex appeal of an early morning run in February.

So where do we start? There's Lisa, about thirty-two and dressed in a nice blue suit just like mine. We've both just watched *Standing By*, a romantic comedy by Norman Barasch. Now we have a drink and some nibbles from local restaurants.

'Hi,' I say. 'You look like you might enjoy LA?' Lisa gives me a look that takes in my physique and the cut of my suit. She's doing big-time calculations about my sanity and I notice my question wasn't on her prepared menu. 'Sorry?' she enquires. Which is what a polite, upper east-sider says instead of, 'What the fuck do you mean?'

Whoops! – be more direct says my internal voice – she's American and probably an accountant. 'LA, that's where they started out – the two in *Standing By*, the play we just saw, they met on a flight from LA to New York. Have you ever been there?'

'Where?' she says, dropping a stuffed mushroom.

Either I no longer speak English or Lisa's ganglia have strangled her cerebral cortex. Maybe she is really from Alabama. 'Oooh, LA. Sorry, I'm a bit nervous,' she stutters. 'This is my first time.' At last, Lisa and Lisa's brain have made contact, but now I'm the wreck dropping his food. It's hot in here and she's checking out the sweat on my brow. God, this is not easy. 'Are you OK?' Lisa gives me a sweet smile and a napkin to mop my brow. And yes, she's an accountant, she loved the play and she gives me her card. 'Call me at work.'

That's passing 'Go' in the New York dating game as played by the city's overworked professionals. No home numbers on first meetings, which should always take place in a 'safe' environment – like a theatre after the play has finished. No running to a bar and slugging down five cold ones to wake up in a warm sweat on a set of sheets you don't recognize.

'These theatre evenings have been just great,' purred Joe De Michael, Managing Director of the York Theatre and a man making serious money out of lonely people. 'We have a singles night the first Friday of every production. That gives us about five a season. The second Friday we have a singles event for gays and lesbians. We find everybody loves the evenings because they automatically have something to talk about. The play breaks the ice.'

It does. Here comes Andie and I'm between her and the smoked salmon. 'Excuse me.' 'Sure,' I say. 'Have you seen any other Barasch plays?' Half an hour later the salmon has curled with the brown bread and we're on to Shakespeare. I look around and see at least twenty other couples doing Coles notes and close eye contact.

'Nobody needs a pick-up line here,' says De Michael. 'The theatre singles are not a meat market. Everybody has something specific in common, and when you come here you know you'll get a literate group of people. This is our ninth season and every year we get more professional people wanting tickets. That's the echelon of partners that most people want to meet.' It sounds like what they all need is a manual on masturbation, or maybe tickets to somewhere warm where their brains can thaw out — but instead they dip into their Hermes leather wallets for $300 a night and they are not alone.

The York Theatre is part of an industry with estimated revenues of over $100 million. Singles are a serious business because nobody seems to remember how to chat people up any more. The New York State Chamber of Commerce has registered over 200 dating agencies since 1980. Agencies are popular, but for many they're a total admission of failure. Singles nights are a halfway house; you're still free to choose your date from a room full of real people and there's lots of variety.

'We started up five years ago,' said Ruth Leach of Single Booklovers, which holds its evenings at that hot Barnes and Noble on 86th Street. 'It's been a huge success. People who like to read are a special group. We arrange dinners for about 100 members at a time. I'm always amazed at the interaction. The conversation is always totally frenetic, we never seem to have any lemons.' Leach said her group helps people who are too busy to meet through more random channels. 'We had a marriage last year. The two people both worked in the same office building and had gone to the same university but they met through Booklovers.'

Back at the York, Andie has just given me her card and it's time to move on. At first I'm shocked by the apparent polygamy of the evening. Then the penny drops — time is short and this is all about sampling. Mr or Mrs Right may be out there, but you won't know unless you cast a wide net. 'I never go home with anybody from the theatre nights,' says Paul, a banker who I meet at the bar. 'That's a waste. I want to collect numbers and take my time getting to know a few women.' A bit later I look around and see him talking to Andie and I know he'll get her business card.

Sharyn Woolf, who runs a New York dating service for lonely executives, applauds the theatre singles. 'Just showing up takes lots of courage but for a professional woman it's much easier to go to a play than a bar. The conversation is built into the evening. People should enjoy themselves and make friends of both sexes. Everybody has a list of people you probably don't already know and meeting them is the start of meeting their list.'

Joe De Michael says the type of play is important. 'My perception is that tragedies generate better singles conversations than comedies. I don't quite understand why, you'd think it would be the reverse.' Maybe if you laugh too much it's impossible to take the singles scene seriously, but De Michael has a different view. 'I think the tragedies scare people into thinking about making their lives better.'

'We don't have singles evenings, that would be crass.' Dan Lacovara is based at the Lincoln Centre for the Performing Arts and runs the snobbish Centre Circle, one of New York's most popular singles clubs – but don't call it that. Andie and Paul both belong to Centre Circle. 'This is a way for high-class people to meet and know they'll have something in common. For singles, New York is a candy shop. Every hour hundreds of new faces arrive in the city so you must be selective. Our "Meet the Artist" events are especially popular.'

This doesn't sound like the best way to pick up anybody but Mr Lacovara is adamant. 'At these evenings people get to discuss the play with the performers. You can tell a lot about a person by the way they ask a question about Wagner or Mamet and that's a lot more revealing than their choice of pick-up line. Young professionals don't have time for a lot of bull.'

Not every New York singles group is quite as highbrow. There's the Country Music Club, the Black Leathers and there's the Well-Rounded Club for large ladies and the men who love them. This group does not discuss much Beckett. They meet in a West Side bar once a week. The men are mostly normal size whilst the women are, well, big or even huge. The club was founded by Diane Ilic and boasts 700 members. 'I was this supersized woman, just divorced. I was thinking of going back to the clubs, knowing that would be tough.' Diane's 5′ 5″ frame carries just over 16 stone. 'I thought it would be nice to have a place where they already preferred heavy girls, so I started this club for women of girth.'

My York Theatre conquests, Andie and Lisa – well, I did get their business cards – would not be welcomed at Diane's club, they spend too much time at the gym. Kim also has well-buffed calves. We met here in Barnes and Noble on 86th Street. This place really is hopping with hormones. Bright lights, hard chairs and lots of twenty-somethings locked in early literary love. Kim is Jewish and says New York Jews have the biggest singles scene. 'It's so organized and it's encouraged by the Rabbis. The synagogues fear there's too much assimilation with Jews marrying outside their religion.'

Kim's story is familiar. My friend Cassie got married a year ago (she was motivated by desperation) and before that went regularly to the Jewish singles clubs. 'I was forty and running PR for one of America's biggest media companies,' she told me. 'I was so far out of the dating scene my favourite pick-up line was: "Didn't I zip up your fly at Woodstock?" The singles clubs seemed the only route I could take, and thousands of New Yorkers feel the same way.'

Cassie would wince at the memory. 'It was dreadful, the first thing you'd talk about is how awful these evenings are, then you'd talk about jobs. In New York, your career is the only currency that counts.'

Now I tell Kim about Cassie. She says the experience is typical for young Jewish women – bad food at New York hotels with over-anxious men in suits. 'But Cassie got married,' says Kim. 'Did she meet him at a singles night?' No, Cassie met Steve at a Sit Shiva, the Jewish equivalent of a funeral. 'The only person I knew there was Steve's best friend Mark and it was Mark's father who had died,' Cassie told me. 'I really liked the look of Steve but how do you get introduced at a funeral? It's not tasteful to get the dead guy's son and ask, "Who's the cute friend?" So who knew? How could I tell I'd meet my match at a wake?'

Kim hands me her business card and I ask why she started coming to the bookstore. 'I paid $2000 for a dating agency. They promised me six dates in three months but nothing worked out so I didn't renew my subscription. The agency started calling me on Friday and Saturday nights, they'd say how sorry they were that I was alone at the weekend. I didn't want to pay again but the calls made me depressed. I like to read, so this was a good solution even if I don't meet anybody.' Maybe Kim should try funerals.

'It's getting harder out there,' says Sharyn Woolf. 'I run seminars in New York for single people and in twelve years it has never been tougher.' Or easier, if you like plays and know a little literature. As I left the York Theatre a laughing couple had just agreed to share a cab downtown. They already seemed comfortable in each other's company. 'Have you seen *Cats*?' asked the man. I waited, anxiety mounting. 'No,' she said. Phew, I thought. That's at least one more date.

Looking at the way so many New Yorkers find their perfect person, it's easy to think the city has lost its legendary power to bring people together, but when these couples fail to make the grade some turn to revenge, which the city can still do with unmatched skill.

New York and anger were made for each other. Sure, the place has parks and picture galleries but it's on the streets where the city steams. That's where cab drivers and bike messengers joust with tyre iron and bike chain, where ordinary citizens turn crazy over the slightest insult, imagined or otherwise. This is the 'in-your-face' town; its people are direct. Mayor Guliani gave the city its slogan for the nineties: 'New York – We can kick your city's ass.' Some people say New York's a romantic town but New Yorkers thirst for revenge as much as love. It is all this high-pressure time spent too close to people we often don't like.

When you've been to one singles evening too many, thank God for the anti-personals. This latest addition to the city's tool-box of fury is just the job. Let's say you were being mugged on the subway and someone close by did nothing to help. No problem, just dip the pen in poison ink. 'To the insensitive boob in the blue business suit and black sneakers who watched me get mugged on the A-train last week without doing a damn thing to help. Pig.'

The anti-personals began small. In January 1998 a shopping magazine called the *Manhattan Pennysaver* invited its readers to 'give the gift of hate' by attacking their enemies in its 'anti-personal' ads. 'Spew forth your anger. You'll feel much better afterwards,' the paper said. The ads were the brainchild of the *Pennysaver*'s commercial director, Eric Naher. 'I just got tired of all those lovesick desperate pleas for companionship that make up the singles ads,' says Naher. 'I just wanted to do something for the dark side of New Yorkers. Believe me, everybody who lives here for long has one.'

The hate ads cost 50 cents a word (about thirty pence), which is the same price as their romantic brethren. According to Naher, the largest number come from jilted lovers, the next biggest category is from people angered by bosses or colleagues. Like this one: 'To my new SOB of a boss. What goes around comes around. No one will stay with you because you do not treat people with the respect and courtesy they deserve. You are ripping us off. I'm going to report you to the proper authorities.'

When it started, the *Pennysaver* got about twenty submissions a week and published an average of ten. The truly offensive were rejected. Now the weekly total is close to 500.

'People are starting to read the magazine just for the anti-personals,' says Naher.

Do the ads work? Do they make the author feel better? For a jilted lover they seem a poor substitute for a slap in the face or a tossed drink. 'I'm not aware of any evidence that people can get rid of aggression symbolically,' says New York psychiatrist Dr Joyce Brothers. 'I don't think these things are therapeutic at all. In fact, aggression tends to breed aggression.'

But hold on – an anti-personal is not a loaded gun, the other favourite means of dispute resolution in the USA. The sender can tell a disagreeable colleague he's a jerk from a safe distance, whilst still smiling at him round the coffee machine. 'It's perfect for our modern times,' says Naher. 'It's a safety valve.' Yup, and it works for both sexes. 'To the woman I could have loved forever. I'd rather split than endure the "Us Talk" No.403. I'm committed now all right, to an asylum. Sorry, I can't be a slave to your biological clock,' and, 'Sex with you was bad, sleeping was worse and your eating habits even grossed out my mother. You can edit books but women aren't for you.' Ouch, I'd guess that these people did not meet at the theatre.

Walking away from the theatre singles night the air was cold and crisp. The light was sharp with an aggressive quality that dragged the eye towards the Chrysler building and its white arrow of lights, like a road sign pointing to Mars. At the corner of 45th Street and Fifth Avenue a guy was propped up on a fire hydrant. He had a sign, requesting money: 'Navajo Indian – Needs Money to Return to Reservation'. I stopped. 'Where's your reservation?' I asked. The guy, called Charlie, looked shocked. I asked again as he rattled his cup. Four quarters got me an answer. 'It's in Arizona.' 'Great. C'mon, let's go,' I said. 'I'll take you there.'

5. Charlie Horse

When I first met Charlie, the Dow Jones Industrial Average had just broken through 7000 points for the first time. I knew that because his bedding for the night was a newspaper with the Dow's epoch-making record as its front page headline. Charlie had no appreciation for this historic event because he can't read. He had his sign made by another guy in the homeless shelter. He figured it would appeal to white folks' guilt, but he was beginning to wonder.

'There are too many Indians with casinos now, man,' he said. I had settled by his side to push my case for taking him back to Arizona. 'There's a tribe in Connecticut. They all be millionaires, be buying back land stolen by the pilgrims. It's stirring up a lot of hatred amongst white folks.'

He was right. The Mashantucket Pequot tribe owns the biggest casino in America. It's in Foxwood, about halfway between Boston and New York. Each day the descendants of Americans who committed genocide against Native Americans turn up by the busload. They have all ruined their bodies with fast food and tobacco but they have strong forearms, the result of daily workouts on the slot machines. This polyester army chucks its pension away on the Pequots' slots and always comes back for more punishment. It is like fighting the battle of Big Horn all over again with quarters against trios of cherries, and the odds faced at the tables are about the same for the white man as they were when Sitting Bull screamed over the hill at Crow Agency, Montana.

In 1991 the US Congress passed a law permitting gaming on Indian reservations where the tribe held the legal status of a sovereign nation. These small countries within a country are dotted all around the US. Some are the nation's most desperate pockets of poverty, because the tribe has yet to win a gaming permit or is too far from big centres of population to run a profitable casino. Others, like the Pequots, have become billion dollar powerhouses. The Pequots made a big contribution to Bill Clinton's re-election campaign and employ comely paleface females as waitresses in their shiny casino, dressing them in tiny replicas of squaws' costumes that must have General Custer spinning in his grave.

In 1998 the Pequots will make a profit easily in excess of $1 billion. In 1997 they bought enough land to double the size of their reservation and they want more. The newly purchased tracts fall under Pequot law and are policed by Pequot cops, and the local white men are sick with rage. All this makes Charlie nervous. 'The white man tried to annihilate us in the eighteenth century,' he says. 'As a percentage of our race it was a much bigger genocide than the holocaust. It was the worst ethnic cleansing in history. I fear the Pequots may make some whites so angry they will try and finish the job started by the settlers.'

Ralph Makin is a fine example of how angry the Indians can make some whites. He is the last of the Mohegans, give or take a dozen. Apart from the spelling, Mohegans differ from Mohicans in one other respect – their traditional hairstyles are more seventies' disco than punk. The Mohegan tribe are from the northern reaches of New York state, their reservation is about ninety miles from the Pequots. When I met Ralph, three years ago, he was living in a trailer. He was working hard to get the Mohegans sovereign status and a casino permit. After we had lunch he took me to the tribe's burial ground.

Ralph looked like a vacationing bank clerk as he stepped from his car in blue slacks and a beige Wal-Mart windbreaker, with steel-rimmed glasses, but he would soon be transformed, at least from the neck up. As the wind whistled across the graveyard and its teepee-shaped headstones, Ralph took off his spectacles and applied war paint to his face in patterns sacred to the Mohegans. He then plucked a feather headdress from the trunk of his car. It was magnificent, not like the tawdry replicas found in reservation gift shops. The red eagle feathers soared high towards the sky, offset by white and green feathers in complex patterns.

With the headdress in place, Ralph checked his look in the wing mirror and he was ready. With the disco hairdo, I thought he looked like one of the Village People, at least until he began to dance. He started slow but was soon whirling like a fairground waltzer, every limb moving in what looked like opposite directions. He was dancing for his gods, hoping they would be on his side at a meeting scheduled in Washington five days hence. As he danced to the drummer in his head, a grey-haired denizen of the nearby housing estate appeared, walking a collie dog. She came within ten feet before a look of disgust crossed her face. Muttering under her breath, she tried to leave but Collie Dog stood rooted, watching Ralph. The woman tugged, Collie Dog tugged back, his ears standing upright as if he could hear Ralph's drummer too. The woman resigned herself and stood with her eyes averted as Ralph's dance was reflected in the dog's eyes.

'Animals have always been close to us,' said Ralph. 'We treat them with respect, understand their souls.' Ralph looked after Ms Disapproval as she finally hauled Collie Dog away, the look on the animal's face suggesting he had been to some other place with Ralph, where the sun rose on a land untouched by concrete.

Ralph's dance seemingly worked with the gods as well. Congress approved the Mohegan application and the Mohegan Sun casino is now the second largest on the east coast after Foxwoods. Ralph dances these days on a twenty-acre estate in front of his twelve-bedroom mansion – and there is a legion of Ms Disapprovals who would like to see him brought down.

Charlie's tribe do not live in mansions. They are housed in trailers which look like they have been left behind by tornados. Stripped of paint and battered, they get so hot in the summer that eggs can be fried on the carpet, a cooking surface that would be more hygienic than most of the trailer's kitchens. Charlie has no real desire to return there, despite his sign. Charlie would rather be Ms Disapproval's collie dog than actually on his way back home.

'You have got to be shittin' me man,' he said when I asked him again to let me take him home to Cow Springs, Arizona. 'They'd kill me, I'm a wanted man.' Charlie said he would actually like to go home but couldn't, on account of 'the killings'. He refused to enlarge and told me to go, I was holding back people from giving. I put $20 in his cup. 'That's got to be more than you make in an hour,' I said. 'So that gives me sixty minutes to persuade you.'

'Why the fuck you want to visit Cow Springs wit' me?' he said. 'It is the worst shithole on God's earth.'

I knew Charlie was wrong. Cow Springs is a small town in the midst of extraordinary scenery just south of the majestic Shonto Plateau, at the edge of Arizona's painted desert. A man could fill his head with so much beauty in a day that his ears would bleed. Maybe that's why Charlie ran away and now rides the dirty undertow of quarters from the waves of disapproving stockbrokers who pass his pitch every day.

'Ain't got nothin' to do wit' it,' he said. He shook his dirty jet black hair, held in place by a Navajo-style headband. 'What you sellin' anyway?'

I explained I was acting on a whim, a pure impulse. He

advertised a desire to go somewhere I'd always wanted to visit and I was willing to take him there. 'OK. Here's the deal,' he said. He had stood up, revealing he was well over six feet tall. 'We fly first class, on Pan Am. We spend a night in Las Vegas before we get to Cow Springs. Then you fly me back, first class again.'

It was hard to see what Charlie could do with the Vegas part of the trip. He read my mind. 'I have plenty of cash,' he said. 'I just don't choose to spend it on accommodation.' I agreed to his conditions. We set two days hence for our departure. 'I even have some good clothes,' he revealed. 'Just no point wearing them out here.'

The sun was barely over the parapet of New York's skyline when Charlie climbed into my truck. He was dressed in a pinstripe suit that was a perfect fit – for a man six inches shorter. Luckily Charlie filled the yawning gap with the most elaborate pair of cowboy boots seen outside a John Wayne movie. They had a silver background and etched into the leather with knife and red dye was a scene from Custer's last stand, in which the unfortunate colonel was swallowing a Sioux war spear.

'Nice boots,' I said.

'These are kinda conservative,' Charlie shot back. 'I have a gold pair which show Sitting Bull in heaven, on a piebald stallion, surrounded by his blood brothers.'

I'd had a tough time explaining to Charlie how a decade's worth of criminals and loan sharks had brought down Pan Am. He couldn't believe that something so grand and important as an airline could just disappear. Being a conservative, he was not happy with the thought of flying any airline that hadn't been started when Power was Propellers. We settled on United.

The flight was full of gamblers. They all had optimistic faces. Since they last dumped their paychecks on the craps table, their hopes and dreams had been washed clean and now were packed on board with their fresh underwear. By the time their trip was over everything would be soiled again. There are three immutable truths of Vegas: you sweat, you piss and you lose.

We hauled ourselves into the smallest first-class cabin I'd ever seen and Charlie immediately thought I'd cheated him. He said the seats must be some kind of economy deal with two inches extra leg room. I looked around for a flight attendant who could verify we were in first class. When I turned back to Charlie he was in the cockpit, waving feathers in the captain's face, chanting something in Navajo.

Back in economy the gamblers mostly had fixed expressions of horror on their faces. They obviously viewed Charlie as some kind of ill omen. Two guys in grey suits with backsides like overstuffed coal sacks were on their feet, as if free chow had been offered to the first man off the plane. Before they could bolt, the pilot announced he was pleased to welcome Chief Sailing Hawk to his plane, who had just blessed the flight crew. The pilot said he expected an especially smooth journey to Vegas, turbulence permitting.

Charlie sat and closed his eyes until an attendant appeared with beverages. For the next three hours drink and words fought for the use of his mouth and I'm still not sure who won.

He had been born in Cow Springs, in a trailer. His mother was so exhausted by the birth and his father was so drunk, it was a day before Charlie got any food. He believes the spirits looked after him until his maternal grandmother came by and took him away. She was a Sioux Indian and took him to live in Crow Agency, Montana. Nearby is the Little Big Horn battleground where Custer died with two hundred US troops.

Custer's killing field is a national monument, dedicated not to the Sioux and Lakota who won the battle, but to the US soldiers killed 'while clearing the district of Yellowstone of hostile Indians'. Sure, they were hostile – it was their land. As a teenager Charlie would go to the monument with his grandmother and derisively tap the obelisk and graves with sticks, an Indian ritual called 'counting coup', which is essentially a celebration of triumph over the vanquished. They would be chased away by the US Army veterans who maintain the monument. Ten years ago Charlie's grandmother began a campaign for a Little Big Horn memorial to the seventy Indians who had died there, which could also represent the thousands of Native Americans who had been slain across the west. She began receiving death threats.

Charlie abruptly stopped reminiscing and began talking about his New York street life. He said he was a spy, not a panhandler. 'New York is the home of the white man's demon spirit,' he said. He paused to empty a vodka in one sensuous movement. 'I sit there watching, assessing how close it has come to corrupting itself. The end will come soon.'

He sounded like any street bum with a doomsday sign until he began talking about his status as a fugitive. 'The white man's laws are a mockery. They are made to protect the powerful. Don't you think we know? This America was built on genocide, our land was stolen, our lives destroyed. Yet the white man's history says it is us who were the hostiles. That's what happened when I killed two people.'

Charlie's voice had risen somewhat. The last four words of his sentence punched the air like well-struck golf balls just as the attendant came by, and the look on her face said Charlie had got four holes in one. She visibly jumped and headed for the chief steward to convene a crisis conference. I could see her point. Charlie and I had finished a dozen of those tiny aircraft bottles which only encourage a drinker to have more. A half hour earlier the bottles had become ten pins and our tray tables a miniature bowling alley. We had bet raucously on the outcome of three games, throwing dollar bills about and laughing like hyenas with a bad peyote problem. This good clean fun had made an IBM executive across the aisle fit to be tied. His requests for peace and quiet were given the same rapt attention as the safety announcements which precede airline flights and he was a not a man used to being ignored.

His pudgy white face soon displayed all the innate racism which lies behind the majority of WASP Americans. If he had been in his country club locker room, he would have been slapping his buddies' backs and saying how he'd never met an Indian worth a moment, and whilst we were at it, shouldn't we have finished off the Japs when we had a chance. Every US minority knows the look he had on his face before he finally complained to the flight attendant. The curled lip was holding back a torrent of contempt that we could all too easily read in his eyes. Before long WASPs will be a minority in America. In California and Florida WASPs already run second to Hispanics so Mr IBM will only find life more taxing as he tries to justify his minority's grasp on the bulk of America's power centres. Mr IBM's future is a volatile mix which includes guns, anger, white separatists, poverty and privilege.

Charlie looked like he'd enjoy putting an arrow in Mr IBM's gut before scalping what was left of the executive's hair. I stood up and approached the attendant. Taking her to one side, I explained that Mr Sailing Hawk was a famous Native American actor who had just finished a film with Mr Robert De Niro, that his remarks about killing were a reference to the movie. Celebrity is the universal currency in the US and is respected like religion, celebrities venerated as if they know the secret of eternal life and the recipe for Coca-Cola. The attendant could not have recognized Charlie as a star because he isn't one, but she took my arm and whispered, 'Wasn't he in *One Flew Over the Cuckoo's Nest?*' 'Right,' I said, winking. She told me it was one of her favourite films. I compared the IBM guy to Nurse Ratchett. She smiled, and from that moment Mr White Executive had about as much pull on that flight as a one-legged dog with mange.

Whilst I was making peace with United, Charlie had become reflective. 'It gave me no pleasure to kill those kids,' he said. 'I was not much more than a kid myself.' He said it happened five years ago. Charlie was back in Cow Springs, riding horseback for a rancher whose great-great-great grandfather had fought with Custer in Wyoming. At night he'd go back to the reservation, a broken-toothed circle of trailers surrounded by satellite dishes and a wire fence. One evening he arrived to find a dozen neighbours outside his 1975 Airstream, the flames from their wood fire reflecting off the trailer's polished silver exterior.

The group were planning a posse. A twelve-year-old Navajo girl had disappeared on her way back from the school bus that dropped her at the end of a five-mile dust road leading into the reservation. In the pitch black a set of car headlights had been seen racing east to the Black Mesa. Earlier, two guys in their twenties had been seen hanging around, leaning against a shiny new red Jeep Cherokee and swigging beers. Charlie knew the girl. Her name was Susan Flowing Stream and he liked her. She wasn't any kind of beauty but she had a nice look and could run like an express train.

The plane was starting its descent into Vegas. Charlie paused to look at the neon lights of the strip flashing redundantly in the hot afternoon sun. The scene looked like my brain felt after five hours of non-stop drinking at 35,000 feet: random explosions of red, green and gold against an electric white background. I knew we either had to sleep or drink more as soon as we left the plane.

Vegas has become a family town. Husbands and wives lose their life savings with their kids in tow. Whilst Mum is putting her son's college tuition fund into the blackjack dealer's pocket, the unsuspecting boy child can get his kicks with every cartoon character on the planet. We were staying at the Flamingo Hilton, one of the hotels that opened when Vegas stood for vice, and the only kids you saw were pretending to be twenty whilst they turned tricks in back alleys. Now it was like camp. Pre-teens ran through the casino unsupervised whilst the adults sat glassy-eyed before their inevitable fate.

Charlie likes to play craps. Two dice, a seven or eleven to win. Two, three or twelve loses. Everything else you throw again. We sat with tumblers of vodka and began giving the Hilton our money. To the left was a woman in her thirties. She was drop-dead gorgeous except for the frozen look behind her eyes. There was a small pile of chips in front of her which had probably been much larger once. She rolled and got a three. Dealer's pile. She looked at me and Charlie. Now she only had four chips left. She leaned in and whispered. 'You want it? Three hundred dollars for anything.'

Her name was Connie, at least that's what she said. She was a housewife with a part-time job in telephone sales. Once a month she and four friends came to Vegas and gambled with other men's money, which they got by sleeping with them. Connie said she never went home with less than she came with. She had a rule: she never gambled the cash from her last trick. 'That way I always have three hundred dollars to go home with and no hard feelings.' I looked around and suddenly noticed there seemed to be at least a dozen women who looked like they might be on Connie's self-financing vacation plan. She meanwhile had begun explaining to Charlie she would sleep with him, no problem, she had no hang-ups about race.

We escaped to the bar. Charlie deviated from the pure white spirit we'd been pickling ourselves in and ordered a scotch. 'Susan Flowing Stream would never have ended up like Connie,' he said. 'She was an artist. A good girl.' Charlie said he had led the posse hunting for Susan. Up into the looming dark of the Mesa, the stars like holes picked in a curtain, hinting at a brighter light in a better universe just beyond. Except, like most things in the Navajo desert, that was an illusion.

It was almost midnight when he heard the laughter and the screams, two sounds dancing with each other across the wind-sculpted rocks. Charlie was with another Navajo, Pete Howling Dog, a man in his early thirties, two years older than Charlie. They reined in their horses and dismounted. Tying the animals to a bush, they crept closer.

A guy in a Green Bay Packers sweatshirt bumped his way to the bar, knocking Charlie's whisky from his hand. It was a clumsy act but when the Packer fan saw Charlie was an Indian it was clear he wouldn't mind if everybody thought it was malicious. Drunkenly he put a fat arm on Charlie's shoulder. 'I could kick your redskin ass and — ' It is not easy to lift a 260lb man by his balls, but Charlie did it as if he were in a circus and the Green Bay grey was his partner in a tumbling act. You could tell Green Bay had been warned by his doctor that he had a heart attack in his future and the dumb son of a bitch was wondering if his time had come.

We were almost twenty feet away from the bar when Green Bay began vomiting. The casinos keep their victims near the gaming tables by laying out free buffets of food in every corner. The amount of stuff coming out of Green Bay suggested he'd been told the buffets would stop being free at midnight. A chunk of pizza hit a nasty-looking Italian guy in the face to be followed shortly after by pork rinds and steamed dumplings. As we walked out into the air, the bespatterd De Niro lookalike was punching Green Bay's face like a man kneading dough.

Hackberry, Valentine, Sloth Cave, Tuba City — the small towns of the desert slipped by, each one lasting for about six of Charlie's snores. He slept, I drove. He was bent in his seat like a collapsible sofa but seemed completely comfortable. Practised in the ways of sleeping anywhere. We had a thousand dollars of winnings and a bunch of Green Bay's friends looking for us, so we figured it was time to hit Cow Springs. At dawn we were in Tonolea, population 239. We slept until the sun felt hot then looked for some breakfast.

'They had her tied to stakes,' said Charlie. He was sipping water, rolling ice cubes around his mouth. 'She was naked. We got our first sight of her just as one of the guys shot her in the head.' Pete Howling Dog was ready to rush them but Charlie held him back. The girl was dead. Now his job was to get these guys hooked to the crime. Charlie and Pete crept around rocks until the rapists' jeep was between them and the white guys. Then they got in close. The two men were both urinating on the girl.

'Howling Dog's great-great-great-grandmother was raped to death by continental soldiers in 1876,' said Charlie. 'I was amazed he kept control.' Both men had guns. They stepped forward and told the two guys to freeze. The men complied. 'We told them to lie down. They was on the floor when Pete got hit.' Neither Charlie nor Pete knew there was a third man in the raping party. He'd been in the back seat of the truck when the two Navajo arrived. Before he could get off a second shot Charlie nailed him with a lucky bullet that went in between the eyes. He was turning around when one of the two guys from the floor jumped on Charlies back. He grappled with the assailant and got him in a headlock. 'I snapped his neck, couldn't help myself. He just went.'

The last rapist had no stomach for a fight. He had already run into the night by the time Charlie finished shredding his pal's spinal cord. The Navajo was left with the stars and four corpses. Charlie sank to his knees ready to pray for the first time in his life. Indians pray to their ancestors, not directly to the gods. Ancestors intercede for those left on earth. Charlie had plenty of dead ancestors, but they were useless to him.

'I realized I could no longer speak Navajo, not that I ever really could,' he said. 'I couldn't pray to the ancestors in English, they wouldn't understand a word.' There were once 300 Indian languages, when the European settlers arrived in America. Fewer than twenty are still taught to newborns. There was once an official policy of 'language extermination' in America, to complement the killing of whole tribes. Charlie's grandmother spoke Crow but not to him, and his own parents couldn't get off the booze long enough to feed him, let alone teach him a complex Navajo language they barley knew themselves.

'I realized I had been amputated from my culture, that it was hidden now behind an iron curtain. I wept.'

Soon after Charlie found both horses had run off. He began to walk home. He was two miles from his trailer, sun above the horizon, when Arizona State Police and the FBI picked him up.

'The three guys who did Susan were cops, from Flagstaff,' said Charlie. 'The guy who ran went back to his HQ with a made-up story. Said me and Pete had been the killers of Susan, that the cops found us and two died in a firefight that also took Pete. With everybody but him and me dead, whose word were they going to believe?'

Charlie was taken to the lock-up in Flagstaff and beaten. He was interrogated for days as they tried to get his confession but he said nothing. Finally a lawyer interceded. Then Charlie got his lucky break. The FBI wanted him taken to Phoenix for a hearing, they planned to make it a Federal case. The night before, he was given a change of clothing and allowed to use the shower. Whilst in the bathroom he escaped.

'I guess they never thought I could get through that window,' he said. 'It was pretty tight. I walked from Flagstaff through the reservation and into Utah. Then I made my way to Salt Lake City and hopped freight trains to Chicago. From there I stole a car to get to Buffalo, then took a Greyhound into Manhattan. It took me eight weeks on the road.'

I was suddenly scared for Charlie. We were just a few miles from where the killings had taken place. I asked why he'd agreed to come.

'I speak Navajo now. I need to say a prayer for Susan Flowing Stream. C'mon, let's go.'

We drove to the place where Susan Flowing Stream had died, her twelve-year-old body violated by the descendants of men who had oppressed her race for four generations. Now Charlie was risking his freedom and maybe his life to pay his last respects. Out of the car he walked to a slight depression on a rock ledge and sank to the ground. He spread his limbs as if he were Susan tied to the stake and began to sing.

It was a Navajo burial song and its words rose into the air as if carried by zephyrs. The sounds were more complex than a dozen Shakespeare plays, as if every thought in the language could be compressed into four rhyming verses. Birds that had been chirping seemed to stop, and some flew to perches around where Charlie lay, marrying his soul to his dead ancestor. A stiff breeze began to blow. Charlie responded by standing and lifting his arms to the sky. His song now changed to a guttural series of chants, each word hitting the air like a rifle shot. He crossed his arms over his chest and began to sway.

On the plane back to New York Charlie was silent until we were over Pennsylvania. 'I had to change my identity, everything,' he said. 'They stole my self. I decided to live on the streets because it's honest. People walk past and don't see me, to most of them I'm invisible. That's the price of my freedom. My sign is ironic. I did want to go back to my reservation, for Susan. I did need help to do it. Now I've been. So now I can leave the streets.'

I thought about whether I should investigate his story further once we were in New York, find out if he was telling the truth. See if I could find ways to get him back on some kind of track. I decided that would be a violation of his trust. It didn't matter whether Charlie's story was true, because he believed it and that's what made him free. His spending in Vegas showed me he could leave the streets any time, but for now he was where he wanted to be, watching the white man, waiting for a sign that Mr Paleface was about to get his comeuppance.

'What are you going to do next?' I asked.

'I think I'll go find Heather Tallchief.'

6. Trust Me,
I'm Perfect

I had talked to Charlie about Heather when we drove away from Susan Running Stream's sacred spot. Heather is also a Native American, a Cheyenne. Unlike Charlie, she had been a devoted professional, but she was assailed by one too many lifestyle aspirations she couldn't afford and one day the love of the good life and Gabriel García Márquez got the better of her. She decided to join the growing list of middle-class American women who choose a life of crime over suburbia.

The FBI special agent in charge of Las Vegas can't help liking Heather Tallchief. 'She seems to have executed the perfect crime,' says Joe Dushek, with grudging admiration, looking at a picture of a smiling Heather pinned to the wall of his Las Vegas office, which, like everywhere else in town, has a slot machine. This one was confiscated from a casino that let one too many mobsters join its top management. 'We really have no idea where Heather is now. Three years ago she took $4.1 million that belongs to the Loomis Armored Car Company, all in unmarked notes. That will buy a lot of disguises and air tickets.' Which doesn't mean that the FBI has given up on her. The bureau has had twenty-something Heather Tallchief on its most wanted list since 1997 – at number three, the highest position for a woman in twenty-three years. Lloyd's of London, insurers of the armoured car company, have offered a reward of £200,000 for her capture.

Most fugitives on the FBI's wanted list are career criminals with a history of violent felonies. Heather is not one of them. Her crime was her first and, seemingly, her last. She had no criminal record when she took Loomis Armored for a king's ransom. In fact, her career, credit and school records were all above average. It appears that her crime was motivated by a love of ceramics and poetry, and a desire to escape from bad memories of friends dying from AIDS.

Heather Tallchief was born in Buffalo, New York, a gritty industrial town which shivers under sub-zero temperatures for six months of the year. Buffalo is typical of a hundred American industrial towns which have been left behind. Orders for its shuttered factories now go to the Far East and computer moguls would rather live somewhere more pleasant. Heather hated every moment she spent in the decaying town. Intelligent and sensitive, she suffered as the child of an allegedly abusive father. Almost every day she begged her mother to leave. In 1988 she got her wish. Ann Tallchief packed up everything and took her only daughter to San Francisco, travelling by Greyhound bus.

In California Heather flourished. She was already pretty. The soft San Francisco air quickly made her beautiful. She had ambitions to work in medicine, obtained a nursing qualification and in 1991 was hired by an AIDS hospice, the Kimberly Quality Care Center. 'She was a great worker,' says a senior Kimberly nurse. 'She had this amazing empathy with patients. Even the ones closest to death would be smiling when she left their bedside.'

In the fourteen months she was at the Kimberly twenty patients died, people who had become close friends. Her sadness and sense of despondency were kept well hidden, but in late 1992 she told a friend that her life was making no sense. She told her mother that she wanted more. 'She began to wonder why she couldn't be happy, have nice things,' says Ann Tallchief. 'She said she didn't want to worry about money, or people dying.'

At the same time, Heather, who had always been interested in ancient Mexican art, began to make a close study of Mayan ceramics. This was not unusual for her. Ann Tallchief says that, as a child, her daughter collected any beautiful objects she could afford. During her last six months at Kimberly Heather began making some unusual plans. In mid-1992 she began to lay the foundations for a multi-million-dollar rip-off, using a level of meticulous planning that still astounds the FBI. Her first move was to establish a series of fake identities. 'That's not hard, although it should be – it just takes patience,' says Joe Dushek. '*Soldier of Fortune* magazine is a good place to start.'

Heather thought so. She used the monthly crib sheet for wannabe mercenaries to contact 'passport collectors', men who sell virgin passports for defunct countries such as Yugoslavia. America is full of such subversives who want to help citizens avoid what they see as an overbearing government. Paladin Press in Colorado publishes six different guides to establishing fake IDs and sells more than 60,000 copies of the books each year. They have tapped into a deep-seated desire amongst many Americans to feel they could, if necessary, run and hide from their past lives. There are more missing people in America per 1000 citizens than in any other country in the world. The late-twentieth-century American likes to go walkabout, and in many cases they know how to do it with exceptional competence.

Heather Tallchief would travel to small towns and get driving licences in the names on her fake IDs. The driver's licence is the universally accepted ID card in the US and anyone who doesn't have one is persona non grata. By the beginning of 1993 Heather already had legitimate driver's licences in twelve different names. She then used her exceptional work record at the Kimberly Hospice to apply for jobs as an armoured car driver. It may have looked an odd choice to some of the cash carriers she contacted, but she had a disarming explanation. 'She told us she wanted a career in the security industry,' says Mike Tawney, of Loomis Armored, which Heather chose from three companies that offered her a job. 'She said she wanted to start at the bottom, to learn the industry inside out.'

'I'm not surprised Loomis were fooled,' says Dave Chipman, a bounty hunter who is following Heather's trail, attracted by the big price on her head. 'She had perfect credit and Kimberly gave her a glowing reference. She was way above the average for the security industry. It was only natural they'd give a sweet girl like her the keys to the safe.'

Heather had not arrived in Las Vegas on her own. 'She was travelling with this guy called Roberto,' says Ann Tallchief. 'It was bad enough when she quit nursing, but we had a bad row about Roberto.' That was because Roberto Solis is a convicted bank robber, who won early release from prison because he began writing ersatz Marquez-style poetry that won attention and praise from some prominent literary figures in San Francisco. Heather seems to have hand-picked Solis. She wrote to him while he was in jail and arranged an early meeting when he was released. 'I think she could have been using him for professional advice on bank robberies,' says Chipman. 'Witnesses who saw them together say there seems to have been nothing romantic about their relationship.'

In Las Vegas the couple lived in the Mark One apartments, a high-rise building full of gambling industry employees. The building stands stark off the main highway to Las Vegas airport, a glass monument to impermanent lives. It's a place where asking too many questions would probably lead to a beating. Heather and Roberto blended into the background. All that anybody remembers of their five months in residence is Heather swimming endless laps and Roberto writing on a laptop by the side of the pool whilst overhead a jet took off every few minutes. It was as if they chose the place to tell themselves they too were on the way to somewhere else.

Every day Heather drove millions of dollars around the Las Vegas strip. She began on the casino house runs, carrying new notes for the gambling tables. These easily traceable dollars proved to be no temptation. Heather was waiting for a promotion, to the cash machine runs where employees left the depot with a minimum of $6 million in used, unmarked bills. The runs were given only to the most trusted employees, and soon Heather was just that. 'I'm amazed at her patience,' says Agent Dushek. 'I can't imagine a man being the same way. She had plenty of opportunities to pull the job, but she wanted the perfect moment.'

Loomis's management were extremely pleased with their new employee. In her second week Heather took a firing-range test to qualify for a side-arm, and achieved record scores. Her colleagues say that they were charmed by her sense of humour, and impressed by her dedication to the job. Anyone who knew her in San Francisco would have been hard-pressed to recognize her in her new job. Though blessed with 20/20 vision, Heather wore what looked like thick glasses whenever she was in her Loomis uniform. She also wore her hair pulled back tightly and tied with a bow.

Heather's two closest colleagues were Steve Marshall and Scott Stewart, guards who rode with her in the armoured truck and handled all deliveries. They both liked Heather, who made a considerable effort to be nice to them. She asked about their homes and families; she helped them to keep track of anniversaries and birthdays. Before six months had passed, Heather had won their trust. This was crucial to her plan. It seems that she was determined not to injure anybody when she pulled off her robbery. That meant winning Marshall's and Stewart's confidence, to the extent that they would allow her to drive the truck without them if they were making deliveries to casinos where the parking was bad.

As 1993 progressed Heather began applying for credit cards in the names of her new driving licences. She also took flying lessons, and made her first solo flight in a Cessna in August 1993. She applied for places at law-enforcement colleges, which increased the trust placed in her by Loomis. It was as if she had a mantra: be patient, be perfect.

In September Heather was rewarded when Loomis promoted her, Stewart and Marshall to the cash machine runs. As soon as her promotion was through, Heather chose 1 October 1993 as 'action day' for her plan. She had obtained detailed lists of convention schedules and knew the check-out times for all the big hotels. It is when the casinos 'change over' between one convention and another that the traffic is at its heaviest. The lobbies fill with sweating conventioneers working off last night's hangovers and trying to decide what they will tell the wife about some of the more dubious entries on their credit cards. Parking at some hotels, such as Circus-Circus and MGM Grand, becomes impossible. The first of October was one of the biggest change-over days in 1993. Heather knew it was the perfect day to implement her plan.

Two weeks before, in the second week of September, Heather, disguised as a nurse, pushed Roberto, disguised as an ageing, wealthy gambler, on to a chartered Lear jet at Las Vegas airport. She was establishing a pattern that would remove suspicion after the robbery. On 24 September Heather booked the same jet for a flight at midday on 1 October. At around the same time, she used another alias and took a lease on a garage under a fake business name, 'Reinforced Steel', and announced that her operation would be building and repairing armoured cars. Heather had business cards for the company made in the names of Nicole Reger and Joseph Panura. On 18 September, using the name Myra Calandra, Heather called an apartment building in Denver that specializes in furnished rentals for corporations. She reserved a small unit for use from 25 September. On 28 September she wrote a letter to her mother, regretting that they had become estranged. It was left in the

Las Vegas apartment. Heather wrote that it was doubtful she would ever see her mother again, but told her mother 'not to fret' for 'we have never been true friends'.

It's strange that Heather attached such finality to the note in which she broke with her mother. She must have known Loomis would unleash the dogs of hell to track her down and would be happy to take her, dead or alive. Yet there seems to have been something Heather had got from Vegas, with its pounding heat and neon impermanence – a sense of her own immortality, maybe; or a controlled fatalism, a belief, derived from her Cheyenne ancestors, that death only matters if it is met with a cowardly face.

On 1 October, Heather left the Loomis depot with more than $6 million. By the time she arrived at the rear of the Circus–Circus Casino, at 9.20 a.m., there was $4.5 million left. Stewart and Marshall were due to deliver $400,000 to five ATMs inside, which Heather knew would take them at least forty-five minutes. There was no parking. The two men readily agreed to let Heather meet them at the front of the hotel at 10.15 a.m. As they went inside Heather drove away, heading for Reinforced Steel, not the front of the casino. From debris found at the Reinforced Steel garage, it is clear that Heather had also planned how to get $4.1 million out of Las Vegas without carrying twenty suitcases. Packing materials and blank waybills show that Heather and Solis packed the cash into boxes and had the money shipped to Denver as machine parts.

At precisely 11.20 a.m. Heather, using a fake nurse's ID, helped Roberto out of a rented car at Las Vegas airport. She settled him into a wheelchair and pushed him to the private charter area where, twelve minutes later, their plane pulled away and took up position on the runway. As her plane climbed towards 35,000 feet, staff at Loomis were alerting the Las Vegas Police Department with a panicky report, claiming that Heather had been abducted. 'We thought for sure we'd find her body out in the desert,' says Sergeant Duis, of the LVPD. 'Maybe with the burnt-out truck alongside.' He adds, with hindsight, 'I hope there aren't too many like her out there – we rely on our criminals to be dumb.'

It was two weeks before the owner of the garage leased to Reinforced Steel became suspicious and forced open the doors. There he found the Loomis Truck, $3,000 in single-dollar bills, a pair of thick glasses, packing material and telephone numbers for businesses in Miami, the Bahamas and the Cayman Islands. There was also information about yacht charters out of San Diego and Acapulco. It was another week before the FBI located the apartment building in Denver. Since then they have had no reliable sightings of Heather. 'She seems to have been a unique character,' says Loomis's Mike Tawney. 'When somebody is such a master of disguise I'm doubtful she'll ever be caught.'

The FBI found one other intriguing piece of evidence at Heather Tallchief's Las Vegas apartment: there was a stack of art magazines. Many of them contained articles on Mayan art, but those pages had been cut out. 'We think she and Solis may be posing as art dealers,' says Dushek. 'We have some indications that recently they travelled to Europe. They could even be in England.'

Heather's crime was an all-American story for the information age. She used sources available in new venues like the World Wide Web to outfox slow-witted authorities. She proved that any American with patience and intelligence has a good chance of pulling off the perfect crime. To her sister Elaine, Heather is a hero.

Elaine came down to Manhattan for a meeting with me in spring 1998. We wanted a venue where we could talk without being overheard by the FBI, who have the Tallchief family's phones tapped. Elaine is just seventeen and remembers her sister as an inspiration.

'She came home once before she disappeared,' says Elaine. We are in Nell's, a New York nightclub where a man of my age can take Elaine and her seventeen-year-old friend without arousing suspicion. In fact, there are half a dozen tables nearby with trios similar to ours, except the other guys look like they have the money to keep their nubile chums interested well into their late twenties. Elaine has noticed the set up and begins to laugh. 'Heather would have loved this place,' she says. 'It would have appealed to her dark side.'

Elaine thinks about Heather every day. On that last visit Heather painted Elaine's room. 'It's like a Mondrian,' she says. 'All these cool lines and squares. She could have been an artist.' Elaine has been on Oprah, Gerry Springer and the Sally Jessy Raphael Show and has enjoyed every moment of the fame purchased by her sister's notoriety. It doesn't bother her that Heather's face is not on the front of glossy magazines but on FBI mug shots in every US Post Office. Elaine, like most Americans, regards fame as a valuable coin however it is minted.

We move on from Nell's. Elaine wants to go to an African-American club. Although she's a Cheyenne like her sister, Elaine says she doesn't know many other tribal members in Buffalo. 'So I hang with the blacks. I call myself a red nigger,' she says. 'It's where I feel most comfortable, hanging with another minority. I'm going to move to New York and be with my bitches.'

The next day Elaine and her pal Shona meet me in the Bronx, to get their hair fat for the weekend. Carmen Gazillo has styled hair in the Bronx for twenty-three years. She's a big-hearted blonde who has modelled lingerie and now tries to keep her teenage clientele out of trouble. It's not easy. The Bronx retains its rough streets, whatever New York's mayor might do with Disney on 42nd Street. Susan Mustick, Jeanine Bruno and Brianne Murillo are all Tremont Avenue Bitches (TABs). Elaine Tallchief and Shona are honorary members. They say it's not really a gang. 'We all hang out together, look after each other, so that's what some others call us,' says Elaine, relaxing in Carmen's salon, which looks like it hasn't changed much since Elvis Presley first sang 'Jailhouse Rock'.

The TAB girls have their own language. They 'sweat' over a

boy who takes their fancy, especially if he has a 'fly ride' (smart car) and looks 'fat' (stylishly dressed). They don't like people who are always 'gibbing' (making up stories). To them they will say 'talk to the hand' (I'm not listening to you) or 'see ya' (I'm never listening to you again). Their hairstyles are part of their language, a symbol of who they are. This year spiral perms are the big thing, a collection of tall tight curls around the top of the head, constructed using a mass of curlers. The perms are hard to maintain so this spring the Bronx TABs have been at Carmen's salon once a week, kicking their sneakers against the hairdresser's worn linoleum floor and chatting about boyfriends. Bronx girl gangs do not shave their heads or have gang symbols carved into short hair like their LA equivalents. They prefer a more subtle look. Bronx gangs say you don't need an outward sign of aggression when everybody carries a gun. 'That's what's scary,' says Brianne. 'These days, any fight that starts is to the death, because so many people carry a piece.'

The TABs recently lost a good friend, beaten to death during a St Patrick's Day Parade. He was allegedly the victim of inter-gang violence. As Carmen teases Susan Mustick's hair ready for a spiral perm, Susan expresses her biggest worry: 'I just don't want anybody else I know to die. We're too young to be thinking about our friends dying.'

'These are real nice girls, good girls,' says Carmen who did hair for the TABs when they had their Sweet Sixteens with long white dresses and is now preparing to style them for their Proms. 'They would never look for trouble but these days it could easily find them.' The TABs giggle at the thought. It's Thursday and the big night for going out to sweat boys and look for somebody with a fly ride and a fat sound system. 'Mostly we just hang on the streets, especially now the weather is warm,' says Brianne. 'That's where anything can happen – and usually does.'

Heather Tallchief is a role model for all the TABs. They think she is about as fly as they come, and Heather's crime has given Elaine honorary TABs leadership. From the way they talk it's apparent their love of Heather fills a deep hole inside every one of them. Each TAB comes from a single parent home – in all but one instance that means a single mother. More than three-quarters of the group have seen their mother beaten by their father or a subsequent boyfriend. The TAB life was probably precisely what Heather was trying to escape. Elaine agrees, and says if Heather is ever caught she won't allow herself to be taken alive.

'Where do you think she is?' I ask.

'Over the Rainbow,' says Elaine. 'She done blown right out of here.'

Ed Morton doesn't share Elaine's view. He's a private investigator who began an obsession with Heather when he saw her wanted poster on an FBI web site. I needed to meet him if only to see his house.

At the end of a 120-foot steel-ribbed tunnel, two suburban lanterns and a 'Home Sweet Home' mat greet visitors to the Mortons' home, a split-level fashioned out of a decommissioned Atlas Atom Bomb missile silo. Yellow marigolds brighten the underground kitchen, built over the former occupants' 'ready room', where they waited for the signal to launch a nuclear powered armageddon. To one side is a big farm table full of computers. There, hidden from natural light, Morton uses the web to hunt fugitives. He has a thousand eyes on the Internet looking for Heather. She has become as much a subject for speculation amongst Morton and his web-nut friends as items like UFOs and Kennedy's assassination. A wood stove adds cosiness to the nearby living room, converted from a launch control unit where Air Force technicians raised and fuelled a nuclear-tipped rocket during the Cuban missile crisis of 1962.

'We love the concept of swords to ploughshares – we hope it will catch on,' says Morton, who moved into the silo with his family last year, when he opened his investigation business after eighteen years in the CIA. He had been a 'remote viewer', hired specifically to try to harness clairvoyance in covert operations.

The CIA spent $80 million on the project before defence cuts left the clairvoyant spooks washed up and without cash.

Morton has become so enamoured of underground life that he has taken out options on the purchase of three more of the nine abandoned Atlas silos that dot the rolling cow pastures of eastern Kansas. Selling them will pay his bills until he gets the bounty for catching Heather. In his new role as silo salesman, Morton now fields calls from people interested in buying these 'sleepers' for post-cold-war uses: as a soundproof recording studio, perhaps, or as a secure vault for bank records, a dark place to raise gourmet snails or mushrooms, or a humidity-controlled cellar for wine.

To the casual observer, the 1990s would appear to be a boom time for recycling nuclear silos: the number of nuclear warheads deployed by the United States has dropped to about 9000 today, from a peak of 24,000 a decade ago, according to a study published in the November issue of *The Bulletin* of the Atomic Scientists Association. Since 1992 nuclear weapons have been completely removed from Kansas and eight other states: Alaska, Arkansas, Florida, Hawaii, Maine, Michigan, New Jersey and New York. With the north-east now entirely free of nuclear weapons, warheads remain only in seventeen states, all in the south and the west.

The United States Air Force simply abandoned scores of Atlas-E, Atlas-F and Titan I silos during the mid-1960s, when technological advances made them obsolete. Atlas and Titan silos were then sold, for just $1 apiece, to school districts, farmers and salvage companies. In Holton, thirty miles north of Morton's home and his Tallchief hunt centre, 150 children now take classes in a decommissioned Atlas silo, owned by the Jackson Heights School District. 'Atlas silos are like dinosaurs – archaeological remains of the nuclear age,' said Robert S. Norris, co-author with William M. Arkin of an authoritative nuclear warhead survey published in *The Bulletin*.

The Mortons have created an atmosphere in their silo that is downright cosy despite a 47-ton garage door – formerly the door to the silo's missile bay — that can be opened only with a hand crank. 'A twentieth-century castle,' chortled Morton, noting that he paid $40,000 to a salvage company in 1996 for an installation that cost American taxpayers $4 million in 1959. 'I am amazed that a private citizen of my means could own a property like this.'

Three pink bicycles belonging to his two daughters Susannah and Ashley are parked casually, along with a lawn mower, beside a $2 million tank that once held liquid oxygen fuel for the intercontinental ballistic missile. And in the huge concrete bay that once held a state-of-the-art rocket, there is now a clutter of wooden propellers, fibreglass cockpits and aluminium wings for the ultralight airplanes Morton makes in his spare time. Above ground, the 1200-foot runway built to ferry in emergency supplies in the event of a nuclear war is now used by pilots who test-fly Morton's $15,000 ultralights.

The quarters for the underground crew, at the end of the steel-reinforced tunnel, were so large that the private investigator needed only a third of the space to create his split-level, with four bedrooms and two baths. A television aerial runs up to an old above-ground military communications antenna. 'The keys are imagination and creativity,' says Ed, who explains that the missile complex flooded with rainwater after abandonment in 1965 and says he first explored it in 1984 with a flashlight and a canoe. Pumped out and dry today, the living room sports trappings that would make Dr Strangelove wince. Above a piano, a decorative plaque reads: 'Love Everyone Unconditionally.'

Morton believes he has just the place from which to track America's most famous female fugitive. 'I was stunned when I first saw Heather's picture on the Internet,' he says. He has just taken a pair of beers from a fridge behind the door of what was once a secret chamber for missile crews to hide if the bombs began to fall. 'She was so beautiful. I couldn't imagine her doing any wrong. I guess I kind of fell in love. Then I learnt she had a half-million-dollar price on her head. I could convert a lot of 'A' bomb silos with that.'

With his battery of computers, Morton e-mails former and present CIA and FBI staff with requests for information on Heather. Despite America's Freedom of Information Act, both these agencies keep most of the truth from the public, according to Morton, but he has an increasingly bad feeling about Heather.

'I keep seeing her skull, in the desert,' he says, going into his remote viewer mode. 'I think Roberto killed her. I can't help what I see.' Shadows are dancing along Morton's walls, beneath ground where Native Americans once hunted buffalo herds a million strong, in a tube that previously held a weapon which could have wiped out millions of Soviets. And it is here that Morton thinks he can see the truth.

7. The Town that has Banned Sex

I saw Charlie again in the spring. He was wearing dark glasses and standing on Park Avenue selling pencils. I put $20 in his tin and whispered to him that I was going far away. I said I was going to the town that has banned sex. He was still laughing when I lost sight of him.

In Emmett, Idaho, Gem County Sheriff Mark John stands tall for law and order. If any fornicators are brought to his attention he'll put them right where he thinks they belong — in the county jail.

Chewing on a big hamburger at midday in the Cranberry Cup, the sheriff spelt out his attitude to sex outside wedlock: 'Moses gave us the laws and one of those was "Thou shalt not fornicate." It's that simple.' He puts the hamburger down and points a beefy finger at the restaurant where Emmett residents are working on their cholesterol levels. 'I'm sure some of these folks are fornicators. If I get evidence of that, they go to the lock-up, whoever they are.'

In the Gem County Jail two young men are waiting for trial.

Their offence is fornication, illegal in Idaho since 1921, and each one could face a five-year jail sentence if found guilty. Both men have teenage girlfriends who have given birth – in Emmett that's irreproachable proof of a criminal act. 'I should be at home, fending for my baby,' says prisoner John Wagnon. 'I can't teach him right from wrong sitting in this cell.'

I know there are fornicators in Idaho because I'd met them the night before in the Tin Bail pub. Emmett is a two stoplight town but one of them doesn't work. It's at the end of a street that once led to a railway station, now closed. It's a town in 'dee-cline' as the residents keep telling me.

In the Tin Bail there are two self-confessed fornicators at the bar. Married to other people, they drunkenly reveal their felonious behaviour to the whole room, which is unimpressed. They've heard the same story a thousand times.

Behind the bar two women dispense Boilermakers at $2 each. A shot of whisky and a bottle of Budweiser, the combination is popular and explains why cowboys get the blues. Emmett has been cowboy country for more than two hundred years. At the bar is a descendant of an original cattle wrangler. Twenty-one-year-old Billy Ray Tomb is dressed all in white leather with one exception: the ten-gallon hat on his head is jet black. The overall effect makes the skinny young man look like a spent match but Billy has something to prove. Tonight is Karaoke night and whilst most of the town's residents sleep, his loyal audience of seven will watch his every move. The group consists of our two adulterers, the two barmaids, Billy Ray, his girlfriend Bella Blue, Rex Lanbay, who is high on Boilermakers, and a guy called Baseboard, who does not open his eyes for two hours.

Billy Ray's toughest competition comes from Suzy, one of the barmaids. As she cracks open a beer bottle with what I think is her bare hands, I wonder if the 5′ 2″ woman is 250lb or 300lb. I bet myself 275lb but doubt I'll get the courage to ask her which large number is right. Suzy has a voice full of glass and hot wax. She barks orders and laughs between almost every syllable. It's clear that everybody in the Tin Bail is scared to death of her.

Billy Ray gets up first and sings 'Roxanne'. In his voice there are dozens of dreams, some broken, some unrealized, but none realistic. His eyes shine, as though what he sees in the bleak bar-room are hundreds of glamorous guests all decked out in tuxedos. As he reaches for high notes he strains every sinew, reaching down into some deep store of self-belief that should have been exhausted by Emmett years ago.

The end of Billy Ray's song is greeted by raucous applause from everybody but Baseboard. Then it's Suzy's turn. Using her body as a giant sound box, Suzy blows Billy Ray away. Her voice is deep and sensual and her version of 'My Way' is so much better than Frank Sinatra or Sid Vicious. When she finishes, the six conscious members of the audience stand to applaud. I ask her to sing 'Kung Fu Fighting' as an encore, she obliges – complete with kicks and chops in the right places. The room shakes as if a freight train is running by outside.

Back at the bar I offered her a drink as reward. She requests a Blow Job. Her colleague goes to work loading six different measures of spirits into a large shot glass. After a quick stir she tops off the drink with an inch-thick layer of whipped cream. 'Watch this,' says Susy. With the glass on the bar she put her hands behind her back and lowers her mouth over the foaming concoction. Picking the glass up with her lips she throws her head back and when she comes back upright the Blow Job is gone. 'That was fun,' she says. 'But then there's not much else to do around here, except sex. That's how my brother John ended up in jail.'

For seventy-five years the Idaho fornication law has lain dormant. In 1996 it was revived after seventeen-year-old Amanda Smisek became pregnant. In New York her pregnancy would not have raised an eyebrow. In Emmett it caused a moral earthquake. The small town has been overwhelmed with teenage pregnancies. More than 15% of its teenage women are pregnant, about twice the national average. Emmett's welfare resources are stretched to the limit. When Smisek came looking for assistance to raise her child she was given handcuffs to wear instead. Teenagers in Idaho are not permitted to have sex until they are over eighteen. Amanda was charged with fornication, her boyfriend with statutory rape

'We need the fornication law,' says Sheriff John, who occasionally still chases cattle rustlers on a thoroughbred stallion. 'As a town we do not believe in our daughters openly having sex before they are married. We do have too many teenagers with babies who depend on the state for money, but in my mind that's not the main point. This is strictly a moral stand. We have decided to live by our principles.'

Deanna Patnaude is sixteen and she has a five-month-old baby girl called Dakota. The police have an arrest warrant out for her twenty-one-year-old boyfriend, but he has fled from Idaho and may be in California. The Emmett prosecutor has not yet decided if Deanna will face trial. 'The town gossips found out I was pregnant and they told the cops,' she says, bumping Dakota from knee to knee with sweet efficiency. 'They set a trap for me. I didn't know you had to be eighteen to have sex, I though it was sixteen like the rest of the US and I certainly didn't know you had to be married.'

Deanna first got pregnant just after her fourteenth birthday. 'I think the age when you first have sex should be based on your readiness, not on the law,' she says with a perky tone that would have Sheriff John choking with rage. 'This is a very conservative area. There is no sex education in the schools but we can all watch soap operas that glorify fornication.'

Local teenagers say they all know friends who are still having sex, despite the new hostile climate. Like Deanna, many of the young women are not always concerned about contraception. 'We didn't use anything because my boyfriend wasn't cheating on me and he wasn't somebody who slept around. I was more worried about AIDS than pregnancy. Without more sex education in the schools, how are kids supposed to know that it's illegal to have sex until you are over eighteen and married?'

Deanna says she became a fornicator because of peer pressure. 'Seeing all those fancy relationships on the soap operas made me feel sexy and it made me feel you couldn't be cool without sex in your life.' After her arrest she was forced to make a full statement about exactly how she had got pregnant. She says she thinks that was a deliberate attempt to humiliate her for doing something that is commonplace in the rest of America.

Sheriff Mark John has set himself up as the moral equivalent of King Canute. He says that he can't let people get away with fornication just because they can see it on TV every day. 'The parents have to take a stand or I will lock up their children,' he says. 'I caught two teenagers fornicating in their car over by the railroad yards. They were buck naked in a Chevy truck. I could have charged her, but instead I decided to let the family talk it through. I hauled the girl back to her mother and she screamed at me – for interfering in her daughter's life. With that kind of nonsense going on in families the law has to take a stand where the parents won't.'.

The sheriff has the full backing of the courts and the local prosecutor, Doug Varie. 'The law has it in black and white,' says Varie, picking up a copy of the Idaho state statutes, as if it were a document that really meant something to panting adolescents who can watch soft porn on afternoon soap operas any time they please. I tell Varie this. I can see he is wondering for a second if there's something he can arrest me for, then seems to decide he has his hands full enough with disgusting natural impulses. 'It says "...any unmarried person who shall have sex with an unmarried person of the opposite sex shall be found guilty of fornication". That's why we have half a dozen people waiting for trials. They broke the law.'

'What kind of message would we send if we tolerated sex between children?' wonders Sheriff John, even though he lives in a part of the US where hearing that kids are spending their days fucking, has to be a relief. They could be oiling Kalashnikovs instead, ready to turn their schoolyard into a battleground. 'We would be saying: "we condone your promiscuousness, and if you get pregnant and you're fourteen years old, we the citizens will pay for your mistakes." That's the wrong message to send.'

Emmett sits amongst rolling hills thirty miles from Boise, Idaho. Its 4000 residents are mostly working class and depend on agriculture or logging. By 9 p.m. the town's two restaurants are closed, and only a battered fifties drive-in diner throws a welcome light across the dusty highway. Apart from the Tin Bail there are two other bars where men drink deep so they won't remember what they've been trying to forget. Drug dealers can be found in dark corners selling homemade methamphetamine, known locally as 'crank'. There is nothing for teenagers to do except take a cruise, and that usually ends in sex.

'You cruise Main Street in a car,' says Deanna, beginning an explanation of how she lost her virginity. 'You can cruise with your girlfriends but it's much better with a boy.' That's how she met Steve, her first lover. 'The guys with the low riding trucks and the big sound systems get the most attention. They use their low-riders as girl catchers – I was caught.' She laughs and tickles her daughter Dakota. She's not shy about sex. She may be a small-town girl but the TV soaps have given her all the education she needs. 'I wanted to get pregnant so I was happy when we first did it. We didn't talk much about enjoying the sex. It's hard to be too creative in a pick-up truck.'

'Deanna Patnaude's attitude is irresponsible,' says Sheriff John. 'She may want children but we have an obligation to say that's not possible until the person is of legal age. I'm not going to walk door-to-door looking for offenders, but in every case where there is proof of minors fornicating I will definitely prosecute, you can count on that. Everyone who is found guilty will be punished and that will include compulsory classes. They will be taught how to become better citizens.'

Michael Hopkins, Dakota's father, is outraged by the Idaho law. 'I am happy to pay back the state for the cost of Deanna's pregnancy but what if I'm convicted?' he asks. 'I'm not supposed to have any contact with the victim if that happens and I would be banned from many places where kids congregate – restaurants, parks, the zoo. It's hard to see how that would allow me to be any kind of father.' That ban would result from one element of Idaho's fornication law: if the girl in the illegal relationship is less than sixteen years old, the male partner is also charged with lewd and lascivious behaviour.

'We find somebody guilty of that if they touch, fondle or caress somebody less than sixteen years old for sexual gratification,' says Sheriff John. I'm beginning to think he talks about sex too much – as if he had something he can't get off his mind, especially when he makes his next statement with his hand stroking the two guns he carries on each hip. 'Lewd and lascivious behaviour can mean life imprisonment. Guys who are found guilty usually spend at least three years in jail. We believe in trying to protect our children's innocence.'

Seventeen-year-old Rhonda Bushong's boyfriend John Wagnon is charged with lewd and lascivious behaviour. He's already been found guilty of fornication because the couple had a baby in May. Soon after that conviction in July, John was arrested again. 'A girl called Stephanie wanted him to leave me for her but he wouldn't, so she went to the police and claimed they had been having sex,' says Rhonda mournfully. 'John was arrested the next day.' Their child Sean required an operation on his skull last month but John could only hear progress reports over the telephone at the county jail.

Now Rhonda and her father Paul pore over legal documents in their modest home, trying to build a defence for John. There's an uneasy truce between father and daughter enforced by the fact that neither knows who is the most powerful partner in the relationship. The Bushongs' house is full of stuff that may have been state of the art when computers were the size of a transit van. The cigarettes that continually feed Paul Bushong's anxieties have given everything the colour of somebody suffering from jaundice. There are a million homes like this in America, built in the fifties when the country had supreme self-confidence. They survive as mocking reminders that progress is never a straight upward line. America is always changing, its tides shifting, and somebody is always being left behind – their homes, like the Bushongs', left to rot like boats in a harbour that's all dried out.

'When I found out I was pregnant we could have got an abortion and nobody would have known and John would still be free,' says Rhonda, lighting a cigarette from a gas ring on a cooker so old that it looks like Edison made it just before he got busy with lightbulbs. 'It never crossed our minds to kill our baby. We wanted to get married.' In fact, they tried but until a female is over eighteen she cannot marry in Idaho without permission from a judge. That permission was denied because Rhonda's intended spouse had a prior conviction – for fornication.

'It's ridiculous,' says Rhonda's father. 'They could have been wed by now. I'm not saying their marriage would have been easy but the baby would have had both his parents.' The Idaho law classifies fornication as a sex crime, and those who are found guilty must register as sex offenders. That's one reason Rhonda and John want to fight the new charges against him. A guilty conviction would make it nearly impossible for them to live a normal life when John finally gets out of prison. 'His activities with Sean would be very limited and he would have to attend regular therapy sessions. John is not some pervert. We were just two young people who became sexually involved. Millions of Americans do the same thing every day.'

Rhonda's father lost his wife to cancer and found out his daughter was pregnant whilst visiting her grave. 'I felt so alone,' he says, wiping a tear from his eye as he lights another cigarette. 'I was angry with Rhonda for having sex but I couldn't blame her too much. All the girls she runs around with boast about having sex all the time. Still, you wonder where you've gone wrong.'

Rhonda was taking drugs when she met John, who had a bad crank habit, although he says he's now clean. Both blame their bout with amphetamines on boredom with Emmett, the uncertain economic prospects and a fear that life is passing them by. Sheriff John has no time for that. 'I'm so sick of criminals claiming they are the victims,' he says. 'All these kids knew they had a choice and they could have kept their clothes on.'

'It's not that simple,' says Carol Patnaude, Deanna's mother. 'They say they are trying to protect children by stopping teenage sex, but Dee has not been a child since she was nine when her father died. This law was passed in 1921 and you can bet they didn't have Madonna singing about sex back then. It's so much more difficult to be a parent now than it was in the fifties. Deanna has been raised by MTV and talk-show stars – Madonna is a more important influence than I can ever be.'

If Sheriff John's bold stand was supposed to stop sex out of wedlock, it hasn't. Sarah Van Ocker is living proof. She got pregnant ten weeks after the first fornication trial and at first she wasn't even sure who the father was. Sixteen-year-old Sarah had two boyfriends and at one point had permission from both to see the other man. 'I didn't mean to get pregnant,' she says, drinking a soda at the Country Kitchen Café, owned by her mum and dad. 'The condom slipped off.'

The Van Ocker greasy spoon retains the original décor from the 1950s. The booth seats are the colour of day-old coffee grounds. The tables have Formica cracked into a mosaic from four decades of cowboy fry-ups. There's grease on the ceiling that's thick enough to hide a stack of Bibles. Behind the counter, one of the few black males in Emmett is bending over a bucket of potatoes, preparing them for a mashing machine that gleams with the chrome self-confidence of America's first industrial age, when people drove cars that did six miles to the five-cent gallon.

Sarah's values are more contemporary. 'People will have sex if they want. The cops should spend more time chasing drug dealers. It doesn't help to punish teens for having sex. The more we get punished the more we rebel.' Sarah's boyfriend

Jeff is also in the county jail and faces a trial in December. Her parents were angry when they found out she was pregnant, but have since decided to support her completely. 'Both men want to marry Sarah,' says Frank Van Ocker as he fries bacon and eggs. 'That should forgive the sin of fornication, at least in the court's eyes. Leave the rest to God Almighty.'

Sarah is a frail-looking girl with almost transparent skin. She says she is scared at the prospect of marriage. 'I may decide to raise my child alone. My parents will support me. I have a loving family. Just because I'm having a kid doesn't mean I can't fulfil my dreams.' A low-rider races past the diner, stereo system pumping a bass line right through the cheap wooden seats. Sarah looks up wistfully, a gleam in her eye as she recognizes the driver. 'That's Billy, he's cool. I know he's been fornicating.' She laughs and takes her mother's hand. 'It's so unfair, they could send Jeff to prison for five years.'

'She already knew it was wrong to get pregnant,' says Frank. 'We didn't need the court butting in and telling us. Like any parents we wanted our daughter to get through college before she started a family but accidents happen. When they do you support the person, you don't punish them.' Susan Van Ocker believes the town's determination to enforce the law will have some undesirable consequences. 'It means that any girl who gets pregnant will have to have an abortion, because she knows if she applies for help or welfare she will be prosecuted. If Sheriff John wants to prosecute people for fornicating he can go to any bar in town and arrest thirty adults right now.'

Sheriff John accepts the law has been applied selectively but he has no qualms about that. 'With moral issues you have to start when people are young, when you can nip the worm in the bud.' The Sheriff is no hypocrite. Whilst rumours persist that Prosecutor Doug Varie got his wife pregnant before they were married, Sheriff John married his wife twenty-eight years ago and their two sons were born in holy matrimony. At his 500-acre ranch in the hills above Emmett, the Sheriff takes in teenage foster children and uses the tough life on the range to teach them values. 'Most of these kids would end up in jail,' he says, saddling a horse for Chad, the latest of sixty teenagers to live with the Johns. 'The fornication law ain't easy for some folks to swallow but it will make plenty of teenagers clean up their lives.'

The town stands firm behind their sheriff. In supermarkets and diners worried parents say that almost everything else their kids have contact with tells them to have sex, that virginity is uncool. A group of twelve teenagers at the De-Ann Diner all said they would wait until they were married to have sex. 'I wouldn't respect a boy who wanted me to have sex out of wedlock,' says Jennie Lynch, a corn-fed 15-year-old with the looks of a young fashion model. Her friend Jill Kirkpatrick, sixteen, agrees. 'If a guy pushes too hard for that I just dump him.'

As the hot sun builds to a 100° heat in the Idaho afternoon, Rhonda Bushong and Deanna Patnaude find some shade to play with their babies. 'Around here girls might say they won't do it but sex is what all the boys want, it's more natural than a wheat field,' says Deanna. 'I am not neglecting my child but the law is forcing Dakota's father to abandon her. That's a bigger sin than fornication.' The babies gurgle as a hot breeze stirs the grass. 'This law was from 1921. People were not real civilized back then. What they're doing here is taking us back to the Dark Ages.'

In the county jail there are four thick steel doors between the courthouse and the cells. In one, a tiny room with steel bunks, John Wagnon slouches beneath his bright orange overalls. On the back black letters spell out 'Gem County Jail'. He belongs to the system now, he's a fornicator. Steel bars separate him from his son and he faces a life of uncertainty. 'I'm sorry if I broke the law,' says John, who came to Emmett from North Carolina. 'This don't help, though. If I'm convicted I won't be able to hold my baby until he's four. How does it help him to have a daddy in jail?'

Sheriff John says he can't be swayed by that. For him a moral stance is not negotiable. Before he's finished many more fathers may see their children grow from the wrong side of prison bars. That's how it is in America, there are places where you can end up in prison for doing something that in another state you could do on a stage for money. There are five states with tougher laws against fornication than Idaho. There are thirteen states where fornication is a felony, punishable by between ten and twenty years in jail. The American Automobile Association should mark its maps with a new set of symbols, just so unwed couples with imaginative sex lives can stay out of trouble.

8. Snakeskin Rhapsody

There was a primeval storm blowing off the Appalachian mountains as I drove into Jolo, West Virginia. Wind-driven rain had fought me for five hours and now it was rallying for a final assault, hoping to sweep my car straight off the desolate hillside. This remote part of the south is still limping into the twentieth century. In rural West Virginia, instead of a Seven-Eleven at every intersection, there's a broken street-light which looks like it might recently have been used for a lynching, and the remnants of a mining village. The people are not friendly In the local dialect the words for 'stranger' and 'enemy' are probably the same.

The road ahead took a sudden turn to the left and as I slithered around the corner my headlamps illuminated a man standing stationary in the middle of the highway. I nailed the brake pedal to the floor and prepared for impact. The car shot through a deep puddle that sent a drenching gush of water over my windshield, reducing visibility to zero. There followed a bump and the car seemed to skip in the air. I began imagining the dead man who must now lie beneath my rear wheels and the probably fatal beating I faced from his relatives. Before I could get any further with that thought a grinning face abruptly appeared at the side window and my stomach jumped high enough to make a hostile takeover of my heart.

The road guy wasn't dead after all, although bearing in mind his maniacal appearance I began to wish he was, fearing that soon *I* might be, if I ever let him get me out of the car. He reached inside a jacket pocket and I expected his hand to come back out with a gun, which would then be waved merrily in my direction. Instead, the hand reappeared with a Jew's-harp which Road Guy began to play, rain bouncing off his nose.

It turns out that Road Guy, Bert Sloan, is largely harmless. He just likes to stand out in the rain. He chooses the middle of the road because that way he gets the full force of the deluge. On the pavement there are too many trees and buildings that offer undesirable shelter. Once you accept Bert's premise it seems completely rational to stand in the way of traffic. A lot of stuff in the Appalachians follows the same back-to-front, sliding-fast-out-of-the-rear-end-of-the-universe kinda logic.

Sloan is a short man and thin. His family say that he suffered a sunstroke in his mid-twenties and never regained his full mental health. Like many Appalachian men, Sloan is an aspiring musician. Although hampered by his illness, Sloan still carries several Jew's-harps, which he made himself from old bed springs. In the summer, when the rains are gone, Bert often takes long hikes on country roads, walking until he passes out. Sometimes the local police pick him up and take him to jail, where they give him food and wait for his Uncle Wayne to come get him, as long as it's not a Sunday. That's when Wayne has to be in his pulpit and he must not be disturbed.

It was Wayne I had come to see. Anywhere else in America it would be surprising to be visiting one man and run into a relative of his as well. In Appalachia it's commonplace. The towns are not much larger than an average-sized Sainsbury's and nobody ever leaves, except in handcuffs or a coffin, sometimes both. A man's brother often looks like his father because they're the same guy. Inbreeding isn't a dirty hidden secret. It's practised openly. After all, what kind of animal has sex with strangers?

Uncle Wayne Shell is married to his cousin Elvira and he's the minister at the Church of Jesus With Following Signs. Elvira's mother is married to Wayne's older brother which means Wayne's wife is also his niece. Wayne has no problem with all this, but then a little mild incest is nothing when you regularly allow venomous rattlesnakes to crawl all over your body. That's the price Wayne pays to lead the Church of Jesus WFS. The congregation are all snake handlers. They draw their beliefs from scripture, specifically Mark, Chapter 16, verse 18: 'They shall take up serpents; and if they drink any deadly thing, it shall not hurt them; they shall lay hands on the sick and they shall recover.'

In Wayne's modest home there's not much evidence that his faith healing has been successful. He prepares for his Sunday service in a room that has been built from a type of corkboard that wasn't top quality when it was manufactured four decades ago. On the walls are photographs of dead relatives in their coffins. These monochrome mementos from recent wakes would give the room an air of a funeral parlour were it not for the garish bedspreads and the leather sofas, which are actually the back seats of old cars that probably belonged to the young-looking dead guys in the photographs. That's what they mean by recycling in West Virginia.

'The Lord is with us tonight,' Wayne says in a southern accent which bears about as much resemblance to Standard English as rural Hindustani. 'I feel the Holy Spirit.' I feel like running, my usual reaction when six-foot-long rattlesnakes start shaking their tails a few feet from my vulnerable flesh. The Reverend Wayne has no such concerns. So long as he believes and is without sin he knows the snakes will not bite him. He says this even though he has survived eight bites in twelve years as a snake preacher. His sister Melinda was not so lucky.

'Melinda was twenty-eight years old,' Wayne tells me, buckling a thick leather belt around his waist. He has thick dark curly hair that would have been the envy of Medusa. 'She'd been handling snakes since she was fifteen years old. She got taken by a timber rattlesnake.' Wayne points to a photograph on the wall. It's Melinda in her Sunday best, tucked up in a coffin with some fancy linen covering all but the top third of her body. 'She were so brave,' he says, flicking at the photograph with a duster he'd been using on his boots. 'About fifteen minutes after she was bit she lost the use of her legs. Even then she refused any kind of outside help. She say she wanted to rely on prayer and faith.'

All that poor Melinda got was a big wooden box – but I don't mention this to Wayne. In the south it's good policy not to upset preachers, especially when they have a large timber rattler in their hands. 'We will go forth in the Lord,' says Wayne, gripping the snake's undulating body as if it were a bunch of flowers. 'The blood of Christ will protect us.'

We would be almost ready to leave but Wayne has to get one more thing, his pot of strychnine. In case the snakes are too docile during the service, Wayne likes to drink a little deadly poison, just to keep his parishioners interested. Wayne and his fellow worshippers cite the scriptures again as their licence to booze on toxic liquids. 'If you have faith it cannot hurt you,' says Wayne in his deep baritone. 'If I die it is a measure of my sin.'

Wondering how on earth a man like Wayne could ever get life insurance, I follow him down the rickety staircase and out into the steamy afternoon. The storm has moved up the valley, leaving Jolo enveloped in a hot thick gas that my lungs keep telling me cannot be oxygen.

'The last time I got bit God had told me to put the snake down,' says Wayne, sweat pouring so freely down his face that he looks like a man with a host of sobbing angels in his hair. 'Ego and pride kept me gripping that copperhead, then I knew I had done wrong and in the same instant the serpent reared back and struck my right hand.' Like his sister, Wayne says he refused to seek medical help. By the next day, the right side of his body was so swollen he couldn't get his trousers on, something that only usually happens after the annual choral barbecue. The swelling subsided two days later after forty-eight hours of prayer. Within a week, Reverend Wayne was back in his pulpit, preaching and handling serpents.

'The bite don't change the word of God,' he says as we enter his church, a garage converted to resemble a small home which smells like a cross between a poorly kept zoo and a gas station. There are fifty similar churches in America, mostly in this region of Appalachia. Some call themselves 'Holiness churches', rooted in the belief that sanctification is the second gift from the Holy Spirit, following conversion to Christianity. Snake-handling churches stress that a preacher or congregation member should feel anointed and protected by God before taking up serpents. Some ignore this good advice and die horrible deaths, their skin turned black with a texture like crêpe paper. Others do not and eventually manage to drape a half dozen serpents over their heads without harm.

'It's a feeling you can't describe,' says Jamie Coots, who pastors a snake-handling chapel at Middlesboro, Kentucky and often visits Wayne's church. 'You don't feel any fear. You know what you're doing, but yet, it's like something's got a hold of your body and you can't control it.'

As Wayne makes his way to the pulpit children are running along the side aisles. There's a holiday atmosphere, made more pronounced by what look like six picnic baskets sitting just in front of the simple wooden altar. The baskets appear to be the old-fashioned sort that are now only available in Harrods, for a small fortune, the ornate exterior suggesting that inside there's silver cutlery and champagne glasses. Up close, it's clear Harrods would only sell these in their exotic pet department.

Each one contains at least three fully grown rattlesnakes, some thicker than a man's arm. None of them look happy at spending their Sunday as the props of a fruitcake religion, but then maybe the snakes don't look at it that way, maybe God has given them 'instruction' as they say around these parts.

'Serpent handlers may be very, very weird, but they're not crazy,' says Andrew Leonard, the dean of divinity school at Wake Forest University in Winston-Salem, NC. 'Millions of Americans say the Bible contains no errors of any kind. Others complain that too many people view the Bible through the lens of safe, middle-class conformity and miss its radical message. Snake-handlers agree, as do the millions of Americans who say that miracles happen, especially when believers have been anointed by God's Holy Spirit.' The bottom line is snake handlers wonder why others settle for less riveting forms of faith when you can have the real thing. What if every time you went to church you knew it could kill you? That would pick up the old Sunday service a bit, wouldn't it?

Wayne climbs into his pulpit and calls for quiet. Behind his head there are boards where the congregation has carefully written the rules of their faith. No Gossip. No Talebearing. No Lying. No Backbiting. I wonder if this last one applies to the snakes, but the stern look of the congregation grabs my attention and the service begins. At first it's a solemn declaration of common faith, but soon Wayne is raising his voice, the southern baritone hitting each word like a hammer so that it drives deep into the head of everyone present.

'People think I'm crazy,' hollers Wayne. One of the congregation yells back, 'You're crazy for the Lord.' A five-piece band that had been still until now begins to play with a hypnotic blues beat. Striding in front of the lectern Wayne spews forth words. 'We got some difficult serpents tonight that like to play games.' The congregation falls silent, anxious. 'You know you can't pick and choose with the Book,' he continues, holding a battered Bible high above his head. 'The Lord hands us what we can take.' The congregation responds: 'Amen.'

Wayne bows his head and spreads his arms. 'It was after they crucified Him,' he declares. The congregation answers like a panting dog: 'Amen, Amen, Amen.' 'But when they went to the grave...' 'Amen, Amen.' '... He wasn't there, He was gone. He was risen again!' 'Amen, Amen, Amen.' 'And do you know what He said? "And these signs shall follow them that believe; In my name shall they cast out devils; they shall speak with new tongues; they shall take up serpents; and if they drink any deadly thing it shall not hurt them; They shall lay hands on the sick, and they shall recover."' 'Amen.'

The music builds to a frenzy, the beat of the band echoing the staccato chanting of the mesmerized audience. The church has grown hotter than a baker's oven turned up high. I feel I can smell the anger in snakes. Around me sweat pours from every face, the floor is slick with perspiration. A low howling noise comes from the chest of a small woman a few feet in front of Wayne. Next to her, a member of the congregation stands and walks to the snake boxes. He is shivering, as though the broiling temperature were actually several degrees below zero. Wearing red boots under a pair of brown checked trousers matched with a yellow shirt, and spinning like a poorly controlled puppet, he slams his fists into his skull as the music suddenly stops. The church is silent except for the man who is now speaking gibberish punctuated with 'Jesus-O-Jesus-praise-the-Lord-O-Jesus.'

Wayne reaches forward and places his hand on the man's head, slowing him down and inducing a testimony that is half sung and half screamed. 'My momma didn't want me to come out tonight, she said please don't go, but I got to go, I said, I got to go. This is a real anointing. There is a real God here tonight. He's a good Lord.'

'Amen, praise Jesus,' comes the reply, now spoken softly, with reverence. Wayne stoops and opens his picnic baskets. Snakes are lifted out and all the congregation look on, spellbound. Wayne holds a five-foot diamond-back rattler in one hand and a timber rattler in the other. They stiffen and shoot their tongues towards the roof. As though passing out Christmas presents, Wayne dips into the snake chests and comes up with bunches of coiled serpents that are tossed to the nearest hands. Soon the whole congregation is handling and passing around snakes. One woman wraps snakes around her neck like a scarf, another man pulls a snake against his forehead.

I catch sight of Bert Sloan holding a cottonwood above his head which then falls on the floor. Calmly it is picked up again and raised to the sky. Reverend Wayne takes three timber rattlers in one hand and straightens them out on a table, stroking them flat from tail to head, like a tailor straightening a row of expensive ties.

Nobody was bitten. In fact, nobody looked in any danger of getting a bite, despite the dozen or so lethal snakes that had been slung around like bits of old rubber tubing. By the time the snakes were rounded up and put back in their baskets, more than two-thirds of the congregation had held at least one viper. As the snake frenzy subsided their faces wore expressions poised between stupefaction and elation. They were all poor people. The town of Jolo cannot afford a full-time police force, its citizens eke out a living from the hills. Half the local homes are built of rough-hewn timber, cardboard and old newspaper. Yet on a Sunday the snakes take them somewhere else, a place they yearn for all week as they make a few dollars from hopeless jobs.

'This makes them feel special,' says Wayne as we leave church. 'That's what my people are, they have more innocence than city people and God rewards them for that.' Although the Lord has occasionally forsaken Wayne. He gave up preaching for seven years from 1986 after serving a stint in jail for assault with a deadly weapon; a woman at another church was bitten by one of his snakes. Snake-handling is illegal throughout the US and Wayne feels he was victimized.

'The woman was transported to God when she first handled my snakes,' he says as we push our way inside a crowded diner on Jolo's only street. 'She was only bit because she was a backslider. I took the blame for her immorality.' We take a table with Bobbie Sue Thompson, one of Wayne's assistants at the church. She wears a blue dress made from a fabric that was big before Japan bombed Pearl Harbor. It's stiff like some kind of recycled cardboard. She's a tall woman but all of her body seems to sag towards a point just above her navel. You'd think she was weak if it wasn't for something remarkable about her eyes. They are clear and strong, green the way moss can be after fresh rain. At her feet is a miniature picnic basket which houses her personal rattlesnakes – some trusted church members are allowed these and Bobbie Sue says she takes hers out for an hour of prayer every night.

'It's faith that makes you handle snakes,' she says as a low hiss comes from beneath the table, like God letting down the devil's tyres. 'I saw demons before I picked up serpents. They possessed me and made me do impure acts. Now I'm pure. Handling the snakes is one sign that you are walking in a state of grace.' The snakes hiss a little louder. I wonder if they sense Wayne seems to have gone a little pink at the mention of Bobbie Sue's bad behaviour. I fancy now might not be a good time for Wayne to pick up snakes. His dirty mind might win him a nasty nip. Wayne clears his throat and finally drags his eyes away from Bobbie Sue, who is trying to explain to me the ecstasy of faith. 'With snakes, I've had the spirit in my arms, in my whole body. I've had it so much, I feel so weak I could fall out. I have to sit down sometimes. I feel so weak in the Lord.'

As Bobbie Sue speaks I look around. The diner is full of Appalachian families. All of them were in church, and now they are lunching on grits and sausage patties with jugs of turkey gravy. Each one has a pinched expression as if life comes knocking on their faces every day with unreasonable requests. The snakes seem to be their attempt to reach inside misery and drag something remarkable from it, to manufacture a contact with the Almighty that money or prestige could never buy. Sure they'd still call blacks 'negroes' and hang them from trees, given half a chance, but serpent-handling is their mad attempt to become angels.

Charlie Horse says his Navajo ancestors used to dance with snakes, twirling them like batons in a marching band. Anybody who died from snakebite was buried with great reverence and his descendant would be asked to send prayers to him, assuming the dead man now possessed great wisdom. 'We just didn't have all that stuff about being bitten if you are with sin and dying if you were without God's grace,' says Charlie. 'That's a white man's invention.'

9. Hunting by Numbers

One American relic of the Old West is bounty hunters — people with no formal training who are encouraged to wear guns and hunt criminals for rewards that are small enough to guarantee these mercenaries of justice are always in a bad mood. Charlie Horse says there are still bounty hunters looking for him, but few of them ever visit New York, let alone give some homeless guy a second look. The city does not encourage a Wild West atmosphere. For that you need something more southern.

New York City has America's toughest anti-gun laws but that's no problem. Drive five hours down Interstate 95 and find some Miami bum with a valid local ID. Pay the guy $50 and he can slip inside a gunstore and come out with an arsenal, no questions asked. Florida markets guns like most states sell postcards of local beauty spots. Every American who visits the Citrus State is expected to leave with at least one deadly weapon. The state is the holder of three coveted records: nowhere else in the US has more acres owned by Disney, more pensioners, or more marriages that end in gunfire.

Florida's heavily armed traditions make the state a magnet for the lawless. Almost every desperado makes it to Florida eventually. I know that because Jeri Gaither told me. Jeri writes me letters from jail and nourishes dreams of being a movie star. She faces an uphill battle. In 1994 a humourless judge sentenced her to twenty years. Jeri was caught driving around with a dead body in her trunk. It was August when Florida gets so hot even the cockroaches head north. Florida traffic cops may be a bit dense, but even they could smell there was something bad in the back of Jeri's Chevrolet. The cop who pulled her over says he still vomits whenever he thinks about what he found under Jeri's luggage. The woman in the trunk may have been dead but that doesn't mean there wasn't anything alive back there. Everybody needs their own Disneyland and maggots had made theirs in the body of Jeri's victim. When the cop opened the trunk, the stench was bad enough to cause an air pollution alert from Tallahasee to Key Largo.

Jeri's arrest was a disaster for Dave Chipman. In America, where there are scumbags there will be bounty hunters, and Dave is one of them. If he'd caught Gaither he would have been paid $10,000. To listen to Dave, you'd think there was a little guillotine sitting above every word he says, because each one is cut crucially short, after a small pause for the linguistic blade to drop. The result isn't really English, it's a whole new language seasoned with a little southern pep. Let's call it 'Chipman', as in 'he lives in a trailer park outside West Palm Beach and he speaks Chipman'.

Actually, Dave doesn't live in a trailer park any more. He's graduated to a house in what used to be a nice neighbourhood before the nice left and moved to where they hear more bird song than gunfire. His new house is quite pretty at first sight, but like a girl guide at a Hell's Angels' party it looks under siege. You just know that absolute degradation is only a few moments away.

At 5 p.m. on a Friday evening Chipman is carefully loading ammunition into his car, preparing for a night's work. 'I love these new bullets,' he says, although what I hear is: 'I lo the nu bults'. From here on I have to concentrate each time he speaks and that's hard work because he never stops talking unless he's about to shoot a guy. 'They blow up inside a perp but don't pass through,' he continues. 'That makes it much safer for any innocent bystanders.'

The killer slugs are tossed inside the trunk of a big brown 1980 Oldsmobile. There they join a small armoury which includes a pair of pump-action shotguns, five sets of handcuffs, three cans of mace, and an anti-personnel device called a Tazer which fires small bean bags that can knock a man clean off his feet. It's just a regular trunkload for a red-blooded Floridian. 'I prefer to use the Tazer before the shotguns,' he remarks, like a true southern moderate. 'It all depends on the fugitive's attitude. If he wants to be an asshole I can accommodate him. I never met anybody who didn't calm down after a nice meal of hot lead.'

Although we know Chipman, forty-three, is a bounty hunter, he calls himself a Fugitive Recovery Agent and that's what it says in bright orange letters on the back of his black T-shirt. He works freelance and gets paid between $100 and $5000 for every man or woman he brings in alive. His targets are indicted felons who have been unwise enough to skip bail in his territory. The bulk of his prey are petty thieves but a few are murderers like Jeri Gaither, big-time drug dealers or pimps with connections to the mob. He works seven days a week for countless hours and in a good year he'll earn around $30,000.

As a warm Florida rain falls on the suburban streets of West Palm Beach, Chipman pulls his shirt off to reveal a muscled torso decorated with four tattoos. He takes a bullet-proof vest from a coat hanger in his garage and belts it on. 'This has saved my life a couple of times,' he says, pulling the T-shirt back on. 'I keep it hidden under my clothes because if a fugitive knows I'm wearing a vest he's more likely to shoot at my head.'

Pausing to load two guns with nine bullets each, Chipman takes the shiny semi-automatic pistols and slips them into concealed holsters. One is slung beneath his left armpit, the other is just below the right cuff of his faded Levi's. Two small blonde girls on their way home from school pass by his driveway as he tightens the holster. With his guns in plain view he gives them a cheery wave. They wave back with placid smiles. This being Florida, they are no strangers to heavily armed civilians. 'It could be a long night,' Chipman observes with relish as he fixes a knife to the back of his belt. 'I have a list of five very bad guys I'd just love to catch.'

Chipman finishes his hunting ensemble with an official-looking badge in the style of a detective's shield. It's inscribed: 'Fugitive Recovery Agent'. It hangs on a chain around his neck and makes him look like a cop, although to many fugitives he's something much worse. The FBI or the police need a search warrant to break down doors, but a bounty hunter suffers from no such restraint. If Dave Chipman thinks his man is inside he can barge his way into any house without invitation or a warrant, although Arizona recently became the first state to restrict this right after over-zealous bounty hunters killed an innocent family of four.

'See this,' he says, pointing to one of his tattoos, a heart and dagger on his arm with a scroll underneath that he reads: 'You can run, but you can't hide.' He laughs hard, revealing uneven teeth yellowed by long nights of coffee and cigarettes. 'I show the toughest scumbags the tattoo once they're in cuffs, when they start to curse me out. I want them to know I can go through any door they happen to be behind.'

At 5′ 8″ in his cowboy boots, Chipman is not a big man but he has an indefinable air of physical menace. He looks like a guy who would take on somebody twice his size − and he often has, earning himself the nickname 'Brass Balls'. In six years as a bounty hunter Chipman has been shot once, in the arm. The healed entry wound is like a pair of puckered lips and sits just above his heart and dagger tattoo.

Despite the risks, or maybe because of them, bounty hunting is one of America's fastest growing cottage industries. It requires a minimum of training, hunters can work part-time and for the more adventurous members of America's struggling lower-middle class it promises the slim chance of big pay days, should they ever catch that million-dollar fugitive.

'I'm training about twenty new hunters every week,' says Bob Burton, who runs the National Bail Enforcement Training School in Tombstone, Arizona. 'They pay about a thousand dollars each for the course. You could say people think there's big bucks to be made.' Burton is planning to move from Arizona to Texas. He thinks his home state's decision to restrict bounty hunters is 'un-American'. If somebody like Burton tells you you're un-American, it's best to run fast and pray you are wearing clean underwear.

For most hunters the reality is eighteen-hour days and meagre rewards mixed with boredom and sudden flurries of potentially lethal danger. The sharp increase in their numbers has intensified the air of anarchy that's been growing in many medium-sized American towns. Increasingly, crime has been driven out of big cities like New York to resettle in areas where the police have less money, the gangs are well entrenched and where a rising number of private citizens have the right to carry concealed weapons. In such places law and order has become an uneasy mix of public and private enterprise, with bounty hunters riding hard in the spaces between the two.

The profession of bounty hunting owes its origins to an 1873 law that was passed by a fledgling Congress when cowboys were still wild and self-employed sheriffs kept order. The law gave bounty hunters the right to enter residences and cross state lines in pursuit of bail jumpers, which allows men like Chipman more power with regard to their quarry than the almost omnipotent FBI.

Bounty hunters may act with the power of federal law but they are all private citizens, and their pay comes from bail bondsmen. These fringe entrepreneurs will put up bail for a prisoner who cannot afford the cash himself. The bondsman gives the court a piece of paper, a bond, that is his promise to pay the full amount of the bail if the accused skips. In return, the prisoner must offer the bondsman collateral like a house or car owned by themselves or a relative.

Once the prisoner has been freed 'on bond', the law states that he has been 'transferred from one jailer to another'. The bondsman in effect becomes the accused's jailer and thus has the right to send his agents to search wherever he thinks the accused may be hiding. As many bail bonds are in amounts above $20,000, the bondsman has a keen interest in finding a fugitive before the courts demand their money, forcing the bondsman into the costly and difficult process of liquidating the prisoner's collateral. For every fugitive he catches, Chipman gets 10% of the face value of the original bond. It's not much, but with enough volume you can survive and even take on somebody else who can help while away the long nights of surveillance.

Ira Berkow became Chipman's partner six months ago. Their physical appearance is football fields apart. Ira is at least three inches over six foot and he weighs about 180lb more than he should. Ira's nickname is Sherman, after the tank, and his job is to protect Dave, who rewards him with endless jokes about his waistline. 'C'mon fat boy,' he shouts as Ira arrives at Dave's house and climbs out of another ageing Oldsmobile with slightly less grace than a hippo rising from a broken sofa. 'If we hurry they may have some fried pastry left at Dunkin Donuts.'

Ira looks like he's already had a few weeks' worth of lunch from Dunkin Donuts on his way over. Suspicious looking crumbs are trapped in the folds of his sweatshirt and they cascade like snowflakes as he helps Dave load some heavy leg irons into his car. Ira lets loose a fusillade of burps loud enough to scare some kids across the street, and then we are ready to begin the night's hunt with a session at the gun range, just so that the two men can get their wits sharpened. I join Ira in his car for the drive. When he turns on the ignition, mournful country music blares from eight different speakers. 'Sorry, man,' he says, revealing for the first of many times that he is a gentle giant. 'My girlfriend and I just broke up and our song came on the radio. I had to turn up the volume.'

Ira's car is a showcase for the bounty hunter's glamorous life, the endless days spent chasing bad guys and mourning good women turned fickle. There's a photograph of his ex on the dashboard, mug shots of four fugitives from justice are taped to the sun visor and the car is awash with partially emptied containers from fast-food restaurants. A box of half-eaten hamburgers sits between us on the bench seat whilst my feet share space in the floor well with a dozen empty coffee cups. Crushed cigarette packets litter the back seat along with walkie-talkie headsets that Dave and Ira use when they are closing in on their prey.

Dave employs Ira part-time so he also works at a local gas station. That's where Ira began his career in the shadowlands of law enforcement. 'There were drug deals going on all around the station,' he says, pulling the car hard to the right as we see his partner's rear lights make a sudden turn. 'I became an informant and Dave came to see me for some leads on a drug-dealing asshole called Snake who ran with the West Side gangs. When he went to arrest Snake he asked me to go as his bodyguard.'

Hooked by the adrenaline rush, Ira signed up with one of Chipman's competitors. 'That was crazy, he almost got me killed,' he shrieks as his memory is refreshed by a long drag on a cigarette. 'That guy was a real Rambo. He'd break down doors just for the fun of it. Dave prefers to talk people out.'

Stopping at a traffic-light, Ira lights a fresh cigarette and muses on his role as a bounty hunter's protector. 'There are plenty of things out here that can get you killed,' he says. 'You start turning over stones and other people get involved. You catch some small douche bag and bang! He suddenly has some connection with the mob and the shit's swirling around your kneecaps. Whatever happens I have to look out for Dave, he's like a brother.'

Does that mean Ira would make the ultimate sacrifice? 'If I had to take a bullet for Dave, if there was no other way, without a doubt,' he says, sticking his chin forward with a bodyguard's surly pride. 'If you are asking if I would save him and take a bullet I wouldn't think about it, yes, I would and he would do the same for me. When it's your partner that's just the deal.'

Ira swings the car into a parking lot, the headlamps illuminating a 12-foot-tall wooden alligator with a sign above its head that reads: 'Gator Guns'. The faux reptile is holding a 3-foot-long machine gun which lights up every ten seconds with lamps that spell: 'Welcome' in bright red neon. Next to the sign Dave Chipman is engrossed in a conversation with a woman who looks about 6 feet tall and less than twenty-five years old. She is both thin and voluptuous in a pair of extra skintight jeans and a cotton halter top that she outgrew some years ago and now wears without a bra. Lest any mad Floridian misinterpret her outfit as an invitation to mess around, she is holding two semi-automatic pistols which are fighting with her breasts for Dave's interest. He may be wondering which contains the most synthetic materials.

'Hey, don't touch that one, it's still hot from shootin',' she says with a sharp southern accent. 'Look at this, it's a Glock with a re-engineered barrel.' Chipman and his gal-pal gunslinger move to one side and become conspiratorial as Ira begins to collect bullets from the trunk. He lights another cigarette after he's finished. I ask him if he's ever killed anybody. 'Yes,' says Ira, without hesitation. 'When I was eighteen. This guy was attacking my mother with a knife.' Before he can finish his story Dave is back, flushed and excited.

'That was Mary Jo from Boynton Beach,' he whispers, as though that should instantly mean something to me. 'She told me this guy we're after will be at his girlfriend's just after nine tonight.' As we walk inside Gator's, Chipman explains that he gets more than half his leads from informers. He buys them a drink and occasionally gives them $20. Most spill the beans because they have a grudge against a fugitive and want Dave to rough them up a little on the way to jail.

'The big mistake every fugitive makes is he talks,' says Dave. 'He gets drunk and talks to a drug dealer or a prostitute. The name of their game is money. They come to us and say, "What's this guy worth to you?" There's no honour amongst this kind of thief, for a few bucks these people will give up anybody.'

The proprietor of Gator Guns is a guy named Bascart. He looks about fifty years old although he could be younger. His shrivelled skin and tired eyes may be the by-product of eighty cigarettes a day and a bad whisky habit. If I wanted to buy a gun here I need to show him some ID, but he gives me the impression I could hand him a Star Trek badge from a kid's toy box and he'd sell me an Uzi with a discount. Bascart lives to sell firearms. He thinks everyone should have at least two and then the world would be a better place.

'I think a gun gives its owner a sense of responsibility,' he says, an arthritic hand on my shoulder. 'I've known people turn away from crime because of guns.' I've known people like that too, only my examples generally only did so after a bullet through the brain. Bascart claims his converts develop a mythical relationship with their firearm. 'A gun changes a man,' he whispers before heading back to his counter where a guy in green fatigue trousers and a 'Guns and Roses' T-shirt is waiting to buy something really deadly for when he next gets drunk and his girlfriend starts to piss him off.

In the back rooms of Gator Guns there are target ranges, full of intense-looking southerners with bad attitude and a good aim. Dave and Ira hoist pulleys with paper targets. They depict the form of a charging gunman and the bounty hunters position them 30 feet away, where they sway from side to side. Each man empties a clip of nine hollow-point bullets then pulls the targets back to check their score and change them for a fresh 'assailant'. They repeat the process three times with an intensity of concentration that a brain surgeon would die for. Ira's rounds scatter over the target's torso. Chipman puts each one of his first shots dead centre into the forehead. The rest of his clip is all in the heart. The firing stops, leaving the smell of gunpowder and testosterone.

'Good shooting, Dave,' says a tall burly man who has just walked into the gun range. 'But you'll remember, I prefer my fugitives to come back alive.' Chipman chuckles and shakes hands with the new arrival, who is called Big Mike, one of the leading bail bondsmen in West Palm Beach. This blond-haired behemoth was obviously built with a grant from Burger King and he makes Ira look like Kate Moss. On this Friday evening he's dressed in the height of Florida fashion, combining tight white slacks with a tight white polo neck that makes him look like a *boudin blanc*. Big Mike gives Chipman more than 60% of his jobs. He owns a store that's all neon light and misery just opposite the court house. Signs in his big glass window scream 'Big Mike, Bail Bonds – 24 Hours'.

Mike shows Chipman a polaroid of a runaway and hits it with a stubby finger as he calls the fugitive a few bad names. Apparently the guy is at an aunt's house just half a mile away. The intrepid duo swing into action. We run to the cars and both men check their weapons, safety on and one round in the chamber. Then they put on their headsets, so they can communicate as they surround the target's home. The men look like a couple of kids. The headsets were designed for domestic use by people with big houses. If Dave gets more than 20 feet away from Ira all he can hear from his partner is broken words drowned in static, which is not that different from how Dave sounds up close. The hunters want to get proper radios but they're too expensive, so for now their lives depend on these toys.

The target is Tyrone Wastley, a young drug dealer, a black man in his early twenties. He failed to show up for a court hearing and the judge called in his $5,000 bail. Dave and Ira get $500 if they track him down. As we approach the fugitive's alleged hideout both Dave and Ira cut the headlamps on their cars and we coast up in the dark, like CIA agents in a bad movie. The street is part of a dingy neighbourhood called Tavern and there's an air of genuine menace. Almost all the street-lamps have been broken and the ones that remain just make the shadows look more threatening. The homes are small three-bedroom bungalows with tangled gardens. For anyone who knows the neighbourhood, there are plenty of places to hide and lots of cover from which to let off a shot.

Ira's headset crackles. Chipman tells him to go around the back. Dave takes the front. Dogs begin to bark. They sound large and angry. After a full minute of knocking, a scared-looking woman in her forties opens the door. She's wearing a floral print dress and socks with holes around the toes. Behind her head is a big-screen TV which looks like it cost more than her house. On the cineplex-sized screen there's a National Geographic special about the mating habits of whales. After a softly-softly interrogation that does not lack charm, Chipman satisfies himself that the fugitive is not here. The aunt's house is collateral on her nephew's bond and when Chipman explains she could lose her home she looks stunned. A few minutes later we're on our way to a new location. 'The aunt gave Tyrone up,' Dave says, chuckling softly. 'She's pissed about the house. She says he's up at his girlfriend's.'

We drive around the new location a few times to case it out. It's a different proposition. The fugitive's car in the drive but so are six others and at least two belong to known dealers. Clumps of young men and women are hanging out on the porch. We move off and Dave stops around the corner at a telephone booth. He wants to alert the local police that we are making a bust and the subject may be armed. 'Damn,' yells Dave, kicking at the base of the phone. 'The darn thing is smashed. Oh, well.' Those last two words mean we are going in without an escort. I remember Gator Guns and their *laissez-faire* policy towards arms sales. To calm my nerves I make bets with myself that Dave's target is one of Mr Bascart's best customers.

Chipman and Berkow stop the cars behind an abandoned church and take shotguns from the trunk. The adrenaline is flowing now. It's their drug. It's obvious from their eyes that this is what they live for. Each day they wake thirsting for these moments when they get to be Wyatt Earp, dressed to the nines in deadly hardware. As Ira straps on extra body armour his breath is coming in short little pants, like a man engaged in vigorous sex. Dave seems to have grown smaller and tougher all at the same time. His lip is curled with a look that combines anger and lust.

The assault begins with Dave again heading straight to the front door as Ira goes to the back. In seconds there's mayhem. Screams from young women at the front door send Tyrone Wastley running out the back where Ira tries to lay him low with a clumsy tackle that the drug dealer ducks before heading into the dark of the bushes around the bungalow. Ira goes down slowly, like a large building and from 60 feet away his lungs can be heard complaining about the impossible task of getting their owner back on his feet.

Dave switches on a bright police torch and chases crazily over other people's property, exercising his rights as a bounty hunter and making everybody along the street angry. Tyrone and their $500 prize are still eluding them but the mood is turning ugly. Half a dozen young men are gathering near the hunters' cars and muttering about harassment. I have an image of all six youths leaving Gator Guns laden down with the store's gaudy carrier bags, Mr Bascart waving happily behind them. I wonder if it hurts to get shot.

Ira can be heard wheezing loudly from somebody's garden. He's cursing. He bumped straight into Tyrone behind a bush but the young fugitive again escaped his portly pursuer. Dave jumps over a fence behind Ira and immediately takes his anger out on the crowd. Far from trying to placate them he tells them to get the fuck away from his car and he makes sure they know his gun is already out of its holster. There is plenty of adrenaline in his system now and the hostile crowd seems to know it is heading straight for Dave's trigger finger. They back off, understandably muttering about vigilantes and racial harassment.

'Let's book,' he says, using New York police slang for making a retreat. As we move off I notice that Ira's kiddy phones are dangling in two bits on his chest and he's breathing asthmatically. Sweat is pouring down his face as he puts his car right behind Chipman's tail-lights. 'Oh, man, I was that close to him,' he says, holding up a pinched thumb and forefinger, oxygen struggling for space in his constricted lungs.

Chasing around like that, on hostile territory, doesn't Ira ever get scared? 'All the time,' he replies, lighting a cigarette to steady his nerves. 'Every night, every house. Every person, every footstep behind you.' We are heading to a diner to regroup. It's called the Gun Club Café. 'On a job, I concentrate on the area around me, where I am and where Dave is,' Ira continues. 'I always look for somewhere that if, God forbid, anything should happen I can get some cover. Like tonight. I was sure those sons of bitches were going to start shooting.'

At the diner Chipman gives Ira non-stop grief for losing his headphones and not staying in touch at all times. He's really angry that the target escaped, but it doesn't last long. A waitress sits by his side and starts offering information, about a child molester they've been hunting for six weeks. Chipman gets all fired up again and wants to head out, even though Ira has only just started working on a 12 oz hamburger with a full plate of fries. 'Hold up, man,' says Ira. 'Let's plan a little.' Translated, this means, 'Stop while I stuff my face in case I lost any calories back there.'

For the next thirty minutes Chipman makes diagrams of the child molester's house whilst Ira uses french fries and mashed potatoes to persuade his lungs they should surrender a little more room to his stomach. 'The pervert has a fence back here,' says Ira, putting a fine spray of food on Chipman's sketch. 'I'll be back there.' That reminds Dave of a job last week. 'We had the cars hidden off a lane, watching for this guy. We had been there for eight hours. We had drunk a lot of coffee and I think Ira had eaten beans. We both get out and walk up the slope to take a leak. We can't be seen from the house but a car driving up the lane would see us. We're pissing when a car pulls into the lane. I run for cover through a hedge and Ira follows, but he gets stuck between the branches. The guy drives past and there's Ira's butt and legs waving in the air.' Chipman laughs like a mad dog and Ira looks genuinely hurt until his partner puts an arm round his shoulder. 'I gotta love all this bulk if there's a bullet coming and Ira's in front of me.'

Chipman's beeper goes off and after a call from the pay phone outside – cellular phones are way outside their budget – he comes back, a little shamefaced. It seems his wife needs his car to take their daughter shopping. The twin avengers of West Palm Beach will have to make do with one set of wheels for a while. The exchange goes smoothly, and almost immediately after we are all snug inside Ira's trash can on wheels Dave's beeper peals again. Another pay phone and Dave is all excited. He comes back to Ira's side of the car and has him move over. 'It's Tyrone,' he says. 'I have another lead on the sonbitch.'

We scream away from the pay phone and the reason for the driver switch is immediately obvious. Chipman has gone insane and plans to kill us all in a fiery smash. At least that's my impression as we all but drive beneath an eighteen-wheeler just to get in front of a petrol lorry that has to brake hard or run right over our roof. As I look back, the lorry driver appears to be sorry he didn't choose that option, but there's no time for reflection. I have to begin a new set of prayers as Demon Dave slips between a trio of cars travelling abreast and thus makes four lanes out of three. That's when we hear Ira's voice, raised by an octave or two above normal.

'Dave, I need a bathroom,' he says with enormous conviction. 'I have to take a dump.' This is unquestionably a side-effect of the spicy chicken–wing appetizer he recently scarfed in the Gun Club Café. Chipman ignores him and swerves in and out of another line of cars that is only going at 80 mph. 'Dave,' says Ira, voice another octave up. 'I have to go, man.'

A quick glance at Ira's face reveals some bad news. Ira's sphincter and his need to dump are fighting a hard battle but the panic in Ira's eyes reveals his sphincter is hopelessly out-matched. One more hard punch from deep inside Ira's intestines and Mr Sphincter will be down for the count. I tell myself I will hold down my dinner whatever happens, but I know I'm lying.

'Dave, there's a Dunkin Donuts at the next exit,' moans Ira. 'Give me five minutes, man.' Chipman is in an agony of indecision. A delay may mean missing Tyrone but Brass Balls seems to have grasped that his partner's sphincter is made of malleable material. In a flash he swings the car across the inside lanes of traffic, and to the sound of car-horn opera we skid off the highway, sliding largely sideways down the exit ramp on which the speed limit is roughly one-third our actual pace.

We make it in the nick. As Ira heads through the Dunkin Donuts, customers scatter at the sight of a 20-stone man running whilst unfastening his pants. A minister eating with his family actually crosses himself as the big man lumbers by, the two loose sides of Ira's trousers in his hands ready for immediate action. The horrified look on people's faces a few seconds after Ira passes suggests he is leaving olfactory clues to go with the visual indicators of his distress.

When Ira re-emerges from the men's room the Dunkin Diner is much more sparsely populated. Encouraged by the short counter queue, Ira stops for a dozen assorted donuts. By the time he reaches the car he's already eaten two, and Chipman is banging his head against the steering wheel.

Tyrone is where we were told he'd be, and this time does not hear us coming. We park around the corner and sneak along the street until the fugitive can be seen bent over the engine of a souped-up Camarro. Chipman's gun is in Tyrone's back before he has time to spin around and Ira has the handcuffs on him in less than five seconds. 'Bingo,' says Ira, using his spare hand to give his partner a high five.

Tyrone is searched. His pockets contain $25, three condoms and a pack of cigarette papers. He agrees to leave these with his girlfriend. 'Good kid,' says Chipman, after the property exchange. 'That will save me a lot of paperwork at the jail.' For that is where Tyrone is heading and where he will now spend a month before his trial. Big Mike does not forgive skips, one chance is all he'll offer. Tyrone has just realized that he will not be out in a few hours and he's pleading, offering information if Dave will let him go. 'Too late, big guy,' says Ira. 'You should've thought of that before you pushed me into that tree.'

In the prison car park, friends of people just taken inside are solicited by thuggish-looking bail bondsmen in long leather coats who promise a quick release. In America the invisible hand of capitalism reaches everywhere, to the bottom of each and every barrel.

It's midnight. Tyrone is processed back into the system, but gunshots a few blocks away suggest the hunters have not yet made Florida safe for the law-abiding. We're drinking bad coffee outside another Dunkin Donuts. 'I wonder where Shark is tonight?' says Ira, toying with a chocolate cruller. 'That bad ass really hates you.' Chipman shrugs and loads sugar into his coffee, a cigarette between his chapped lips. Shark is a 'drug king pin' in FBI speak and Dave arrested his lieutenant and hit man two weeks ago. Since then, Shark has put out a contract on Chipman's life. FBI agents were guarding Dave's wife until two would-be assassins were arrested outside one of Dave's favourite bars. He doesn't know if the contract has been lifted yet, but he's damned insulted that his 'price' was only $2000.

'Cheap threats are an occupational hazard,' says Chipman. 'People say I'm a cop wannabe or an adrenaline junkie. I don't give a rat's ass. I get a good feeling when I put somebody like Tyrone away and that's what it's all about. Keeping the scum off the streets. A lot of the kids on the street make $400 a day. I don't make that – I'd like to make that. I drive a 1980 Oldsmobile and then I see a seventeen-year-old kid driving a $35,000 BMW. What am I doing wrong? It's like the American dream turned inside out. If you're a criminal you do well, if you are a working guy you don't.'

A police car screams past with its lights and sirens engaged. Dave and Ira watch it and look a little wistful. 'I just wish I had their technology,' says Dave. 'Then we'd catch us some bad guys.' His beeper goes off and it's pay phone time again. He's back quickly with another indefatigable smile. 'That was another lead on the child molester. He's been using the card.' Chipman sends out free phone cards in the name of his fugitives to addresses where they once lived or to their relatives. Often they get sent on to the target and when the 'dumb son of a bitch' makes a call with his free card, a central command centre traces the fugitive's exact location.

'He's at Boynton Beach, at a strip joint on 134th Street,' Dave yells as he runs for the car. We take another white knuckle ride along the freeway. Without the benefit of lights or sirens we screech between lines of traffic, testing the skill and nerves of late night drivers who are probably on the dangerous edge of drunk. It takes eight minutes to go twelve miles. We pull into the lot behind Pussy Galore and jump out into a pool of yellow neon light that makes Ira's head look like a Halloween pumpkin.

Inside there's no suspect. A guy answering his description left about ten minutes ago. 'Jesus,' shouts Dave, banging his hand down hard on a table. The fugitive was out on a $20,000 bond. That would have been a $2000 reward. Enough to meet the rent and a few car payments. Maybe Mrs Chipman would have been able to lay off the overtime next week. The barman sends over drinks and gives a friendly wave. Two women in minimal clothing come by and give both brave boys a squeeze, although I promised not to say where. 'We were here for two weeks once,' says Ira. 'We were waiting for a woman fugitive, a stripper and scam artist who was missing on a $15,000 bond. Two weeks, just sittin' here every night. You see, this job ain't all hard work. I won't die rich but I'll know I've been alive.'

10. Freud and the Reindeer

New York is full of fugitives. People run here from their dreams and nightmares, which usually manage to come along for the ride. Charlie Horse brought his and every time he sits down to panhandle he says the spirits find room right beside him on the sidewalk. With the snows of winter lining up to coat Manhattan I figured he'd be ready for another nice warm plane ride to a place where we could finish our gambling spree. I was so wrong. 'This is the best time for me to be in New York,' he said, adjusting some tinsel that he has woven inside his Navajo headband. 'I get lots of cash. People think I should be home for the holidays, so when they sees my sign they open their wallets.'

Yet Charlie is angry. His usual spot, outside the up-market department store Barney's, has been usurped by crowds. 'There's some guy in the window,' he growls. 'It's not natural. When I first panhandled on Fifth Avenue – it was traditional, Father Christmas. What kid wants to sees some pyschotherapist where Santa ought to be?'

In New York children still see Santa Claus, but adults see the father of psychoanalysis. That's why at 4 p.m. on the Saturday before Christmas I'm lying on a battered leather couch in the window of Barney's, a luxurious Manhattan department store. Outside, hundreds of New Yorkers pause to peer through the glass as a Freudian analyst asks me about my dreams.

Barney's is a store like no other in New York. The staff are undoubtedly all aspiring actors, but when they treat you badly it's the real thing. You could cut their disdain with a knife. Impeccably dressed in fashionable black, they treat the majority of customers with a mixture of contempt and pity. 'I'll accept your grubby credit card,' their faces seem to say, 'even though I know you are unworthy.'

A store with such *haute* pretension could never just have its display windows sullied by a regular Father Christmas and a few fairy lights. Barney's has to have high concept windows which plough an erratic course through twentieth-century history. There's Martin Luther King, a venerable man, but hardly an Advent character, and Mae West, who would never ask anything as small as an elf to come up and see her some time.

The twentieth-century windows, including the Freud tableau, were conceived by Simon Doonan, the store's creative director – who would never call them anything so prosaic as 'window displays'. Doonan's 'shopping scenery' is comprised of striking pieces of art mixing several different mediums, but only the Freud diorama includes a real man who hates Christmas. He's in the window entitled 'Neurotic Yule: An Homage to Sigmund Freud.'

It was the peak shopping hour when I began my session with David Rakoff, Barney's fenestrated Freudian. The son of a psychiatrist father and psychoanalyst mother, Rakoff is an amateur therapist who dresses like a 1930s shrink, complete with tweed jacket and horn-rimmed glasses. To reach his couch it's necessary to navigate behind a counter that sells lady's lingerie at prices which would wipe out the limit on at least two of my credit cards. Two Amazonian sales assistants ignore me for the statutory eight minutes before asking what I need. When I reply, 'Dr Freud's office', I'm surprised they don't call security, but let me through and direct me behind a wardrobe.

It's there I find a small door, and soon Rakoff has me on his couch, ready to begin one hour of therapy behind plate glass. Outside, the world walks by, swinging expensive-looking bags. About one-fifth of the flow stops and gawps for it seems the spectacle of such a public glimpse of a private moment has gripped New York's imagination. Some Manhattan shoppers claim they have been to visit several times. The same people probably like going to zoos and rubbernecking at road traffic accidents.

Rakoff is not a classic Freudian. He wants to talk too much. As I take in the 80 square feet of his 'doctor's surgery', he tells me how surprised he is to have an English visitor. 'It seems to me peculiar,' he says in a clipped accent. 'An Englishman in therapy. Isn't that an oxymoron? Like a vegetarian in a steakhouse?'

Ignoring the stereotyping of Brits as anally retentive and repressed, I asked him for his take on Christmas. 'It's all about guilt and control,' he says. 'We give presents because of the hate we feel deep down for the recipient. Whatever they say about the gift, we will regard their response as phony.'

Outside on the pavement, a pair of small children have their noses pressed against the window and both are making faces, desperate to attract our attention. Rakoff ignores them like the Scrooge fan he certainly is, staying resolutely in character. Following his suit, I inquire about Father Christmas. 'Do *you* believe in him?' Rakoff asks. 'Not a bit,' I reply, 'except on Christmas Eve.'

'Let's look at the name: "Father" Christmas,' he says emphatically. 'It's obviously an Oedipal fantasy. Santa Claus is supposed to come down a chimney which is clearly a simulacrum for a vagina. Then he leaves presents and children are always anxious about what kind. So it's really all about parents engaged in sex, an act that necessarily excludes their kids. It's no accident that Freud and Father Christmas became popular at the same time.'

In front of me, as Rakoff speaks from behind the couch, I can see a video screen that alternately shows a monochrome picture of Sigmund Freud followed by a skull and then the word 'Daddy'. Rakoff seems to sense the theme of death has caught my eye. 'Presents are a non-violent form of assassination,' he says. 'Haven't you felt enraged by someone to the extent that you bought them a present? You have to do something to that person, but it's illegal to strafe their body with bullets, so instead you do the next best thing, buy them a present. You take the moral high ground. Christmas is a wonderful opportunity to make your enemies feel small.'

We've all opened gifts from loved ones on Christmas Day that do nothing but disappoint. 'Doesn't she know me yet?' we think secretly, tearing paper from a John Grisham novel or a bottle of Brut. Rakoff has analysed this problem. 'There is an underlying agenda in gift giving,' he says. 'The giver has an explicit objective. It's not simply, "here's a gift". The giver is demanding to be liked. A gift is also an attempt to curate somebody else's taste. Women use this as an opportunity to punish men. We are beneath them so our gifts can never be adequate. If a woman lavishes praise on a lover's gift it means she doesn't care for him any longer. He can expect the heave-ho, or to find his girlfriend in bed with another man.'

The pavement outside is now crowded six deep with onlookers. They point at us and then prod each other. They all have cheery seasonal faces. It's a good job they can't hear what we're saying. They would probably storm the window and lynch both of us for molesting the innocent spirit of Christmas.

'There's nothing innocent about it,' says Rakoff. 'Why do you think so many people commit suicide at this time of year? Many of the patients I've seen in here say the season just rubs their noses in the inadequacies of their lives. If you're not a perfect WASP family with a turkey the colour of krugerrands, the twenty-fifth of December just makes you feel like last week's garbage.'

The surprising fact about Rakoff's window is that a few of his sessions have turned into genuine therapy. 'I have people confess stuff they have never told anybody before,' he says, ignoring a large blonde woman in a fur coat who keeps taking our picture. 'I have had tears. I have had decisions made.'

Does that mean the window, with its public setting, creates an effective environment for therapy? Rakoff thinks it does. 'I think the fantasy element convinces some people to share confidences here that they would not trade with their own therapist.'

A man dressed as Father Christmas has taken up a position near our window. He's ringing a bell, soliciting money for the Salvation Army. 'This is outrageous,' says Rakoff. 'I long for a Santa-free zone. Did you ever sit on Santa's lap?'

'Of course,' I reply, remembering department store queues and tacky gifts handed out by gruff men who smelt like my father's drinks cabinet. 'I found it humiliating,' says Rakoff. 'Why should he ask me if I've been naughty or nice? I think Christmas is the start of neuroses for many children. They are forced to consider how the love they get from their parents measures up to what their friends are getting. If you do worse, you risk insecurity. If you do better, you become a narcissistic brat. Let's say I get a new train set but you get a train set too, with twice the amount of track and faster engines. In my childish mind I realize I'm worth less than you. By the same poisonous token, you believe you are worth more. If we remain friends through life, this poison will always be there until the day I make a pass at your wife.'

Above my head, five television screens are showing scenes from Freud's life. Alongside them is a tiny bed, like a child's cot. Freud is most remembered because he taught us dreams have meaning, and bananas can be symbolic of something other than fresh fruit. It is only in New York that such a character could win a prominent association with Christmas. The city is full of transplants, people who are refugees from the big skies of the mid west or the interminable swamp of the south. They come here for remodelling but they never quite lose the feeling that they don't fit. New York is wired for its own special kind of electricity and most people don't have the right kind of emotional plugs. The result is lots of minds with blown fuses. Despite their hardboiled reputation, New Yorkers are amongst the most insecure people in the country. That's why money is so important to them. It's the only thing they really trust as a measure of somebody's worth.

'New Yorkers are inherently neurotic,' says Rakoff. 'Gifts necessarily inspire suspicion. Give a New Yorker a present and he or she will wonder what you want. There is a pagan justification for the season. We seek light and warmth in the depth of winter, but that has long been irrelevant for city dwellers. It has now become a triumphant parade – how could any of us enjoy Christmas if it weren't for the poor, there to remind us how fortunate we are.'

Lying on Rakoff's couch I begin to get depressed. I feel I have hidden from myself the real motivations of Christmas. It seems all those carefully wrapped gifts under my tree are actually emotional time bombs. Seeking release, I ask him to play a word-association game. 'Red,' I say. 'Blood,' he replies. 'White.' 'Cocaine.' 'Snow.' 'Heroin.' 'Ho, Ho, Ho.' 'Chinese Food.' 'Reindeer.' 'Sex.' I jump at this last connection. Surely Rakoff cannot be linking the adorably red-nosed Rudolph with carnal behaviour?

'Look, it's obvious,' he says. 'Santa Claus is pulled by reindeer through the sky. As Freud has taught us in *The Interpretation of Dreams*, flying is symbolic of sex. A dream that includes flying is an allusion to an unfulfilled sexual longing. We never see a Mother Christmas. No wonder that guy is always up in the sky, he's looking for an elf with breasts and a easy way with her underwear.'

Our session is over. As I stand I can see looks of disappointment on the faces of our audience. Then I notice they all have bags full of gifts ready to wrap. Rakoff has opened my eyes. These people are psychic shock troops, ready to do untold emotional damage to their friends and family, proving that Christmas does more harm than good, except for the retailers. Passing back through Barney's, I'm ready to spread Rakoff's message. I can feel the words 'Bah, humbug' forming on my lips. Then I pass by some carol singers on a street corner and suddenly I'm singing the song I would beg my mother to sing at all seasons of the year, the only one that could always put me to sleep: 'Then one foggy Christmas night, Santa came to call. Rudolph with your nose so bright. Won't you guide my sleigh tonight.' Humming happily, I realize Freud was right about one thing – conditioning runs deep. We can never escape. 'Resistance is futile,' I mutter as I buy an excessively high-brow friend a *Star Trek* video and ask to have it wrapped in garish red paper with holly sprigs the colour of artificial grass.

11. *Black Pudding*

In its chequered history as a slave state and bastion of the south, Kentucky has seen many trails of blood, but few have been more bizarre or chilling than the one left by five teenage vampires who haunted Florida and Louisiana in the spring of 1997. They wormed their way into people's dreams, sowing a wild crop of panic that overwhelmed the minds of many God-fearing southerners who, at the best of times, can be a bit on edge.

The vampires' most public victims were Richard and Naoma Wendorf, a middle-aged couple from Eustis in Florida, about fifteen minutes from Orlando's Disney World. Given the anaemic effect Disney's cultural bloodsucking has produced in the American consciousness, a few real vampires should have been a welcome diversion, but one of those accused of the murder was the Wendorf's fourteen-year-old daughter Heather. Her alleged accomplices were Dana Cooper, nineteen, Scott Anderson, sixteen, Charity Keese, sixteen, and Roderick Ferrell, also sixteen. Ferrell used to be Heather

Wendorf's boyfriend. Apart from Heather, all the group came from Murray, Kentucky, 260 miles away. Wendorf was eventually acquitted but the rest are serving life. They left behind a conviction in Kentucky that vampirism is widespread, especially in Murray.

In spirit, this small western Kentucky town could not be further from the dollar-coloured landscape of Orlando which Rod Ferrell chose as his killing ground. Murray is in a land of rundown shops and bowling alleys. Its strip malls resemble a poorly maintained museum of fifties architecture. The homes are small and poorly maintained, but it's also a deeply religious community which was shocked by details of how Heather's parents met their death.

'The Wendorfs were bludgeoned to pulp with a metal bar,' says Sheriff Stan Scott, who speaks with an impediment constructed from a golf-ball-sized wad of chewing tobacco. He was called to the Wendorf house after Heather's seventeen-year-old sister Jennifer had found the bloodied bodies in the family dining room. Jennifer's mind had been so pulverized by the techno-convulsive therapy of the Internet and cable TV she at first thought the death scene was an elaborate hoax, until she slipped and fell in her mother's blood. 'This was not a quick killing. The wounds were inflicted by at least three different individuals.' Scott says there was no evidence of satanic rituals at the Wendorfs' pretty bungalow, but he says that does not mean none took place. 'These five individuals are part of a group that's about thirty strong. They have been under investigation for about two months. We always have vampires in this community, goin' back to when my great-grandaddy Jimmy Black wore the silver star.'

The fear in Murray is fed by the fact that the town has profound religious convictions. The small churches that dot the largely rural landscape preach a version of Christianity which acknowledges the devil as a real and powerful force. 'Evil is a reality,' says Matther Edgar at the Murray Baptist Mission. 'There are demons in the world and Lord Jesus Christ is our only saviour from them. I am praying for the souls of these young people.'

Edgar claims he sees vampires in his dreams. 'I have been with them at the altar, blood dripping from their ugly fangs into the communion cup.' Like most southern preachers, Edgar is a part-time freelancer. By day he sells second-hand cars and fantasies are a big part of that life too. Edgar told me he dreamed of my buying a very ropey-looking 1987 Cadillac with yellow paint, and implied failure to purchase could damage my mortal soul.

After work, Edgar's voice booms around a small church that looks like it might once have been a public lavatory or an abattoir. 'I love the way my voice bounces off all the tiles,' says Edgar of his religious home, before confessing that he was once arrested in England for drunk driving – 'before I saw the light'. Included in Reverend Edgar's recent revelations has been a claim that vampire author Anne Rice is a bride of Lucifer, something which Rice's agent must be unaware of, otherwise she'd be using it in publicity material.

Some residents in Murray say the slaughter of the Wendorfs is evidence of how evil has seeped into their community from mediums like television and the Internet, which are outside their control. Perhaps the most frightened man in town is Rod Ferrell's grandfather, Harold Gibson. 'What if they come after me?' he sobs. 'They're saying Rod is a monster. He's not, he's a nice kid. I'm scared that he has been set up by vampires who now will want my blood.' Gibson is a member of Reverend Edgar's church and may have heard too many tile-amplified sermons for the sake of his sanity. 'My dreams are drenched in blood,' he says, shivering on the rickety stairs of his trailer home, taking a hit of cheap whiskey to greet a clock chiming 9.30 a.m.

Sheriff Scott's vampire probe began after Rod Ferrell broke into a dog rescue shelter and attacked more than fifty animals. Murray is the kind of town that can make such behaviour seem like a fine way to spend a Saturday night. Ferrell killed two pooches and one was put to sleep because its hind legs had been ripped off. The legs were never found although the perpetrator claimed he sold them to the local pulled pork barbecue restaurant. When Ferrell was questioned he had small cuts all over his arms, which he admitted were the result of vampire rituals. He told police he belonged to a group called 'The Vampire Clan', and he showed them a blood-stained edition of Rice's *Interview with the Vampire*.

Ferrell is also the link between Kentucky and Florida. In 1995 he went to high school in Heather Wendorf's home town and it's there that the couple met and he introduced her to vampire worship. 'She was a real nice girl but deep down you could tell she had emotional problems,' says Joe Barrett, a fifteen-year-old friend of Wendorf's, a youth who seems genetically unaware of the ironies in his own understatements. 'When she started hanging out with Ferrell she changed. She was dying her hair purple or red and she wore all these long black clothes. Most people around here wear shorts and T-shirts. She went around telling her friends she had "crossed over" and become a vampire. I thought it was kinda strange.'

Jeremy Hueber dated Heather for two months and also confirms that she had become different from the girls he usually hung out with, all of whom were on the high school cheerleading team. 'She enjoyed and got pleasure from drinking her blood and other people's blood,' he says. 'It grossed me out, but she said you could have the best sex only after a blood drink. I'm happy to say I never got to find out. I still have trouble eating hamburgers.' For a southerner to make that admission suggests Heather had got to Hueber in a really big way.

Ferrell's murder conviction left many questions unanswered. Law officers in Kentucky doubt that the sixteen-year-old was the cult leader. They are investigating a number of adults who are suspected of initiating Ferrell and dozens of other Kentucky youths. 'We have just scratched the surface of vampirism in Kentucky,' says the Murray sheriff, Stan Scott.

'There are many more involved in the valley than just Ferrell's group. Right now, I think most of them are lying low.' Presumably in coffins with the lids ajar.

In October 1995, local police officers stopped a car with a faulty tail-light on the secluded road between Murray and the neighbouring town of Mayfield. It was three days before Halloween. Inside were four people dressed in black with their faces painted white. A fifth passenger, a girl, was in normal clothes but wore a blindfold. The travellers said they were going to a fancy dress party. The police had no reason to detain them but they checked the driver's ID. He was a local man, Kile Bayton. The Kentucky authorities did nothing more, until they received a call from police in Tennessee. A fifteen-year-old matching the girl's description had gone missing. She had left behind letters from Dean Frank, a Murray resident and friend of Bayton's. They were full of references to powers the girl could have if she 'crossed over' and became a vampire. One letter described blood rituals and human sacrifices. After reading one of the girl's letters, investigating officers in Tennessee discovered Bayton's real first name was Andrew. Dean Frank had written that 'Kile' is a name taken by men who believe they have become 'undead'.

The girl is still missing. Kile Bayton says he had never met the girl before that night nor seen her since. Like Dean Frank, he has been interrogated but not charged. No body has been found nor any evidence that the missing teenager has been physically harmed. Yet some locals believe she was killed in an initiation rite at the Vampyre Hotel which went wrong.

'That's what I believe,' says Cindy, a seventeen-year-old local girl, as we examined the concrete shell that has such a dark reputation. Inside and out the walls are daubed with spray-painted messages that are an incongruous contrast to the beautiful surroundings. 'Me Killa', 'Follow me to Death' and 'Please Deposit Dead Bodies Here' are just three of the ungainly scrawls that are mixed with strange symbols, many of them Egyptian in origin. There are also dozens of discarded fast-food containers, suggesting that vampirism is hungry work and that the blood meals are really just appetizers to fried chicken.

'This is where I had my initiation,' says Cindy, a dark-haired waif with piercing brown eyes. 'I stripped to my waist and they painted a pentagram, upside down, between my breasts.' Probably for my benefit, she seemed to shudder briefly at the memory before continuing: 'A tall blonde woman I'd never met before made three cuts on both my arms. They let the blood flow a little then collected it into a cup.'

Cindy said she felt a little light-headed at the memory and needed to sit down. She found a spot by the structure's entrance. Inside, the floor was littered with gaudily coloured candles which jogged her memory. 'We had big red candles when I crossed over,' she said as I notice some old cut marks on her forearms. 'They placed a drop of my blood in the flame of each one. Then they mixed the blood in the cup with water and everybody in the circle drank some, there were nine people in all.'

Once that was done, Cindy says everybody made cuts in their own arms and drained some blood into a separate cup that was again mixed with water. 'I was given the cup and told to drink every drop,' she says. 'Once I'd done that I'd "crossed over", I had become a vampire. Then everybody began sucking at each other's wounds.' Maybe that's what the fried chicken pieces were for: to dip in all this blood, like bread in spaghetti sauce.

Cindy says one of those present at her initiation was Sandra Gibson, the mother of Rod Ferrell. Gibson allegedly led one of the competing vampire cults that brought a new kind of fear to the Kentucky valley. She has fled the area but before she left Murray police charged her with sexual assault. The thirty-six-year-old woman had allegedly tried to seduce a fourteen-year-old boy as part of a vampire ritual. Murray police have released part of a letter from Gibson, written to the teenager. 'I long to be near you for ever, to become your vampire bride,' it reads. 'You will then come for me and cross me over and I will be your bride for eternity and you my sire.'

Gibson apparently led young people into vampirism through a game called 'Masquerader', which is loosely based on the books of Anne Rice, especially *Interview with the Vampire*. (The book was made into the 1995 film which Rod Ferrell has rented more than twenty times from his local video store.) The game is an elaborate fantasy serial that players make up as they go along, its characters endowed with different powers, depending on their place in the hierarchy. It's supposed to be make-believe, but Gibson and her friends encouraged Murray's teenagers to take it seriously.

Kathy Lee, a fifteen-year-old from Mayfield, played Masquerader with Gibson's group. The girl met the older woman in The Wag, a Murray coffee bar which Sheriff Stan Scott identifies as a meeting place for members of local vampire groups. Kathy Lee claims she, like Cindy, was initiated in the Vampyre Hotel. Since then she says, without a trace of irony, 'I prowl on moonless nights. My character was Lynthia, that's a gangrel, a vampire who can change herself into an animal or vapour.' Kathy Lee alleges she was taught by Rod Ferrell that female vampires are the strongest, but that male vampires live longer. 'He told me women are always chosen to lead vampire groups, because they have the power of life in their wombs.'

Part of Masquerader's rules say that a vampire who spots a rival blood-sucker must attack, anywhere or any time. Friends of Ferrell, who do not want to be named, say he'd become convinced that his girlfriend's parents were vampires from a rival group, that they were trying to turn his girlfriend against him. Whilst these thoughts are probably delusional, nobody has suggested Ferrell exhibited bizarre behaviour before he became involved with the Kentucky vampire cult.

'I think there are two rival cults here,' says Cindy. 'Rod's group were led by a woman from New Orleans who was a friend of Sandra Gibson's. The others follow two women from

Houston, Texas. They are really vicious and I think Rod was afraid of them.'

Police in Houston confirm that since 1994 there has been a series of 'ritual biting' incidents. Marshall Varis, a Dallas psychologist, says that in 1997 he treated fifteen teenagers who said they were vampires. Patricia Seymour, a psychiatric counsellor, says that in the last three years she's had fifty clients from the Houston region who have emotional problems that stem from practising vampirism. All of them say they've met a shadowy woman who calls herself 'Clyte'.

'It's a form of mass-hysteria, on a small scale,' says Varis. 'People get in a group and convince themselves supernatural powers are there for the asking. Once they believe that, few have any qualms about drinking blood.'

That's what happened to sixteen-year-old Amanda from Houston, a patient of Dr Varis. 'Being a vampire gave me everything I craved,' she says. 'Clyte instructed me to sink my teeth into my victim's back, in the fatty tissue close to the heart. The rush that followed was amazing. I showed no mercy. I wanted it bad. It made me feel I could do anything.'

Amanda was part of a group she says was led by Clyte, who disappeared after three other members were arrested for torturing a seventeen-year-old boy during a vampire rite. Police say Clyte's real name is Alice Lynn Shapiro and she is wanted in three states for assault and fraud. Clyte's alleged victim was in a coma for five days after living through four days of terror. He was sexually assaulted by women in the group and a man threatened to cut out his tongue. The group then set the boy on fire.

Amanda says she became addicted to the blood high, mixing sucking sessions with sex. 'I made myself believe I needed blood to sustain my life,' she says. 'I truly believed I was a vampire.' Amanda spent so much time in vampire rituals she became anaemic. After fainting at school, a nurse spotted the bites on her back and the cuts on her arms. Once, in therapy, Amanda described a series of bizarre rituals, including the night she was forced to climb inside a cow's carcass to be 'reborn' in its uterus.

Ferrell's night of animal mutilation and torture was the first sign Murray sheriff Stan Scott had that vampires were well entrenched in his town. Then he began to spot other evidence. 'It's pretty easy to tell who's been a vampire for any length of time,' he says. 'Most of them are going to have self-inflicted razor cuts or knife wounds.' How that distinguished the vampirists from other Kentucky residents wasn't clear, but Scott has looked for links between his blood-suckers and those in Houston or New Orleans but he's found nothing concrete. That doesn't surprise Gordon Welton, who edited *The Vampire Book: Encyclopaedia of the Undead*. 'There are about two hundred committed vampires in the US who are trying to build a nationwide cult, and they belong to three different groups,' he says. 'Each is at war with the other. These are fanatics in the strongest sense of the word, like Moonies or Scientologists. They keep their tracks hidden and, given their beliefs, commit violence against their enemies without remorse. As with most cults, they are especially hostile to members who try to escape.'

Rod Ferrell's grandfather, Sandra Gibson's father, urged him to leave the vampires, but his grandson said he was too afraid of reprisals. Charity Keese, one of those convicted of murder with Ferrell, also claimed her life was in danger. 'She was a good child until this,' says David Keese, her father, a man with a southern accent thicker than treacle. 'I told her to get out of the sect. She said, "They won't let me. They'll kill me."' Keese is an old-fashioned man, a religious fundamentalist who uses archaic expressions. When he fetches a pen he calls it a 'writing stick' and his views on evil are Old Testament. 'I believe the devil has my daughter's soul,' he says. 'I can't explain her behaviour any other way.'

Charity Keese was with Rod Ferrell when he committed the Florida double murders. According to police reports, Keese, Ferrell and the other Murray vampires spent the hours before the killings in blood-drinking rites at a friend's house. When they were arrested numerous fresh cuts and scars were found on their arms and necks.

The Federal Bureau of Investigation say they are reviewing the Kentucky group and several other cases around the US, especially in the south. They are likely to have plenty of work. The Vampire Information Exchange in New York says the number of vampires is growing, helped by the Internet, where their message can be easily spread. Staff at the exchange say vampires have a real physical need to drink blood but do not live for ever, they have a longer life span, proportional to the number of feeds they take, and prefer to seduce their victims rather than make random attacks – which makes them sound like stockbrokers. The exchange notes that vampirism has been a factor in southern folklore since the eighteenth century, when many alleged vampires were burnt at the stake.

Kentucky is well suited to nourish the cult. It has a long history of strange religious practices. Once a troubled teenager has embraced vampirism, challenges to their belief in the power of blood sucking can inspire violence, just like it used to with the KKK. The vampires' lurid practices require cult members to keep secrets about each other, and in the sometimes paranoid atmosphere of small-town life that can breed murderous suspicions.

'I think Kentucky, and the whole south, is more susceptible to vampirism,' says Gordon Welton. 'These are Bible-thumping people. Kids there are raised to believe in Christ and the devil. It's a scary place, almost medieval. Many southerners believe there are real demons in every dark corner.'

As the sun sets over Kentucky Lake, I am standing by the entrance to the Vampyre Hotel, supposedly the starting point for Rod Ferrell's fatal odyssey. I see shadows dancing inside as the wind blows through the trees and I know what those southerners mean, although there's a way they can all stay safe. The Vampire Research Council issues an identikit of the average vampire. If he's male he should be around twenty-six,

5' 10" tall with very dark brown eyes and black hair. Females have the same hair and eyes but look about twenty-three. Both are thin. The average male vampire weighs 11 stone, the average female, 8. I noticed, as I accelerated out of town, that most of Murray's residents were a good match for this description.

12. Million Dollar Southern Belle

In the deep blue of Dorothy Hutlemyer's eyes there's a hint of steel that warns the world not to mess with her. Margie Lynne Cox could not have seen that sign, for she stole Hutlemyer's husband Joe, at least that's what Dorothy and a North Carolina jury believed. The latter awarded Dorothy $1 million in damages after the forty-year-old mother of three boys pursued Cox with all the power the law allows, which in the small southern town of Greensboro is a lot. A God-fearing community of 21,908, they don't look kindly on a bottle-blonde cheat like Lynne Cox.

The judgement against Cox was an American record for a case involving the theft of a spouse. Cox must pay or face bankruptcy. The first Mrs Hutlemyer's lawyers are examining ways of forcing Joe Hutlemyer, now Cox's husband, to pay part of the debt, which, unless paid, will stand for twenty years. When William Congreve said 'Heaven has no rage like love to hatred turned', he must have had Dorothy Hutlemyer in mind. The case is unlikely to be settled for a decade.

'Cox acted maliciously towards Dorothy,' says sixty-eight-year-old jury foreman Gene Grimley. 'The defendant went out of her way to destroy a genuine marital relationship. Once we on the jury had agreed on that, large punitive and compensatory damages were inevitable.'

Grimley lives up to the first syllable of his name. He's the character you hope not to meet at the Pearly Gates wearing a name tag that says 'St Peter'. Grimley has no interest in forgiveness. A sin is to be punished, hard. If Lynne Hutlemyer had been hoping for sympathy from a jury, her heart must have sank when she saw Grimley's face, which seems to have disapproval etched into every deep wrinkle. Like many elderly southern gentlemen of his type, there's probably not a single human pleasure he rates as innocent, except maybe wearing bedsheets and burning crosses. He probably dreams about angels in thigh-high boots whipping the backsides of sinners, stopping only when their wings begin to ache.

'I feel Americans have to make a stand against the immoral tide of filth sweeping this land,' he says. 'I blame the Japanese, they made it possible for us all to buy TVs with their cheap little sets. In this state we won't let a brazen hussy steal another woman's man.'

Grimley's reading of the law is right. North Carolina is one of only five states in the US which retains ancient 'alienation of affection' laws. They were written originally when men treated their women like household goods, and if another man enticed a wife away he could be found guilty of stealing the husband's property, as if he'd borrowed the guy's CD-player without asking permission. Although Dorothy Hutlemyer receives generous alimony from her ex-husband Joe, she felt that wasn't enough. The scarlet woman had to pay as well. All Dorothy had to do was prove her marriage was jogging along smoothly until a wanton intruder came along to wreck it with her devilish charms.

'When I heard about the alienation of affection law I was so pleased because it gave me a choice,' says Dorothy, in a voice that's doesn't quite seem real. Like the sounds that come out of a talking Barbie doll. 'I could either accept what she had done or I could stand up and say, "Wait, we had a wonderful marriage with three children and you broke it up", because I truly felt it was Lynne who pursued Joe. I felt for the sake of my own mental health I had to go after her. I couldn't just sit back and accept what she did.'

The action in the Hutlemyer case took place in the towns of Gibsonville, Burlington and Graham, places where people still talk to their neighbours but no longer leave their front doors unlocked. Economic decline has left a greasy film of decay over parts of the area, beneath which crime and drugs have begun to fester. In secretly rented apartments, motel rooms and restaurants, forty-three-year-old Joe Hutlemyer, president of a multi-million-dollar marine insurance company, began to transfer his affections from Dorothy, his wife of eighteen years, to Lynne, his secretary since 1991. Although the jury found in favour of Dorothy, Lynne says the truth is more complex than the law could understand. The new wife claims Dorothy drove Joe away with cruel emotional indifference, leaving him lonely and afraid for the future. Lynne says Joe chased her after he realized he no longer loved Dorothy.

For Dorothy Hutlemyer the problems in her marriage began when Joe rejected a tuna sandwich, an act that amounts to treason in suburban America, and should have signalled that her man was now with Satan. Joe had been away on a business trip – actually he'd been having a long weekend of adulterous sex with Lynne – which he'd extended by twenty-four hours. 'He came home, I was in the kitchen,' says Dorothy, who likes to portray herself as the ideal wife and mother. 'I'd just had a tuna sandwich and prepared snacks for the children, which I did every day before they got home from school. I gave him a hug and offered him a sandwich. He said no, we had to talk and led me by the hand into another room.'

Dorothy says what followed was a bolt from what she had

thought was the clear blue sky of an idyllic marriage. 'He said he couldn't live with me any more. That he felt ill and had to get away,' she says with curiously little emotion in her voice – in fact, Dorothy says she hasn't cried once since that day. It's an even bet her lawyers, whom I'm sure being part of the American legal profession have no interest in earning exorbitant fees, will soon claim she has post-traumatic shock syndrome and needs another million dollars in damages for pain and suffering. 'I sat there, stunned. I kept on waiting for the punchline. I couldn't believe it. I was functionless. He cried but still I couldn't believe it, I just sat there and he was talking and I was listening to him, but I was like a blob. I was there but I wasn't responsive.'

Joe and Dorothy had tickets for a ski vacation due to begin four days after this bombshell, which was dropped five days into the New Year, whilst the Hutlemyer home was still wreathed in festive Christmas decorations. 'He left his key and said he'd be back the next day to tell our three teenage boys. When he left I immediately began taking down all the decorations. I could not have the boys hear about Joe leaving with the tree still up because I thought then they'd always associate Christmas with something sad.' I thought of giving her David Rakoff's telephone number, but tuna sandwiches had just arrived. I had to eat or be identified with the enemy.

Joe Hutlemyer never returned to tell his boys; according to Dorothy she had to do the job three days after he left home. The four of them went on the ski trip as planned and Dorothy had a week in the mountains to reflect on her marriage.

'We met on a blind date in 1978,' she says, her sing-song voice becoming more pronounced, like a greeting card commercial. She embarked on some sentimental reminiscences. 'We really hit it off, I thought Joe was so sweeeet and haandsome. We got married eighteen months later. After I met Joe I didn't date anybody else. Ours was a very romantic marriage. He wrote me poems and sent me little cards, even when it wasn't my birthday.'

The couple began married life in Pennsylvania, the north-east state where both were born. Joe came from a working-class background, steeped in hard work. Dorothy's family were millionaires, her father a partner in a construction business. She has a sister three years her junior and their mother never worked. 'That's what I wanted so I could always be with my children,' says Dorothy. 'I was teaching, but in 1983 when Joe got the job in North Carolina it meant a promotion and much more money. It was just after our first son was born, so moving south meant I could give up work.' Two other children followed in the next four years. The Hutlemyers became pillars of the community, Dorothy especially. Chairing the local Parent-Teacher's Association, the Library Committee and playing the supportive wife to perfection.

'As Joe moved up in the company I offered to entertain a lot,' she says. 'We always had people at home. Once he became chairman of Seaboard we held the company's annual Christmas party at our house, with about a hundred guests. I think it made a difference to Joe professionally that we were such a good couple and a stable family. That impressed his business colleagues.'

In 1986 Dorothy began hearing the name Lynne Cox, who had just joined Joe's company. In 1991 Cox became Hutlemyer's personal assistant and a more common topic of conversation in Dorothy's household, but she never for one moment considered Joe's PA was a rival. 'Not for a second. Joe and I were very happy. We took trips to Hawaii and to London, twice. He called me every day whenever he was away on business and we'd talk for a long time.'

On her strange holiday without Joe, surrounded by snow and happy vacationing families, Dorothy began to question if she had done anything wrong in the marriage, if there were any signals she might have missed. 'My impression was that we had been fine, right up to that moment when he said he was leaving. We had a normal intimate relationship until the end and I was very happy. I thought he was happy, but I sat down in our ski lodge and went back to think from memory if there was ever a time we had a problem. I wanted to be honest with myself so I would always know if I missed something. I thought and thought but there was nothing. I was wondering if I had seen any early indication and ignored it but I just didn't. I wondered, what did I do wrong?

'Then I started thinking, even if it was something I'd done, like forgetting to kiss him goodbye one day, there was nothing I did that could justify him leaving three wonderful children. I was devoted to him, the children were devoted to him and that's all I could think. This was something he chose to do to me for no reason.'

At least that's how it appeared until Dorothy returned from the slopes. Then the small-town gossip mill began pumping out dozens of juicy titbits. With Joe publicly separated from Dorothy, the women at his company felt free to let the wronged wife know that her husband had been snapped up by the town siren.

'I started getting calls from Joe's work telling me about him and Lynne,' says Dorothy, the steely glint of indignation shining bright again. 'They said I hadn't been told before because they were afraid for their jobs.'

What Dorothy heard seemed like a tale of calculated seduction. The witnesses from Seaboard called at Cox's trial told with relish how Lynne suddenly changed her behaviour in 1993 when Joe Hutlemyer became the $100,000 a year president of the company. The allegedly scheming Cox promptly divorced her husband within five months of Joe's promotion, had a fashionable haircut and began wearing short skirts with see-through blouses. A female shark in transparent polyester.

'She had chased him, that's what I heard,' says Dorothy, still managing to sound shocked by such brazen behaviour. 'She was always in his office, leaning over his desk. She wouldn't let anybody else near him. One woman told me she'd caught them kissing. Another said it was known they'd been sleeping together. I was told she'd sit in Joe's desk chair with her skirt rucked up and her legs apart, just staring up at him.'

Stunned by these revelations and believing the vicious gossip, despite her husband's denials, she hired a private investigator, one of those bottom-feeders who usually have one hand on a whiskey bottle and the other rooting around in someone's trashcan. This gumshoe picked up a paper trail of hotel bills, airplane tickets and restaurant meals which ended in a local jewellery store three days after Joe had left home. It was where he'd bought Lynne a $3,000 engagement ring with his Mastercard. Like many before him, Joe Hutlemyer discovered that itemized phone and credit-card bills have taken all the mystery out of having an affair.

'I went into shock for a few days, I was numb,' says Dorothy. 'It was like somebody had knocked the stuffing out of me. The last time I'd seen Lynne I'd carried dinner over to her house after she'd had surgery, and all the time she was trying to take Joe away from me.'

Joe and Dorothy were divorced in March 1997 and Joe married Lynne in May. The first Mrs Hutlemyer filed her alienation of affection suit in March 1996 and kept pushing it forward even after her husband began paying her $4,000 a month in alimony and child support, a figure that's 76% of his take-home pay. 'I know, and I also got the house,' says Dorothy, who strongly contends this has nothing to do with money. 'I knew from the start I'd probably not get a cent from Lynne. I just wanted her to sit in the courtroom and hear the judgement. When the jury found for me I felt vindicated.' That's because Dorothy believes if it weren't for Lynne she'd still be married to Joe. 'He is a good person who got enticed,' she growls through gritted teeth. 'I believe he still loved me and the children, which is why they carried on for so long in secret. I believe she was pressing him to separate. I think she gave him some kind of ultimatum which is why he suddenly left, even though we had a holiday planned.'

It's rare for two women who have fought for the same man

to be in court together. Most divorces are far more bloodless. In this case Lynne had to endure a two-day interrogation that exposed every soiled sheet in every hotel room where she met her lover, whilst Dorothy looked on. Lynne said she felt mounting anger and disbelief, unable to match the nice stories she had been told about Dorothy by Joe with the cool, calculated avenger sitting twenty feet away. By contrast, Dorothy says she felt little emotion, just a calm sense of satisfaction, although there was one piece of courtroom theatrics she especially enjoyed.

At the suggestion of her lawyer, Lynne came to court in a long dress wearing granny glasses and no make-up. It was a tactical mistake. 'My attorney found a really glamorous photograph of Lynne from a local paper,' says Dorothy, smiling hard, relishing the anecdote and the way it made her rival look bad. 'He asked her if she always dressed in long skirts and glasses. She said yes and then claimed she never really wore make-up. Then he showed Lynne this dolled-up photograph and asked if it was her. When she said yes, he asked her to step down from the witness box and stand in front of the jury. Then he put the magazine photo alongside her face and almost all the jurors burst out laughing. I did too.' Game, set and match to the avenging angel.

Dorothy says she doesn't hate Lynne, but if her ex-husband's new wife were to publicly apologize for her behaviour Dorothy would not drop the million-dollar claim against Mrs Hutlemyer II. 'She did this to me and my children,' says Dorothy. 'She can't just walk away like it never happened. "Sorry" is just a word.'

'Joe and Dorothy's marriage was over long before he and I began seeing each other,' says Lynne Hutlemyer, née Cox. 'We want to appeal but we doubt we can raise the money.' She is sitting in the kitchen of the Hutlemyers' modest $500 a month apartment in one of the less safe parts of town, a far cry from the $300,000 house Joe left behind. 'I earn about $400 a month from a part-time cleaning job, the rest of the time I'm finishing my law degree. Joe has about $800 a month left after paying Dorothy and we have a lot of legal bills from the first case.'

Lynne Hutlemyer is dramatically different from her rival. Where Dorothy seems to exist on a single, placid, emotional plane, Lynne's passions apparently span the full spectrum from cold to red hot. Dorothy's voice never seems to change its volume. Lynne can go from shouting to whispering and back again in a single paragraph. Where Dorothy makes one think 'genteel', Lynne brings the word 'earthy' to mind. Whilst Dorothy and Barbie dolls seem like soul mates, there is nothing plastic about Lynne.

'Joe made the first approach to me, I didn't chase him,' she says. 'In 1993 the company was being pursued by several merger suitors. Joe and I had hours of extra work to do, providing written answers to questions from the suitors' lawyers. One night, late, he leaned over and kissed me. I was terrified. I pulled away as quickly as I could. I thought I'd lose my job and I couldn't afford to do that, being a single parent with two little girls.'

According to both Lynne and Joe there was no follow-up kiss for several months. 'My dress did change around this time,' admits Lynne, who claims she tried to keep her relationship with Joe on an honest footing from the start. 'I divorced my husband the year before our first kiss. We had got married when I was fresh out of high school. I was eighteen, he was my teenage sweetheart. I was a virgin when I married him. So I went from having my mum tell me what to wear to having my husband tell me. Once he and I split I began to find my own style. I had this awful southern-style big puffy hair-do, so I cut it short and I bought some fashionable work suits.' Lynne says the new suits were a reflection of her social status in the company. Seaboard has sixty employees in Burlington, fifty-three of which are women, and all had clerical jobs except Lynne who was hired as a management administrator. Whereas the other women spent their days with each other, Lynne worked in the management suite. 'I saw female clients come in with smart outfits and I thought I should look like them. I bought four or five, but none have micro leather skirts or see-through blouses. I'm a very modest person and I would never dress in a revealing way.'

Joe Hutlemyer says he sensed early on that the other women in Seaboard were jealous of his assistant, especially as Lynne had been hired from outside the company against a list of internal candidates. That envy increased, according to Lynne, as their workload made them inseparable.

'We began having dinner together,' she says. 'He asked me and it all seemed professional, or at most just a developing friendship, but Joe did begin to tell me about the problems in his marriage and there were plenty, whatever Dorothy says. Once he told me they hadn't had sex for seven years and only twice in the three years before that.'

Joe Hutlemyer confirms this detail with an agonized expression, as if he can't believe his libido was in the ice-box for so long. In contradiction to Dorothy, he says the intimacy in his marriage disappeared soon after their tenth anniversary, which was spent in Hawaii. He found she would not talk about any problems they were having. Dorothy says they never discussed going to a marriage guidance counsellor; Joe says he begged her many times to go with him to a psychiatrist. 'She refused,' says Joe. 'In October 1992, she took me to a hotel for a night, so we could talk without the children hearing. I told her then if it hadn't been for the boys I would have left her a long time ago and that was a year before I first kissed Lynne. Unfortunately, my ex-wife is one of those people who lives in her own world, she doesn't want to think there's a bad world outside. Whenever I wanted to talk about our troubles she would go shut herself in the bedroom.'

Lynne heard some of this from Joe at their dinners and their relationship intensified. 'There was no definite pattern,' says Lynne. 'Joe was very involved with his children. I liked the fact he was so dedicated to his kids. In July 1994 he told me he had spoken to an attorney about a divorce. I felt sorry for Dorothy but the relationship did sound dead. We began meeting. When we did first have sex, I was told he was no longer living with his wife. He'd taken an apartment and there were some of his clothes there, but I became suspicious. I called the attorney, who said Joe had not approached him about divorce. I stopped seeing him immediately.'

Lynne's outrage about Joe's lie could be interpreted as a morally proper decision. Or a calculated attempt to put pressure on him to get divorce proceedings under way. Lynne claims it was the former. 'We went back to a working relationship for the next four months and I did not sit at home pining,' she says, her voice full of passion and emphasis. 'I saw plenty of other people. I was having a good time.'

When 1995 began, Lynne and Joe started having their dinners again. They say it's because they enjoyed the friendship, both felt that a love was developing that went deeper than either of their previous marriages. Throughout the year they met when they could, but had a further disagreement just before Christmas, based on Joe's reluctance to get the divorce he claimed he wanted.

'That Christmas was the most unhappy time of my life,' says Joe. 'I looked at Dot on Christmas Day and I was scared. I worried that I would be stuck in a loveless marriage for the rest of my life. I couldn't bear that.' He waited until all Dorothy's relatives had left on New Year's Day 1996 and then began calling Lynne. 'I wouldn't answer the phone to him, I kept hanging up,' she says. 'He came around to my home and begged me to let him in, which eventually I did. That's when we went away.'

Lynne is not proud of that part, that she was having sex with somebody else's husband when he was still married. 'We have asked forgiveness many times. We have been on our knees crying many times,' she says. 'We know what we did wasn't right. We've made mistakes. I think I didn't take action soon enough to make our relationship public because of my upbringing, and there were three kids involved on his side and two on mine, but I know I've been forgiven. In my religion, Pentecostal, if you ask for forgiveness and you're repentant you are forgiven. The sin I committed was adultery, not theft. I am not guilty of stealing Joe. If you have a wonderful marriage, as Dorothy claims, nobody can get in between.'

The new Hutlemyers now face an uncertain future. Both were fired from their jobs when the affair become public, although Joe was re-hired by the new owners when Seaboard was taken over. Their apartment is tiny and sparsely furnished compared to Joe's big house. They no longer have the money for the dinners that began their relationship. Instead they get by with simple pleasures like riding a fairground carousel and eating popcorn.

'We never thought Dorothy would go through with it, once she got the alimony settlement,' says Lynne. 'What she gets every month puts her in the top 5% income bracket for North Carolina, so the suit was pure revenge, but we are trying not to judge her motives because there are five children involved.'

The million-dollar judgement gathers interest – Dorothy Hutlemyer originally asked for $6.7 million – and will hang over Lynne Hutlemyer like a burgeoning dark cloud, unless the woman scorned moderates her fury. 'If Joe dies tomorrow the proceeds of his life insurance policy will all end up with her,' says Lynne. 'I'm financially persona non grata. I cannot own property, take out a loan or have a joint bank account with Joe. We've just heard that Dorothy's lawyer is trying to find a way to sue Joe. They've dug up some other old law which says they can prosecute him if he was a willing participant in my actions.'

Despite these worries, Joe and Lynne seem happy with each other, their interactions carefree and relaxed, something Joe says he never had with Dorothy. They even believe the court ordeal has brought them closer and made their love stronger, that two weeks in the glaring spotlight of international media attention has proved to them their love is built on a firm foundation.

Curiously, both Lynn and Dorothy agree about one thing with regard to Joe – that he will never commit adultery again. 'I'm not scared of that,' says Lynne. 'He doesn't have a roving eye.' Dorothy can't see Joe as a professional Casanova either. 'He's a family man. He'd still be in this family if she hadn't lured him away but he's a good person, he's not a womanizer.'

The jury that found Lynne Hutlemyer guilty was mixed, with nine women and three men. Four of the jurors were teachers; jury foreman Grimley owns a car dealership. They deliberated for seven hours before making their unanimous decision. The instructions they received from the judge, based on case law, told them that the consent of the plaintiff's spouse to the relationship is no justification or excuse for the defendant's behaviour. Many jurors say they feel this instruction left no mitigating circumstances for Lynne, leaving them no chance but to find her guilty. Grimley says they also voted guilty because Lynne's lawyer presented little evidence in her favour, opting instead to trivialize adultery and the alienation of affection law on grounds that 'everybody does it these days'. 'He chose the wrong jury to do that with,' says Grimley, who has been married to the same woman for thirty-three years.

Lynne believes the jury chose to ignore her side of the story, which can happen to an adulteress in a town where the merits of slavery are still under debate in some quarters. Dorothy claims the verdict is reassuring. 'The people of North Carolina were saying to me, "You were right to stand up for yourself," and saying to the other person, "You were wrong in what you did, breaking up my family."' Lynne has a different perspective. 'It's ludicrous to say I split them up. The two of them had not made love in seven years. If my husband hadn't made love to me in that long I would not describe my relationship as a "storybook marriage". Until Dorothy can acknowledge she shares responsibility in the breakdown of that marriage, she can never get on with her life and other people will go on suffering.'

In fact, with the million-dollar verdict seemingly written in stone, neither Lynne or Dorothy will find it easy to move on. It will hang over both of them, increasing the ex-wife's bitterness and building anger in her replacement. That's a volatile mix with five children involved and Joe Hutlemyer trying to be a father to his old and new families. Knowing the possible consequences of such sharp emotions may explain why forty-six more enlightened states in the US have removed alienation of affection laws from their books. The irony is that if Joe had met Lynne in Pennsylvania, where he and Dorothy were born and married, the most his ex-wife could have hoped for would be decent alimony.

The most striking aspect of the Hutlemyer's legal triangle is what it says about the intrusion of lawyers into every corner of American life. The US legal system has become like a Stalinist code, impinging on social behaviour that has nothing to do with criminal acts. It calls for double jeopardy across the board because of the way damages are interpreted so liberally. It's not enough to fire somebody for inappropriate behaviour, they must be sued as well for the 'distress' they caused. It's not enough to pay alimony, there must be compensation for 'alienated affections'. Not that there is any consistency in this. Lynne and Joe Hutlemyer suffered their tribulations whilst their President admitted to lying about at least two extramarital affairs.

'I can understand people who say our government has become wicked,' says Joe. 'There's a sense in America laws are no longer made for the people but for the benefit of the few. I'm not going to join a militia group and go shoot somebody, but there are plenty who do, and I'm not sure I can blame them.' Of course Joe's biggest mistake was to reject that tuna sandwich. If he'd eaten the thing, Dorothy might have been more forgiving.

13. The Other Oklahoma

The state of Oklahoma is full of people who take the steps towards violence that Joe Hutlemyer shies away from. There are more armed militia groups in Oklahoma than any other state in the union, apart from Florida. The militias are the biggest threat to peace in America, yet federal authorities have bungled every significant operation against them, including one which, when it failed, opened the gates to the worst act of terrorism in US history.

In the pre-dawn hours of 19 April 1995, a sinister team of eight men loaded themselves into a rented yellow lorry and a battered Chevrolet sixty miles from Oklahoma City. As the sun began to rise over the mid-western plains of America's heartland the men talked excitedly about striking a blow for freedom – one that would kill any sense of innocence the country still retained.

In Tulsa, ninety minutes away, an agent of the Federal Bureau of Investigation called a colleague in Oklahoma City. He wanted to ensure all federal agents had been warned away from work for the next twenty-four hours in anticipation of a terrorist attack. On the man's desk was a top-secret file from a government undercover informant. She had slept her way to the top of a vicious right-wing organization housed in a heavily armed camp on the Oklahoma-Arkansas border. For six months she been had been warning that American terrorists would strike hard at a government building in Oklahoma on 19 April.

As the eight men in their two vehicles drew close to Oklahoma City, forty-six-year-old Kathy Willburn was changing her two-year-old grandson Colton, whilst his three-year-old brother Chase played nearby. The boy's mother, Edye Smith, was finishing her make-up. She had lived at home since her marriage collapsed a year previously. It was her twenty-fifth birthday and she wanted to look special. Kathy's husband Glenn helped Colton into a pair of blue sandals and kissed his forehead. The boys were Glenn's pride and joy. Although a successful businessman with a big Mercedes, he loved Colton and Chase more than anything money could buy. Unlike FBI agents, the Willburn family had not been warned that the normally serene setting of central Oklahoma City was the potential site of an atrocity. By 9.00 a.m. Colton and Chase were playing at America's Kids', a nursery school in the basement of the Alfred P. Murrah Federal Building. Edye Smith had chosen it because she worked nearby. Outside the Murrah, the men left their yellow lorry parked at the kerb. The four men in the second vehicle sped away and the four in the truck ran from the scene. In her office, blissfully ignorant of any danger, Edye Smith prepared to blow out candles on a birthday cake, when the clock reached 9.02 a.m. and one hundred and sixty-seven people died. The terrorist bomb struck the Murrah building like a hammer hitting a ripe melon. In the fiery implosion Colton and Chase were ripped apart. No agents of the FBI or ATF, the Bureau of Alcohol, Firearms and Tobacco, were injured. Saved by the advance warning, they were 'off-base'.

To hear Tulsa lawyer Clark Brewster tell it, twenty-six-year-old Carol Howe knows enough about what really happened that morning to put half the FBI's top men in jail. The Federal Bureau of Investigation has mishandled more than a dozen high-profile cases in the last five years, but Brewster says Howe can prove something much worse than incompetence – that America's top law enforcement agency must share responsibility for the Oklahoma City blast.

'Carol was a federal undercover agent for the last few months of 1994 and all of 1995,' says the wealthy Brewster, arguably Tulsa's top lawyer, a man who holds court in chambers decorated with paintings of million-dollar horses – livestock that he owns. He didn't take this case for the money but because he believes in Carol Howe. 'She spied on domestic terrorists for the FBI and its sister agency, the Bureau of Alcohol, Tobacco and Firearms. From reports she filed, the FBI knew full well the Murrah Building would be bombed on 19 April 1995, and that makes her a big embarrassment for the US government.'

With characteristic spite, the FBI and ATF say Howe is 'unreliable and deceitful' and claims she was eventually fired from undercover work because she was too 'volatile'. These mighty agencies got their chance to prove Howe a liar. She was charged with inciting others to build bombs and make threatening telephone calls. It was a strange twist to events because Howe's allegedly illegal activities were exactly the kind of thing the FBI asked her to do when she was first recruited. The FBI's case was laughed out of court and Howe was acquitted. Now she waits for a much bigger court hearing, which probably will not take place until 2001. That's when twenty-eight families of victims from the Oklahoma City blast, including Edye Smith and the Willburns, will be able to call Howe as their main witness. The bereaved relatives claim Howe's reports from deep undercover in America's right-wing militia movement gave federal agents plenty of time to stop Oklahoma bomber Tim McVeigh. They want the US government to pay $80 million in damages.

The FBI recruits about four dozen undercover operatives

each year. Their shadowy world is usually kept firmly from public view, but Carol Howe's case gives a rare insight into the dangerous, deceitful life of a spy who snoops on her fellow citizens. If her example is typical, it shows that working under-cover requires agents to experience a complex series of psychological manoeuvres that can lead to depression, rage and attempts at suicide. It also shows that with communism's collapse, US espionage agencies have turned inwards, putting more Americans than ever before under the surveillance microscope. Their mendacious tactics have helped spread paranoia amongst the population to an unparalleled extent.

Friends say Carol Howe has a flair for the over-dramatic, but when we met in Tulsa it was easy to see the fear she feels is real. 'I know the group I spied upon wants me dead,' she says, nervously pulling at a thumbnail already picked red and raw. 'I think the FBI would not cry a single tear if I died because they'd like me silenced for good.'

The FBI decision to turn Howe into a spy should have given her some claim to be a hero, but almost everything that led her into the line of fire seems to have had a sordid edge, making her motives seem dubious and those of her handlers evil. Like many Americans, Howe grew up on a diet over-rich in chat-show hysteria, which may help explain why she took on a life-threatening mission so eagerly, as if it were a fantasy computer game. Now, as then, if photographs of her as a spy are a guide, Howe's eyes often have a vacant look, the stare from a mind with a short attention span. It seems like something has deadened Carol Howe's consciousness. It could be TV, it could be the FBI or months inside a stinking, primitive camp full of fanatics. It could be the alleged sexual assault by a prominent American neo-Nazi that made it easy for the FBI to recruit her. The look is increasingly common amongst Americans, as if the brashest and most ubiquitous elements of the culture are inflicting a pernicious form of brain damage.

'I wasn't looking to become a spy,' she says. 'I was looking for justice.' Carol Howe tells me this sitting in a lounge that feels like a furniture showroom. Everything is polished and fresh but, like furniture for sale, it doesn't seem as if it belongs to anybody. There is no sense of an owner's personality. There's a coldness, a sign of a house where emotions are always kept in check. Her mother hovers nearby, cleaning a kitchen that's already spotless. There are plenty of signs that this is a home where it would not be easy to discuss sex, where a young woman like Howe could feel she had to hide the sexual abuse she suffered for fear her socially connected parents would be ashamed.

Howe says she has always felt isolated in her parents' million-dollar home. An only child, adopted just after birth, she claims she was given everything but love. Howe's adopted mother Aubyn is a prominent philanthropist, who for over a year during her legal trials refused to be photographed with Carol, reinforcing her daughter's apparent belief that she was taken on by the Howes as just one more of their charity projects. Lacking affection, she says she looked for emotional support from men and found it with a neighbour she married just after her twenty-second birthday. Neither she nor her parents will discuss her failed marriage, but Howe's friends say the match met with disapproval, especially from Carol's father, an oil company executive known throughout Oklahoma.

In September 1993 Carol was with her husband (whom she divorced in 1995) when she began her journey into the FBI's network of domestic spies. She was resting in Tulsa's Langland Park at the top of a rock outcrop. Her husband and two of his friends had gone for soft drinks. Three black males approached and tried to rob her but the mugging soon escalated to a sexual assault, after which Howe was pushed off a ledge twenty feet above a bridle path.

'I broke both my ankles. They were shattered. I'm still having corrective surgery,' says Howe, whose dreams of becoming an Olympic horsewoman ended that day. 'I found I suddenly hated blacks with all my being, I couldn't be around them. I became a racist. I was pleased whenever I heard about bad things happening to black people.'

Evidence from several quarters, including school friends, shows Howe had no racist leanings before the Langland Park assault, for which nobody was ever charged. Her adopted parents are liberal Republicans. At high school and college fellow students thought Howe was a liberal, but within two weeks of her release from hospital Howe had joined a white supremacist group, White Aryan Resistance. She left her husband, after catching him in an affair, and had swastikas etched on to her ankle and shoulder.

'I still don't know why I got the tattoos,' she says. 'One of my husband's friends persuaded me to join this Aryan group pledged to fight blacks. He told me I'd never get justice from Tulsa's cops. He said they were all black and hated me because my parents have money. I think the tattoo was all about having them accept me, I really wanted to belong to something.'

Howe's sudden conversion to neo-Nazi politics has been analysed by her psychiatrist as an adverse reaction to trauma. It certainly surprised her friends. Before the Langland Park attack, Howe had ridden her parents' connections, becoming a local debutante, a Tulsa beauty queen and a talented horse-woman, making the trials for the US Olympic show jumping team that competed in Atlanta. 'She never spoke much about politics,' says Candi Gillard, who was her friend in college. 'Horses, manicures and boys were Carol's topics of conversation – in that order.'

A prominent member of WAR, Dennis Mahon, soon developed a sexual infatuation for the fetching young recruit, who was so different from the goth-like men who made up the bulk of membership. When Howe decided after six weeks she'd taken a wrong turn, her troubles escalated. 'I think I emerged out of post-traumatic shock,' says Howe. 'I was at a WAR meeting and the other members suddenly looked repellent, worse even than the men who attacked me. I felt I couldn't breathe, it was like a bad anxiety attack. I decided to resign; they wouldn't let me.'

For the next three months, through mid 1994, Dennis Mahon

harassed Howe almost every day. The abuse began with telephone calls. He would leave threats of violence on her answering machine. Then he began sending audio tapes describing what had happened to those who plotted against Hitler. Eventually Howe handed all this evidence to local police, but not before the night her persecutor arrived at her front door.

'I'd been out of the movement for about a month,' she says. 'He had threatened to kill me and said I'd gone to the other side. When he arrived at my flat he said he was sorry and wanted to talk. I refused, then he barged his way in.' Howe alleges that for the next three hours she was subjected to a prolonged sexual assault. 'I felt so dirty and ashamed afterwards, like somehow it was my fault. I didn't feel I could tell anyone. I remember lying in the shower scrubbing my swastika tattoo with a hard brush, trying to make it go away, lying there for hours.'

Three days later Howe decided her attacker would return unless she took action. She went to the local police and filed a petition for a protective order. She placed with the court the tapes from her answering machine, some of Mahon's threatening letters and one of the audio cassettes, all of which gave a good basis for criminal charges against her attacker. Howe's petition, protective order number PO 94 02047, was filed with Tulsa District Court on 23 August 1994. Her handwriting is shaky and adolescent, like a teenager's diary, except one of her complaints has nothing to do with dates or dances: it catalogues a threat that the Aryan group would 'take steps to neutralize' her.

When ATF agent Angela Graham saw Howe's petition it seems she sensed a goldmine. She had been trying to get inside information on Oklahoma's extreme right-wing groups, of which there are several dozen, for more than five years, with little success. In that period the groups had staged eighteen local bank robberies, netting more than $6 million, killed an Arkansas police officer, and were suspected in the disappearance of two civil-rights workers. The American right has what many believe is its national headquarters in north-east Oklahoma, a heavily armed compound hidden in the Ozark mountains. Called Elohim City, it's the home of Christian Identity, an umbrella organization for neo-Nazis that has been a refuge to a score of armed white separatists, including Timothy McVeigh. When Graham was given access to the petition she immediately hatched a plan to use Howe as an infiltrator, putting her on the federal payroll as an undercover agent with the hope Howe could get inside Elohim City.

'I was shocked when Agent Graham called,' says Howe. 'It was the last thing I expected. We met and there was something sympathetic about her. I ended up telling her everything that had happened, including the sexual assault. She told me there was no way to prosecute my attacker, now that so many days had passed. Her solution was that I should get my own back by putting him behind bars as a terrorist. I found the idea instantly appealing. I wanted him punished, I also felt the neo-Nazi movement, from what I'd seen, was a real threat. Agent Graham also made the job seem important, like I'd be doing a real service for my country.'

Howe had considered a military career before her ankles were smashed, but knew her injury put that ambition out of her reach. Graham's suggestion of working for the FBI seemed a good substitute and Howe, who says she had been feeling increasingly depressed throughout 1994, suddenly felt her self-esteem improve. 'Graham made me feel I was really wanted, that I was important,' she says. 'It was a huge boost for my morale.'

Graham's plan was that Howe should go back to her attacker and say she'd had a change of heart, that she wanted to 'fight for the preservation of her race'. Howe doubted she could tell such a blatant lie with much success. Graham's response was to despatch her on a training course where the main item on the curriculum was deception. The FBI trainers allegedly taught Howe every trick of the lying trade, emphasizing the importance of eye contact. She was told, the bigger the lie, the deeper she must look into the target's eyes. For the first of many times she was told to use her sexuality as an asset when probing a male target. By October 1994 she was deemed to be ready.

'I didn't feel I was, I was actually getting cold feet, but Agent Graham made all sorts of promises about the back-up I'd get from the bureau,' says Howe, ruefully. 'She put me on the FBI payroll at $120 per day; her first assignment for me was to film WAR arming hand grenades. She especially wanted evidence against Denis Mahon, who was now the leader of WAR in Oklahoma.'

As part of the plan, Howe and Graham went shopping for a large steamer trunk. During their trip around the stores, Graham continued Howe's education in espionage, describing methods for leaving notes at dead drops concealed in parking lots, shrubbery or deserted houses, and techniques for shaking a tail. Howe says she felt she'd stepped through the looking glass, especially when Graham helped her rig the steamer trunk for a meeting with Mahon.

'We had a tiny surveillance camera mounted inside, with a small hole drilled for a lens,' says Howe. 'We then put the trunk in my apartment.' Howe and Graham bought legal, practice grenades from an Army surplus store. 'I got Dennis talked into turning them live by repacking the grenades with explosive, so he did, on camera,' says Howe. 'That's when I realized these guys mean business, that I could get hurt.'

Graham played down Howe's anxieties and aggressively pushed her to do more. She suggested her new young spy persuade Mahon to take her into Christian Identity's Elohim City compound. It didn't take the WAR leader long to agree. 'I think he thought we were going to be a romantic item,' Howe says. 'I encouraged him to do that, like I'd been taught. It was really hard for me to keep up that act, but by now it seemed more dangerous not to go forward with the surveillance. I felt if I dropped out of WAR for the second time I could get really hurt.'

In November 1994 Howe had won Mahon's trust to such

an extent he was prepared to introduce her to Christian Identity's leadership, so she began preparing for her first visit to Elohim City. The night before she was due to leave she had a nightmare. 'I woke shivering,' she says. 'I realized if they found out I was spying, I might not get out alive, that I might never see my parents again.'

Although Agent Graham would later describe Howe as 'flaky', there's no doubt Howe soon became an invaluable source of information about Christian Identity, universally regarded within the FBI as America's most dangerous right-wing cult. According to Clark Brewster, during her first spell at Elohim City, Howe filed more than forty detailed reports that gave federal agents an unprecedented grasp of CI's politics and personnel.

The CI compound is located six miles off Oklahoma's main highway, East-West Highway, and it's reached by a muddy track full of dips and potholes. The makeshift road is deliberately kept in bad condition to slow down any attacks from the FBI and the ATF, which led the raid on the Branch Davidian compound at Waco. Heavily armed CI 'soldiers' patrol the track and the surrounding woods.

'Those guys are really paranoid,' Howe says. 'To them, every stranger is an FBI agent disguised as a journalist, mailman or travelling salesman. They want you to think they're a well-oiled military machine. My FBI training included role-playing sessions where I was quizzed about my background or directly confronted with charges that I was an infiltrator. I went through two mock interrogations lasting more than nine hours with nothing to eat or drink, but that can prepare you for the real thing. It's an incredible adrenaline rush when you first get away with telling a bald-faced lie to a guy with a gun pointed right at you. It gave me a feeling of power I'd never experienced before.'

At Elohim City, males are the dominant sex. Women in the Christian Identity compound must do the chores, work the fields and bear children, whilst swearing allegiance to Jesus and the movement's men, who nurse a vicious anger towards the government and its agents, especially anyone who, like Carol Howe, might be an informant.

The Elohim City homes are shaped like beehives and were constructed by pouring polyurethane over a hot-air balloon, which was then deflated. Once the polyurethane sets, windows and doorways are cut into the material. These odd structures give the compound a unique sense of menace. The polyurethane, orange in colour, looks malevolent, resembling sulphur bubbling up from some deep chamber of hell. Carol Howe lived in one of these structures for five long months, freezing in winter, roasting in the baking hot midwestern summers and witnessing the CI-membership's psychotic rage. Most of the time contacting Agent Graham was a risky enterprise.

'The CI people know how to intimidate,' she says. 'For anybody who joined, the leaders made it clear betrayal would bring death, for the new member and their family. They said there had been informers killed in the past, their bodies buried under coffins in other people's graves. They told me one woman was buried in the forest, her body booby-trapped with explosives. I was stripped and searched eight times in the first three weeks. I felt bad but I couldn't let that show. I learned that my role demanded I deaden most of my emotions. Every morning I'd spend time in the bathroom practising the kind of extremist statements I had to make to be credible, watching my face in the mirror to make sure my expressions were appropriate.'

Inside Elohim City Howe became precisely the kind of 'honey trap' ATF agent Graham had expected. Men in CI from the leaders down were attracted to her and several made advances. At one point, whilst she was back in Tulsa for a month, Graham suggested Howe visit a psychologist who schooled her in 'male sexuality' so she could better control her 'targets' with a 'flirt/promise/reward' system, in which the reward was always much smaller than the promise.

'The psychologist told me men can be trained like dogs,'

says Howe. 'She said they will do anything for sex and almost anything for the promise of sex in the future. I was told to act like I was always available but never actually consummate anything. There's a lot of sex on the compound. It's miles from nowhere and the members aren't supposed to drink, so there's not much else to do. All female agents in federal organizations are taught that male sexuality can be used as a potent weapon against a male target. I was no different. I used to be quite romantic about men, now I tend to treat male strangers with hostility.'

One of Howe's best sources of information in Elohim City was the Phillips family. 'They were very warm to me,' she says. 'They asked me to stay in their home and I became close with their son, who had just turned twenty. He was keen to impress me and gave out extensive information about CI's arsenal – his father was CI's quartermaster. I felt sorry for him. He was a nice kid and I'd pretend to be so impressed when he told me about this or that gun he'd seen his father use. That made him melt, he'd just start babbling, saying, "You ain't seen nothing yet," and promising to show me some "top secret" rocket launchers supposedly hidden under the compound's church.'

Howe and twenty-year-old Stephen Phillips developed a close relationship full of flirtatious innuendo and the spy says it was a key factor in her survival, until Stephen's mother intervened. 'She took me aside one day and asked me to back off Stephen, for the sake of her husband. I was really puzzled until she revealed that Stephen's father had chosen me as his second wife. Mrs Phillips said her husband was polygamous, like all the CI leadership, and she said she approved of his choice, so long as I stayed away from Stephen.'

Polygamy is widespread amongst the US radical right. Multiple wives and multiple firearms are the two passions of the modern American Nazi and the two are probably connected, if only because the way the men speak to their women suggests they are not adverse to using a gun or two to keep them in line.

Andreas Strassmeir was another Nazi charmer who fell for Howe, whom he called 'a model Ayran'. A German illegal immigrant who claimed to be from a neo-Nazi cell in Berlin, Strassmeir became CI's head of security whilst Howe was at Elohim City. Graham had taught Howe techniques for remembering all she had seen and been told without making extensive notes. Instead Howe marked key words in different chapters of paperback novels, each chapter representing a new day. This tradecraft served Carol well. 'I know Strassmeir searched my room on several occasions,' she says. 'I think he suspected me of being an infiltrator from the beginning.'

Graham had told Howe to get especially close to anyone like Strassmeir who looked like he might have guessed her true identity. Carol was taught psychological games to play with Strassmeir, designed to get his sympathy. She was told to ask him extensive questions about his past, to respond sympathetically whenever he mentioned difficulties in his life and to repeat his opinions in her own words whenever he was near.

These psychological manipulations, originally developed by the CIA, worked. Strassmeir ceased to treat her with suspicion and increasingly drew Howe into the CI inner circle. Throughout late 1994 and into 1995, Howe filed detailed reports to Graham concerning CI plans to bomb federal buildings, including accounts of trips by CI members to 'case' the Murrah in Oklahoma, McVeigh's eventual target. To assess her honesty and accuracy, Howe was subjected to monthly lie-detector tests, a standard routine for infiltrators. According to FBI documents, she passed every one. 'Those polygraph tests were a reality check for me,' she says. 'I used each one to ask myself if I wanted to go on. I only had to think of the way I was attacked by a member of WAR. Then I found the courage I needed to say yes.'

In February 1995, at a meeting with Mahon and Strassmeir, attended by Pete Langan and Kevin McCarthy, two CI 'fund raisers' (they rob banks), CI's leader, the Reverend Robert Millar, announced it was time to 'go to war'. Howe was asked if she was in. When she said yes, Millar told her she could no longer leave the CI compound without permission.

'We were all given notice that our movements had to be accounted for at all times and we began to train extensively in the woods, with all sorts of weapons,' says Howe, who became an expert in small arms with the help of CI. 'They also had us dress in paramilitary uniforms, complete with boots and swastikas. One day when we were in combat dress I almost broke down, because I knew my mother would be so upset if she could see me. I couldn't let anyone know I was feeling so bad because by now everybody was on combat readiness and any sign of weakness would have been suspicious.' This was the hardest time for Carol Howe. Isolated amongst men whom she says think nothing of raping or maiming, she increasingly feared for her safety. 'I often felt completely alone, ' says Howe. 'Even if I spent time with other CI women who I'd become friendly with, it didn't help much, because I was sure they wouldn't be my friends if they knew my true identity.'

Howe tried turning to prayer. 'That didn't help much either,' she says. 'I think I felt God should never have let me be attacked in Langland Park. Then I saw the CI people talking about God all the time and it twisted my sense of Christianity. I think they made it much more difficult for me to believe in God.' A spy in the field is always psychologically vulnerable and someone with unresolved psychological problems especially so, because spies need an exceptionally concrete sense of their own identity to survive. Like Carol in Elohim City, they are far from home and cannot communicate with anybody on an honest level. Many snap and Howe was no exception.

At the beginning of March 1995 Howe, claiming she had to attend to a legal matter back in Tulsa, was given a ten-day leave of absence from Elohim City. She was warned to be back in the compound on time or a contract would be put on her life for desertion. In the week before her departure Howe says she witnessed several meetings that made it clear an attack had been given the green light and would take place on 19 April, Patriot's Day in the US, the most sacred occasion in the white supremacist calendar. She passed this on to Agent Angela Graham, also revealing that the target would be a building in Tulsa or Oklahoma. She was given another polygraph test after her debriefing, which she passed.

A few days later Howe suffered some form of brief mental collapse, and even she isn't sure exactly what happened, although she says her psychiatrist believes it was further delayed reactions to the two attacks she had suffered, combined with the stress of working undercover. The Tulsa police report on the incident notes that Howe was admitted to a local mental health facility suffering from what appeared to be self-inflicted wounds. ATF agent Graham says that when she heard of the incident she had Howe 'decommissioned', but there is no evidence of that in the ATF or FBI records. Both organizations continued to list Howe as an active agent available for duty and pressed her to make a trip back inside Elohim City after the Oklahoma bomb. 'I got a call from Agent Graham on 20 April 1995,' says Howe. 'I was taken to a secret command post near the Murrah Building where I was debriefed by the FBI for the next three days. From the sketches of John Doe 1 and 2, the people who allegedly rented the Ryder truck which carried the bomb, I identified Pete Ward and Michael Brescia, two Elohim City soldiers who had bragged to me about their hold-ups at over a dozen banks.'

Graham said the FBI needed information about who was still inside the CI compound and what kind of weapons they had. 'I sensed the FBI were planning a raid,' says Howe. 'I told them they were crazy, that I'd be killed. Angela told me I'd be fine, so long as I used my "charms" to make them trust me again. She even suggested I tell the CI security guys I'd signed on with the FBI so that I could be a double agent, reporting back to CI the details of FBI operations.'

Horrified by the bomb in Oklahoma City, Howe decided with great reluctance that it was her duty to revisit Elohim

City, although she insisted on taking several small guns with her, hidden in a secret compartment under her car. 'There was a lot of talk about being raided when I got back in,' she says. 'There were a lot of new faces too, guys who were heavily armed and talking about a stand-off with the FBI.' The key fact she reported was that Brescia, Ward and security chief Andreas Strassmeir were all missing. 'I was too scared to stay more than three days,' she says. 'I left and told the FBI nothing I saw changed my opinion that CI were involved in the Oklahoma City bomb.'

Back in Tulsa after Carole had spent the summer trying to get over her grief at the Oklahoma city bombing, Howe's life took another sharp turn. Agent Graham asked her to get friendly with a suspect called James Viefhaus Jr, another member of WAR. Howe was told to play Viefhaus using the same techniques practised on Mahon. She agreed because she felt Viefhaus was not yet a militant and she felt she could still save him from WAR and CI. Now a sophisticated operator, Howe soon had Viefhaus making threatening telephone calls in her presence and buying explosive materials.

At the same time, the FBI 'accidentally' told Tim McVeigh's defence team about Howe's work in Elohim City, blowing Carol's cover. She was sought out by McVeigh's attorney and a victims group that already suspected the FBI had been negligent. 'If they'd listened to Carol my grandsons would still be alive,' Glenn Willburn said when he filed suit against the US Federal Government. 'They let the bomb happen through their negligence and both my daughter's sons were killed.'

'Since Mr Willburn filed his suit, the FBI and the ATF have been trying to discredit me,' says Howe, checking the window as a car she doesn't recognize slows down outside her house. 'They know I can expose their incompetence.' In March 1996 Viefhaus was arrested and charged with conspiracy to make bombs. He was found guilty. To Howe's astonishment she was also arrested and charged with the same offence.

'The charges were always ridiculous,' says her lawyer, Clark

Brewster. 'She was charged with a crime for doing what she was ordered to do by the FBI and ATF. She was still listed as an undercover asset of the FBI throughout 1996 and had only agreed to monitor Viefhaus because she thought he was wavering and she might be able to get him out of WAR. The charges are an attempt to gag Carol.'

Before police put her in handcuffs, Howe says she thought the FBI were trying to lure her and Viefhaus into an illegal act. 'For weeks earlier this year James and I kept getting a document faxed to us, encouraging us to buy machine guns and explosives, along with numbers we could call if we were interested in avenging Waco,' she says. 'The faxes were traced to a number that belongs to Richard Scrum, another FBI undercover who has testified in court that he is paid to infiltrate right-wing groups. I had to laugh. An FBI operative myself, I was being infiltrated. It was absurd.'

Reflecting on her time at Elohim City and the events since, Carol Howe has no doubt that Timothy McVeigh and Terry Nichols did not act alone. She feels her knowledge of CI secrets gives them a reason to hurt her, whilst the FBI's fear of an embarrassing lawsuit made it necessary for them to try to keep her silent, and in her darker moments she fears she's being set up. 'The FBI knew the CI people would like me dead so they arrested me and took away my guns, so I was defenceless. And they forced me to live with my parents, which puts them in danger. Nobody should be surprised if we all end up dead. The biggest irony of all is that nobody at Elohim City has been charged with anything.'

Howe has changed into a pair of blue jeans and a white blouse. The clothes hide her Nazi tattoos, the ones that helped her deflect suspicion inside Elohim City, where they functioned as a badge of devotion. She looks like an ordinary young woman from a nice family, maybe set for an afternoon shopping with friends. Unless they knew, nobody would suspect that if the Oklahoma victims get their negligence suit to court, she could one day become one of the most famous spies in American history. 'I did my job, like they asked me to. I guess like anybody who has spied for America, I thought it was my duty to work for the FBI and the ATF, now I'm no longer sure whose side they are on.'

The Willburns' home is still overshadowed by the tragedy of the Murrah Building. The one-storey ranch – American for bungalow – is like a macabre museum. The Willburns collected celebrity memorabilia before Chase and Colton died. A trio of mannequins stand guard to the lounge, dressed in costumes worn by Elvis, Mae West and Racquel Welch. Once they must have been dusted every day. Since the bombing nobody in the Willburn household has had the will to clean them and they wear layers of dust, like so many tears gone dry. There, the lounge centrepiece is a white piano which Sinatra once played, and a battalion of signed celebrity snapshots. Around the room are glass cases displaying costumes once worn by silent movie stars now long dead.

These fragments from the largely deceased are an unsettling counterpoint to the back bedroom, which has been left as it was on the morning Edye Smith ushered her boys out for what became their last day at school. Toys tumble around the pillows that seem to have ghostly indentations of the lost boys. Edye's mother has kept the diaper she removed from Chase that morning. She knows it must seem odd but it would feel far too final for her to throw it away. To this add one more fallen leaf: Glenn Willburn died a month before the second anniversary of the Oklahoma bomb, from a rare form of lymph cancer. He lived long enough to see Edye remarry but not to see her deliver a new child, Connor, born just before Christmas 1997. Willburn, hitherto a patriot, took to his grave a profound sense of betrayal. He died believing his country had let him down.

'I don't blame him for that,' says Carol Howe. 'Most people have no idea the lengths government will go to when it has secrets. I'm still afraid for my life.' On 10 April 1998, Howe left Tulsa for an undisclosed location. Her lawyer hired a team of ex-cops to help his client disappear. She now lives somewhere in Canada under a new identity but she keeps in touch with Clark Brewster. When the time comes he will bring her back to testify against the FBI.

After meeting Howe I decided to put her charges directly to CI's leader, the Reverend Robert Millar, who is reckoned to be one of the most influential right-wing extremists in the US. The sun seemed to rise sluggishly over Muldrow, the closest town to Elohim City, as I approached from the west. Muldrow is a place so far from anywhere that the days appear in no hurry to arrive. Beyond the run-down houses, dime stores and gun brokers, the Ozark mountains look like a wall, built by God or nature to keep prosperity at a distance. One mile beyond the city limits, a ribbon of two-lane blacktop crosses a river by means of a rusty trestle bridge. The rushing water below looks like it's hurrying to get away.

Just beyond the bridge, at the beginning of an enclosed field, there's a pair of tall T-shaped gateposts which have been blackened by tar and scorching sun. From the front end of each crossbar hangs a chain attached to a plank of wood, painted white. At the rear there's another chain which just swings in the air, making the posts look more like a gallows. This is the area that gave birth to the Ku Klux Klan and it's not hard to imagine that idle chain attached to a noose around the stretched neck of a black man. The white plank carried the word 'Elohim', a Hebrew name for God.

A few yards beyond the Elohim gateposts the shiny black asphalt is scarred with ribbons of brown, tyre marks from vehicles that have been driven out of a muddy lane that slinks up into the tree line and the CI headquarters. The thick trees suddenly disappear about six miles into the CI compound. For a stretch of 50 yards, an area the size of two tennis courts had been cleared from the forest on both sides. To the right there were five ancient Packards, at least fifty years old. The once proud automobiles had rusted to a uniform brick-red, their bonnets open, engines stripped of any usable parts. To the left, a pale green MG, from around 1980, stood beside a 1950s Cadillac Convertible painted bright pink. On the Cadillac's boot a man in military camouflage sat cradling an AK-47. Nearby two men were already rising from makeshift seats in front of a camp fire. When they get near they draw handguns, identifiable at close range as Kel-Tec P-11s, a rare lightweight pistol engineered from aircraft steel and unbreakable polymers. The gun is a sophisticated semi-automatic designed for combat conditions. Unlike most small pistols, it can handle a wide range of ammunition, from 9mm to .38. It's a survivalist's weapon, built for shoot-outs or close-range assassinations.

'I'm going to need you to step out of the car,' said a man with a weasely body and a pock-marked face. 'Can you produce photo ID?' Both requests were made in a tired Texan drawl, sounding like John Wayne after a dozen beers. The ID question was asked with an air of unmistakable menace, as if failure to produce proper documents would result in instant death, whereas the right papers would simply leave being shot as an option, along with a beating or good stabbing. I offered Weasel an international driver's licence and a passport. He sauntered away, dangling the documents from his left hand as two mongerel dogs the size of skinny wolves sniffed at their covers.

Back at the pink Cadillac, Weasel gave the two IDs to the guy with the AK-47. He looked them over like they were tablets and he was Moses, searching for something that would reveal what he suspected was my true identity.

Because the soldiers of CI expect imminent attack by bomb or bullet, the trees have been cleared around their checkpoint to give them a clearer line of fire. I was still two miles from the fortified church where Robert Millar holds court. He'd agreed to a meeting to discuss the Howe's investigation but insisted on my travelling without a photographer or any other companion. It would be a while before I'd see him.

'We're not real happy with your documents,' said Weasel, on his return, waving both in the direction of Mr AK-47. 'I need to make some calls.' The man and his dogs repeated their earlier ritual, only this time Weasel walked past the Cadillac and on into the trees. For twenty long minutes AK-47 cleaned his weapon, checked ammunition and regarded me sporadically with the eye of a huntsman. Then a new figure emerged from the tree cover, carrying the two documents, a mobile phone pressed to his ear. 'The Reverend Millar is ready for you now,' the man snarled, hitching loose overalls around massive shoulders. 'We just have to search your vehicle first.'

Another twenty-five minutes passed in the cool morning air. The men who checked every inch of the truck reminded me of similar quasi-military personnel encountered on the roads around Sarajevo. Their attitudes were bad, their sense of destiny a deadly danger to anyone they perceive to be 'on the other side' and, like the Bosnian or Serb militias, these men, just two hours from Bill Clinton's home-town, also believe in the cleansing power of civil war. Finally, Weasel emerged from the jeep, sniffing suspiciously at the wrapping from an Egg McMuffin, yesterday's breakfast. Deciding the odour was sour cheese and not Semtex, he threw the garbage to the dogs and waved me back behind the wheel. 'Be careful on the road ahead,' he said, with a grin made goofy by a dozen missing teeth. 'It can get real slippy.'

Pulling up the hill toward's Elohim City, more men with guns could be seen moving through the trees, and then the ramshackle compound came into view. Reverend Millar began building here 18 years ago. He's an intense man with a surfeit of charismatic charm that's centered on his piercing brown eyes. When he speaks, it's with absolute convinction, his voice the sound of a true zealot with, absurdly, a legally armed militia to back up his bullshit.

Millar believes the US federal government is run by a Zionist conspiracy, that African Americans are morally and genetically inferior, that miscegenation will lead to a catastrophic breakdown of civil order, and that the FBI is dominated by Zionist cliques who are not loyal to the federal government. The reverend, who has a scholar's grasp of scripture, believes these issues will be solved by a bloody confrontation, a third American civil war. (He counts the Revolutionary War against Britain, not north versus south, as America's first.) Millar has built around himself a paramilitary group of theological revolutionaries who feed their appetite for hate with the memories of dead heroes.

Millar's best friend, Richard Snell, is buried in the garden of the reverend's large trailer home. He was executed in Arkansas for killing a black state trooper and Millar, along with his soldiers', would probably do the same if the opportunity arose. They dislike the police, hate the FBI and nurse a vicious deadly anger towards anyone who might be a government informant. Millar's website on the Internet is one of the most popular, which is evidence that more than a million Americans take his messianic vision seriously.

We meet in the Millar home, me and this man who is probably plotting Carol Howe's death even as his three wives make breakfast. Apart from the extra sex, there's clearly something to be said for this arrangement, at least in terms of efficiency. One Mrs Millar does the toast, one the fry-up and one the tea. The only problem is that the Millar wives have the cowed look of slaves, women who suspect an impromptu beating may be only a spilled cup or a broken egg away.

Millar is in the great American tradition of religious confidence-tricksters. He seems to have in his genes men who made fortunes selling snake oil as a universal remedy to passing wagon trains. For over two hours he uses every nook and cranny of the Bible to justify white supremacy, oppression of blacks and a host of other revolting propositions which are, sadly, increasingly popular amongst his fellow citizens. I feel if I, like Carol Howe, had to spend weeks under his gaze, I would be truly frightened. He denies ever having met Tim McVeigh or any other Oklahoma City bombers, and his alligator eyes dare me to contradict him.

In the end, and I'm choosing my words carefully, he decides to let me go. As I pass the CI church, the membership are filing in for a service, along with many of the compounds guards. I grab a stupid chance to stop and take some surreptitious photographs. A man appears with a gun. I tell him I have the Reverend Millar's permission. Whilst he goes to check this, I leave quietly feeling more scared than I have at any other time since I arrived in America, and that includes when a woman in California tried to make me wear a corset manufactured to fit a 17″ waist.

14. Not Meant for Walking

San Francisco would be a fine place for Carol Howe to hide. It's possible to remake one's identity here in a few hours and then merge into the comfortable camouflage of non-conformity. Charlie Horse got a tattoo here once, a pair of eagles fighting over a dove. He says he was on mescalin at the time and doesn't know what the symbolism means. He has thought about taking the drug for a second time to find out, but knows that wouldn't work. 'My ancestors know,' he says. 'If they wanted me to know they would have told me by now.'

Tattoos are painful for a few hours. Body piercing can cause discomfort for a couple of weeks, but one form of self-mutilation puts both these in the shade. A group of San Francisco women have reached right back way beyond Navajo history into Chinese folklore for this one. They are binding their feet, using a device that looks like an instrument of torture. Their purpose is to make their feet smaller and far more arched, so they can wear tiny shoes with 8" or 9" spike heels.

They call themselves 'modern primitives' and as the millennium drew to a close, they emerged as a potent force in West Coast fashion, claiming women don't take their feet seriously enough. The modern primitive creed says gorgeous feet aren't born, they must be trained, forced into shape with bindings and buckles that can cause excruciating pain – but hell, who said beauty would be easy? And they don't stop at feet. A world-class foot is no good on a chunky body. Feet trained to be fabulous should be accompanied by a tiny waist, preferably one that's less than 18″ round.

'Modern primitives' say their name should be taken seriously. They want it to be known that some of the barbaric practices of the past can be revived by women and used for their own purposes, in the case of foot binding and waist squeezing, to give a woman a heightened sense of her own body and her sexuality. The modern primitives say this is a form of 'feminist empowerment'. They also say their ideal woman is the cartoon character Jessica Rabbit from the 1986 movie *Who Framed Roger Rabbit?*

'We take sexist images originally produced by men and reshape them for our own purposes,' says twenty-six-year-old Sharon Nickle, as she struggles to walk around her San Francisco apartment. The young computer programmer can normally move freely and in the past she has jogged up the city's steep hills, but since January her feet spend every evening squeezed into a modern primitive foot bender, designed to reduce the length of her foot and exaggerate its arch. The more she wears the bender the easier it will be for her to slip into the highest high-heels, shoes that once would have been worn by a gangster's moll or a prostitute, women who are not noted for their freedom from oppression.

'I'm hoping to get my feet down by one quarter of their current size,' says Nickle, wincing with pain on the way to her kitchen. 'I think they will look so much prettier once I've finished,' she says, regarding the crumpled pink skin around her big toe. 'This is something I'm doing for myself. After twelve hours of binding I can wear super high-heels and I love the feeling that gives me. Men just want to fall at my feet.' No doubt, but it's what they might want me to do once they get there that should make Sharon pause for thought.

The foot bender is a fearsome-looking device which includes two metal bars that run side by side along the foot, strapped to a piece of rounded wood that fits under the arch. With the aid of straps around the toes and another set that is bound to the leg as far up as the calf, the foot is bent over the wood, the bindings pulled to the tightest point the wearer can bear.

Nickle began body training after she had got her weight down with the help of a personal trainer. Although the bender looks like something that might be used by a fascist regime to torture suspects, Nickle toes the modern primitive line that body binding is a feminist act. 'Starting with my grand-mother, who was an early women's liberationist, my ancestors have fought against women having to wear tight corsets and foot bindings,' she says. 'Now I can choose to constrict my body, if that's what I want. If I chose that shape, it's liberation; if I'm forced into it, it's slavery.'

Nickle confessed her decision to force her flesh back into a bygone age is a mix of politics and pleasure. She says she likes the way her body looks when her waist is less than 18″ and her feet are curved like a fishing hook. 'I am demonstrating control over my flesh,' she says. 'I'm sending a message that I will not be dominated by my own body. This was a look that once represented the domination of women. Now it stands for their freedom.'

Strangely, there are many women following Nickle's example, especially in Los Angeles and San Francisco. Binding is a cousin of body piercing, but practitioners say it's a distant one. Most foot and waist binders have minimal body piercing. They claim to be looking for a smoother look, although when body binders are dressed in spike shoes and corsets they look more like dancers in a cheap strip club than the vanguard of a new sexual politics – but then, there are those like Demi Moore, who claim many women strippers find the job empowering, that it's men in the audience who are being exploited. The modern primitives buy into this line. They want to be looked at and will go through awful pain to get attention. There's probably a medical term for this condition but the binding ladies would never use it, they're too busy boasting about their many new followers.

'Originally this was just a San Francisco phenomenon but now we have a list of about 100 people in New York who are binding themselves and none are particularly into piercing,' says Autumn Barnes, manager of the Dark Garden, a superficially genteel store near the Golden Gate bridge. 'Women across America are custom-designing their bodies. I think it's part of women's evolving freedom. We can do things publicly now that were once forbidden. Binding is about women testing the outer boundaries of their sexuality.'

In the back room at the Dark Garden three employees work hard, crafting corsets from a mix of silk, leather and stays made from steel. The whalebone stays of old have been ruled politically incorrect – in other words it's all right to dress as a male fantasy made flesh, but don't let any aquatic mammals get hurt along the way.

Barnes shrugs off these kind of remarks. She says they're made by people ignorant of the MPs' true purpose, which is apparently to make the world safe for crippled feet and mangled internal organs. 'I recently made a corset for British actress Tilda Swinton. It was for her latest film,' says Barnes. 'If she wore it regularly and pulled it tight, her waist would shrink to 15″, she'd be like a pinched shrimp.' Which is just what every girl wants.

The Dark Garden workroom is also home to a half-dozen foot benders. Dark Garden has sold more than a dozen in the last month. 'The objective of the bender is to produce enough foot flexibility to provide a radical arch in the metatarsals. That relocates the ankle front and forward, making it the leading edge of the ultra-high-heeled foot,' says Barnes, speaking in a dry tone more frequently associated with computer sales-persons. 'When flat, the toes are the foot's leading edge, with the ankle following between 4″ and 6″ behind.' To make the ankle overtake the toes requires considerable flexibility, which comes at a cost. 'The bender can cause some pain, especially if a woman has flat feet. That's the price they are paying for a more beautiful foot. With the bender it's possible to get into shoes with 7″ spike heels. Many women say the pain is good, it makes them more aware of their body.'

That's how Cheri Wright sees her body training. A twenty-seven-year-old financial planner, Wright says modern life forces people to deaden their sensations, which is not for her. I ask if that means the pain is good in itself, not just as a means to a smaller foot or waist. 'Sure, I don't want to be bland,' she says, wearing a pair of 6″ spike heels that are two sizes smaller than shoes she wore a year ago, before she began foot training. 'I won't take painkillers either, except for something real bad. I want to accentuate the messages from my body, not block them out. Fashion magazines show us too many women who look like young boys, they're androgynous. I want to accentuate my femininity and two things that define women are curves and delicate feet.'

The modern primitive movement says pain can be used to build and maintain higher levels of energy. With the body forced into a more acute state of awareness by the tight bindings, wearers say they get an adrenaline high. A bit like running a marathon but without the nuisance of pounding sidewalks for more than twenty-six miles. All the foot binders say a night wearing super-high-heels makes them long for the moment they can put their foot binders back on, as though they were a comfy pair of slippers and not a device that could snap the wearer's ankle bone if applied in the wrong way.

Wright saw an advertisement for the Dark Garden and has since become hooked on corsets and foot benders. 'My objective, for my waist, is to achieve the Edwardian ideal,' she says as a friend laces her into a red corset. 'Women in that era trained their waists to be no larger than their thighs. I'm almost there,' she says patting a midriff that looks like a tightly squeezed tube of toothpaste.

That was also a time women routinely fainted because the tight corsets had so badly distorted the shape of their internal organs, making it impossible to eat or breathe properly. The MPs say they often suffer from the same ills – in fact, when I watched Autumn Barnes put her silk wasp corset on she had to do special breathing exercises to get the thing closed – but that doesn't stop them holding the Edwardian ideal sacred.

According to Wright, the 'waist equals thigh' equation is the perfect proportion for a woman because it gives maximum play to the curves of breast and butt. 'Women are curvaceous, that's the essence of their sexuality. By pushing breasts forward and butt back we proclaim our power. It's feminism equals femininity.' Men's reaction to the sight of MPs is likely to be something primitive as well, although at a more basic level, which brings us to sex.

Wright says that her love life has improved markedly since she began training. 'Men love this look,' she says. 'What I like is being able to dress like a woman from an era of female oppression, yet I can behave like a liberated woman, I have all my freedoms. That makes for great sex. I find during a period of intense body training I feel any sexual contact much more intensely. The corset concentrates sensation in my vagina.'

Although she claims no adverse side effects, Wright may be lucky. Body trainers are advised to proceed with caution because the waist and feet bindings affect bones and, alarmingly, internal organs. 'A waist-trained body's organs move very easily,' says Midori Herring, a twenty-eight-year-old with a 16″ waist and size 3 feet – her natural measurements are 27″ and a size 5. 'If you are properly corseted, your internal organs should be evenly displaced,' she says, demonstrating that a waist trainer, by bending over while lacing up, can 'feel the bulk of her intestines roll up away from the tightest part of the corset'. Something most of us have only felt when riding a rollercoster after a heavy meal.

'If you overlace or waist train too quickly, you can run into problems such as aching kidneys, digestive trouble (including frequent vomiting), shooting pains, and numb thighs and toes,' says Herring, who admits that when bound in her corset, she doesn't walk far and can only eat tiny amounts. She usually opts for small cucumber sandwiches. 'To properly waist train, you must be consistent. You must wear your corset every day when you first start even if that restricts all other activities,' she says. 'I once wore mine for up to twenty hours per day and took my waist measurement down 11" in nine months. Although I wouldn't recommended this regime for the average person.'

Autumn Barnes has joined with Herring to write a binding guide for the Dark Garden. It's an unusual self-help manual which emphasizes that the discipline required to body train can help a woman in all aspects of her life, making her more 'goal orientated and focused'. Sent out with every corset and foot bender, the manual is also the last word on the physics of flesh manipulation: 'Reducing the waist 3" to 4" is a good goal for a novice; in training, it's not how tight you wear the corset, but how long you wear it each day; don't lace right after eating; don't let someone bind you unless that person is experienced (an overzealous helper can do physical damage); if attending a corset-wearing event, start lacing several hours beforehand, tightening a bit more each hour; avoid beer and beans (or anything that could give you the airs). Foot bending is most painful at first. Novices should not use the device more than two hours a day and never when they have to stand for long periods the following day. But above all, grin and bear it: beauty can be such a pain.'

American academics are beginning to study modern body binding – which must mean some universities have run out of more sensible subjects. Either that, or academics have been lacing too tight and cutting off oxygen to their brains. Raelyn

Gallina, a forty-two-year-old anthropology professor at San Francisco's Berkeley University, claims most body binders are also likely to have suffered anorexia and other eating disorders, possibly as the result of some emotional or physical trauma. In other words, she suspects evenings spent with feet clamped in a vice may not be the act of a well-adjusted person. 'These women desire binding as a means of re-establishing control over their bodies,' she says. 'Binding is an act of empowerment. With things being so out of your hands, out of your control in society, this is a way to exert control over your life.'

None of the Dark Garden patrons will admit to eating disorders and Californian body binder Kathryn Thomas is radically opposed to Gallina's view of binding. 'A corset makes me feel powerful, like a warrior,' she says. 'I feel more confident when men look at my tiny feet and my hourglass waist. I have something they can never have.'

Or maybe want. Men do not look for empowerment in a tight corset or an 8″ heel, unless it's worn by a trophy wife or some other female accessory. The modern primitives may think they are liberating themselves through bondage but it's more likely they have just reinvented a new way of fooling themselves. It's all part of the relentless American search for self, the constant trudge down a road not their own, where the signposts, if they exist, are in a foreign language – the tongues of tribes extinct or barely alive.

15. Stealing the Truth

Spring in New York is my favourite season. The city seems washed clean. There is no more beautiful sight than the 72nd Street boating lake shrouded in early morning mist, its banks lined with cherry blossoms. All this and bagels with good coffee just a hundred yards away. T. S. Eliot, a joyless curmudgeon who hated Manhattan, wrote ironically that April was 'the cruellest month', mocking our pretence to be both happy and sad when the departure of winter forces us to get active. We love the caress of the new warmth but often resent its aspirational qualities, the way fresh life everywhere makes us question if our own miserable existences still have any forward momentum.

This especially applies to love. Charlie Horse says he's tempted to wear a blindfold in the spring, otherwise he'll see some young woman just as the light catches her face in a certain way, and he will be hopelessly in love all over again and he's had his heart broken too many times already.

Twenty-five-year-old Teresa Russo knows how Charlie feels. She is tall, blonde and beautiful. She's also a professional decoy. If a man has a cheating heart she will know and so will his wife, thanks to the tiny tape recorder Teresa wears strapped to her calf. 'I run the wire from the recorder up the leg of my trousers and under my blouse,' she said, sipping mineral water at a sidewalk table outside a smart Manhattan restaurant where she has ruined many a Casanova. 'There's a tiny microphone in my bra that can pick up everything a man says.' Which makes her the anaconda of the dating game, lovely to look at, but never get too close with your mouth open.

Teresa has been a decoy for five years. She works with a team of former New York City detectives who own Check-A-Mate. 'Business is booming,' says former NYPD homicide investigator Gerry Palace, the company's president, a cuddly dumpling of a man with a black moustache that makes his face look like an exclamation mark. 'Men in the nineties seem more inclined to cheat than ever, plus in New York you can never be sure that a guy you meet is telling the truth. That's where we come in.'

Check-A-Mate clients come to Palace with their cheque-books, suspicions and doubts. Teresa's job is to give them certainty and peace of mind. 'My typical assignment is a wife who notices a change in her husband's habits,' said Russo. 'Maybe he's suddenly staying at work later than usual.' That's when Teresa sets up the sting. 'I'll go to a bar or restaurant where he's known to hang out,' she said. 'I'll go stand next to him and get into conversation.'

The purpose of this exchange, with tape rolling, is to see how far the husband or boyfriend will go, if given the chance. The clients often give Teresa a list of questions to ask, designed to test their man's fidelity. 'I tell them how great they look, what a nice personality they have,' she said. 'Then I'll say something like, "A guy like you has to be married, right?" We call this the integrity test. Most married guys under suspicion say, "No, I'm single." That's when I've got them. I've done more than 700 cases and only three guys ever told me the truth. I know most of my married targets are going to fail, because the first thing I notice is they ain't wearing their wedding rings.'

Teresa was Miss New York in 1991 and critics of decoys say she entraps her targets with a figure and a sparkling smile that makes her green eyes all but irresistible. Middle-aged accountants with a paunch must scramble to stuff their wedding rings in their pockets the moment she walks in, the anaconda in 4″ heels. 'That's not the point,' she said. 'They are only a target because they have done something suspicious. If they're married they should still be able to resist temptation, even if I'm Cindy Crawford with no clothes on.'

Gerry Palace usually sends out Teresa with a back-up. He will sit somewhere else in the venue, keeping a close eye on the decoy and the mark. Palace always carries a gun and sometimes Teresa will follow suit. 'I have a 9mm Glock semi-automatic, it's light and fast,' she said. 'Sometimes I have to be in a bad neighbourhood or targeting a mark with a history of violence. Then I'll carry a weapon and you can bet I know how to use it.'

It's eight o'clock on a Saturday night. The venue is Match Uptown, a slick restaurant within catwalk distance of Calvin Klein's headquarters. Models line the walls with faces familiar from building-sized billboards in Times Square. One face is strikingly familiar and he's Teresa's mark.

'I'm really nervous about this job,' she said in the cab on the way. 'The guy is engaged to a supermodel, she's really gorgeous. I can't compete with that.' She fiddled with her long blonde hair and adjusted the velcro that holds her tape recorder in place. 'Gerry hand-picked me for this but I don't know.' She's dressed for the part. All Calvin Klein elegance. Graceful slacks end in a pair of fake crocodile boots. An Armani-style jacket swings open to reveal a curvaceous chest and an athlete's stomach all sculpted inside a tight body suit from Donna Karan. 'Only three guys have ever turned me down and one was a religious fanatic. Tonight could be number four.'

She needn't have worried. Whilst Palace watched from the bar, Teresa went to work. Earlier she had booked a table for two but sat there alone. She kept giving the mark a look with her flashing eyes and soon he was at her side. The tape tells the tale. The underwear model asks Teresa why she's alone. She fakes a story about a girlfriend stuck in Denver airport. He sits down, orders drinks. Then she works the hit. Teresa: 'Where's your girlfriend tonight? Or are you married?' Guy: 'Hah! I ain't married, not yet at least. I have few girlfriends, but somebody special? Nah, there's nobody.'

Nobody except a supermodel fiancée with a big diamond ring who broke down crying when she heard the tape, her suspicions confirmed. Her man is a runaround. 'She was unhappy,' said Palace. 'But at least she knew the truth before she got married. That cost her some sleepless nights and our $500 fee but it would have been more expensive to marry the loser.'

There is is nothing illegal about what Teresa does, which is astonishing given the litigious nature of American society. Her recordings have been used as court evidence and nobody has ever challenged their validity. Gerry Palace has a portfolio of twenty women decoys. He shows their photographs to his clients and tells the wife to chose the face their husband is most likely to find attractive. Teresa gets picked more than anybody else. 'I'm working all the time,' she said, acknowledging that these days she also carries her gun more often than not. 'Some guys have been leaving messages at Gerry's, threatening my life. That is scary. They're anonymous calls but Gerry's tracking them.'

A prime suspect for Palace is a Frenchman called Charles who was pulled down by Teresa in August and lost half a million dollars in the bargain. 'He came here from France with a sob story,' said Theresa. 'He met our client and played hard to get. For weeks this went on. He is very handsome and charming but reserved. When he explained that he was recovering from the loss of his wife and two children eighteen months ago, our client was hooked.' The couple got engaged. She was wealthy with an independent fortune. Charles wanted to open a business, selling high-quality designer leather coats. She helped him get started. Each night he'd bring home flowers and make love with her until the early hours. 'There were none of the usual signs,' says Palace. 'He was loving, he was full of desire for her and his habits were regular.' Perfect? Too perfect for the client. Before she injected another half million into Charles's business and walked down the aisle with him she wanted to know if he was really so good.

'I went to his showroom,' said Teresa. 'I told him I modelled. He said he'd love me to do a fashion show with him. He said I was beautiful, the compliments just poured out of him. He asked me to lunch. I asked if he was involved. He said no and told me he hadn't been out with a woman in two years, not since his wife died. He kind of teared up when he told me.'

With the incriminating tape in hand, Teresa went about the other part of her job – taking the tape to the client, sitting by whilst they listen and then offering help once they've heard the awful truth. 'This was hard,' said Teresa. 'The poor girl started crying. He said to me exactly what he'd said to her. She heard him say how he had this rich aunt who gave him money, that the business was just a game. It turned out he'd been screwing girls in hotel rooms on his fiancée's money almost every afternoon of the week.'

One of Teresa's clients heard her husband say he was a widower, another heard her fiancé make arrangements to meet Teresa in a Las Vegas hotel room. When he turned up he found his wife waiting for him, tape recording in hand. 'These women are worried that they are being betrayed,' said Teresa. 'Often their marriage is the most important thing in their lives and so long as they are suspicious they can't retain their self-esteem.' That explains the questions that most women want asked. 'The wife wants to know if he's going to deny her, if he's going to deny their children, if he's going to ask for my telephone number.'

Teresa is something of an avenging angel. A tall willowy nightmare for any cheatster, driven by her own pain. 'I first met Gerry because I thought my fiancé was betraying my trust,' she said. 'I needed to know the truth. When I found out he was, it destroyed me.' Gerry helped her pick up the pieces, offering her a job. 'I've been cynical about men ever since and this job doesn't make it any easier,' said Teresa. 'I'm not out to hurt any man, I'm out to help the women and give them some peace of mind. For some reason, men don't think they will get caught. They are so wrong.'

Teresa comes from a large Italian family. When her father heard what she was doing, he flipped. 'He said: "How can you do this to men?" I told him: "But Dad, you wouldn't do that. If you did I'd catch you!" My mother thinks it's a wonderful thing, that I'm helping women,' she laughed, flashing the eyes that have undone hundreds of men. 'I go in already knowing these guys are lying and that's not something they have to do.'

Breaking men's secrets can be risky and Teresa's gun shows she knows the danger. 'The most scared I got was with a guy known to be violent,' she said. 'We were in a private club. The mark was real suspicious of me at first but in the end he relaxed. I got what I needed but as we're leaving my tape recorder falls off my leg.' Teresa shivers a little as she recalls the moment. 'I thought I was done, this guy owned the club and had some nasty-looking goons behind the bar. My back-ups were outside. Luckily, I was wearing new Jill Sander boots with a wide cuff and the recorder just dropped down inside.'

In the last year Gerry Palace has flown Teresa to London twice to do jobs. She trapped two prominent businessmen. One at Claridge's, one at Annabel's. The trips were so successful that Palace plans to open a London office. 'In New York men know about decoys now,' says Teresa. 'I think we are having a deterrent effect. We can do the same thing in London.'

The boom on Wall Street has brought Palace a whole other category of business – wealthy single women with stock market fortunes who do not want to get taken for a ride. Love in the millennium requires that potential husbands for these female dollar machines pass thorough background checks.

'They all want to avoid being a victim,' says Palace. 'These women have very structured days. A certain amount of time for exercise, for semi-social business functions, for work, research and time with girlfriends. Finding a mate is often squeezed to the bottom of the pile. If they are going to invest time in cultivating a relationship, they don't want to find out after six wasted months the guy is a lying scumbag with kids in Chicago.'

Or worse. Palace has five clients who all got taken the same way. They met a handsome European at an expensive bar downtown. He said he was from former Yugoslavia and told a sob story about a brother killed in the fighting. The guy said he was a doctor with a flourishing practice at a New York Hospital. On the first date he bought champagne and caviar like it's beer and sausages, whilst doing all the right things, as if he's read all the best manuals on how to seduce women. Then nothing. Not for days. He keeps radio silence, having warned beforehand that pressure of work might make this happen.

On about the fifth day he calls, breathless. He's so sorry, he's been up to his ears in emergency operations, but all he can think about is the wonderful evening he spent on that first date. He is going to be in work-hell for the next week at least, but how about a snack lunch at the hospital. Maybe tomorrow?

The effect on the guy's victims is electric. He has hit the sweet spot. They are bowled over by the prospect of being seen with a high-powered physician, a handsome life-saver who in marriage could provide a nice spiritual counterbalance to their obsessive materialism.

At the lunch date the guy looks like he's done three heart transplants since breakfast and will perform at least a dozen miracles before the cocktail hour. In his white coat with a stethoscope around his neck, Doc MagicMate strides along the hospital corridors, turkey sandwich in one hand, smitten stockbroker princess in the other. As a nice touch, he even greets other doctors as he walks. They are too bemused to ask him who the fuck he is and she is testing her well-honed calf muscles just keeping pace, leaving no time to evaluate if the whole dance is real.

After a few more equally exciting dates punctuated by his beeper reminding her how he's god of the scalpel, lord of cardio-thoracic surgery, Big-Shot starts describing some technique he's invented that could revolutionize heart surgery – if only he had the money that's currently frozen in Belgrade by the bastard Serbs. Mr-Einstein-in-a-Surgeon's-Mask could market the H-bomb of angioplasty, but he needs just a little capital. Of the five women who contacted Palace, one didn't want to say how much money she'd lost to the guy after this pitch but it was in six figures. Two said they'd given him a $30,000 loan, two said they'd given him $25,000 and had sex with him during the hospital lunch date.

'A fake cardiac surgeon who breaks hearts, you can't beat that,' says Palace. He's chuckling as he looks at the perpetrator's mug shot. Teresa got the guy in the end. She hung out at the hospital with one of the victims until he was identified. Then the T-girl, as Gerry calls his top decoy, tracked Surgeon Boy to that week's fishing ground, a swank hotel bar on 57th Street. Gerry turns on the tape.

'I don't have much time for dates,' says the husky voice, marked with more accents than a plate of Californian cuisine. 'I'm a doctor.'

And so he was, a physician of the yearning soul, a salesman of emotional snake oil to the desperate for love. Of American's under thirty, 82% say that the most important goal in their lives is true romance and that they believe in marriage, even though 50% of marriages in the US fails. This gave Surgeon Boy a big pool of gullibles, except now he's serving five years in a place where his romantic encounters may also involve surgery and the victims he left behind won't go on a date with a guy unless they have his bank, health, psychiatric and criminal records first.

I almost did a bad thing walking with Teresa away from where she had told me her story. We passed the end of the street where Charlie Horse usually sits. I thought they could be made for each other. Both were hiding a deep hurt behind a complex disguise. Maybe an introduction? Luckily a cab almost ran over my foot just in time and I remembered that April is only the cruellest month if you let its soft rain and pinky-grey sunsets get the better of you.

16. California Dog Days

There are no people more obsessed with their appearance than Californians, especially those who live in Los Angeles. Half the city seems to be employed making the wealthier other half look good. Los Angeles has more beauty consultants, cosmetic surgeons and personal trainers per square foot than any other place on earth. In some neighbourhoods it is impossible to find a bakery but there will be three dozen places where you can have some part of your body improved. Now the latest addition to the trade in personal glorification is veterinary surgeons who prettify the pets of California's egocentric millionaires. 'People here are searching for perfection,' says Christy Edwards at the Wayfarer Veterinary Hospital. 'A woman who spends a thousand pounds a month on her looks does not want people to think her chihuahua is ugly.'

Susie Dyer was worried her dalmatian puppy was not perfect. The ideal dalmatian has tight skin around its eyes, making the spotty dog's little peepers the most adorable in the canine world. Dyer was worried her dog Cotton had drooping skin around its eyes. 'I had my eyes tucked when I was thirty,' says Dyer, a film editor at a Hollywood studio. 'The change in my appearance was dramatic. I thought, if I can, why not Cotton?'

Although Dyer lives in California, not every vet has caught the prevailing virus of pleasure at any cost. Cotton the dalmatian had to suffer the embarrassment of drooping eyes for a whole week before his owner could find a canine cosmetic surgeon willing to cut out the offending imperfection.

Dr Joy Aaron began conducting cosmetic surgery on animals three years ago. At the time, her practice did everything that might be expected of a normal vet, in the style of the late James Herriot. Now, supported by a large base of demanding clients, Dr Aaron does almost nothing but cosmetic work. An eye tuck is $1000, removal of skin imperfections range from $100 to $1500.

'Dogs get warts and moles on their face as they get older, just like humans,' says Aaron. 'That's unsightly.' Mary Carpenter certainly thought so when her champion golden retriever got two warts on her face. 'I take my dog Candy everywhere. I want her to look the best she can, she's a reflection of me. People I know are well aware that these imperfections can be removed. What would they think of me if I just left them there?'

Most people in Britain would not call the RSPCA on a neighbour who failed to get cosmetic surgery for their blemished hound dog, but then Los Angelenos are not like the British, as the All Animal Referral All Care Center proves. Located on expensive Ventura Boulevard amongst lingerie and diamond shops, the All Animal Center is the Harley Street of Los Angeles pet care. The centre is equipped with more high tech equipment than many developing nations. A worried owner can have a treasured pet scanned through a Magnetic Resonance Imager and a host of other multi-million-dollar machines.

'That was very important to me,' says Charity Kane, a retired actress who now owns a large cosmetics business. 'My poodle Kazaam needed eye tucks, but she was getting a little old. I wanted her scanned through the MRI first, so we could check there were no hidden problems that may have disqualified my little dog from surgery.'

Kane heard about the All Animal Center at a Los Angeles cake shop devoted entirely to pets. The Three Dog Bakery is next to a Petcare shop that sells orthopaedic dog beds, chicken-flavoured dog toothpaste and classical CDs designed specifically for canines. At the weekends Petcare offers doggy massages. The store's car park is jammed with Mercedes and Jaguars from the moment it opens. Kane takes her poodle for a back rub and then next door to Three Dog for her favourite treat, a honey-cinnamon-almond-flavoured treat called a Scottie-Biscotti.

'When you love an animal, you want to pamper her,' says Kane. 'If I buy her dog biscuits that cost $1 each, of course I'll give her plastic surgery, if that's what she needs.'

Stephen Ross took his dog Calvin to the All Animal Center for a different reason. He needed his dog neutered. 'I was worried about the psychological side-effects,' says Ross, a photographer. 'My brother had his English springer spaniel neutered and the poor animal all but died of a broken heart.' Dr Bill Bookout at All Animal had the answer. 'We offered Calvin a pair of artificial testicles. They are called neuticles and the pet cannot tell them from the real thing. We find neuticles completely remove any post-neutering trauma, something that dogs always seemed to suffer from before artificial testicles came along.'

It's good to know that the problem of 'post-neutering trauma' in dogs has been resolved before world hunger or the common cold. Although when this point is put to the inventor of neuticles, he gives a look that suggests he's about to let loose the hounds.

'I've now sold 2000 canine testicle implants to all fifty US states and to seven foreign countries, including Britain,' says Greg Miller, a businessman from Missouri. Miller's mid-western home town sees more than a dozen tornadoes a year and one seems to have blown his brains out. 'After neutering a dog inevitably gets depressed,' he says. 'They wake up and a familiar body part has been whacked off. The animal is bound to become paranoid and suspicious of its owner. That can ruin a beautiful relationship. I'm working on cat and horse neuticles. Heck, I want to have a zoological division with elephant neuticles.'

Miller got the idea after a vet neutered his dog Buck. Miller noticed his hound was depressed, mourning the loss of his 'dominant feature'. After a month of experimentation, Miller perfected his design with help from a local vet. The artificial testicles are manufactured from polypropylene, a government-approved tough plastic. After the dog's real McCoy have been snipped, the neuticles are slipped into the vacant space. Miller offers the falsies in five sizes from small through extra large to jumbo. 'The biggest slice of our market is California,' says Miller, talking bollocks again. 'In Los Angeles they're going nuts for neuticles.'

Greg Samel is one of Miller's West Coast customers. He had a rottweiler, Karl, and needed it neutered, but Samel, a beefy concrete mason, reckoned a full set of testicles was important to the fierce image of his beloved dog. 'I didn't want Karl to suffer the fate of my sister's dog. Her dog Toby, a pit bull, had testicular cancer. He had disfiguring surgery. It was more people than the dog caused the problem. I'm not sure dogs know anything. But people say, "Oh, Toby doesn't have any walnuts." They start laughing. Then Toby's little tail goes between his legs. He gets sad and walks away.'

Samel had his rottweiler neutered and when the dog awoke he was even better off than before, at least in the boasting stakes. Karl would naturally have been fitted with extra large neuticles, but Samel opted for jumbo size, so the dog could have 'a little extra swing'.

'We wouldn't normally do that,' says All Animal Center's Bill Bookout. 'Our expertise is realizing our client's ambitions for their pets. These are people who have their car cleaned every time they go for a drive. That's a person who demands a high level of quality. It doesn't do the animals any harm.'

Some experts are not so sure. 'Post-neutering trauma occurs to owners, not dogs,' says Dr Bonnie Beaver, a vet at Texas A and M University. 'Any cosmetic surgery that involves anaesthetics puts the animal at risk, especially when the pet is older. Owners who have their pets operated on for cosmetic reasons are acting selfishly.'

Animals are inevitably deprived of any self-respect they may have had in a culture that dresses them in diamond waistcoats and pearl collars. If animal cosmetic surgery is suddenly all the rage in Los Angeles that's because it's another form of conspicuous consumption in a town that's always looking for new ways to flaunt its wealth. The pets are the equivalent of the quadrangle in Bishop Berkeley's philosophical conundrum: they exist only because their owners can see them and what they see is an extension of themselves. Naturally, in the state which invented the silicone breast implant, that extension has to be beautiful otherwise all sorts of self-doubts set in, and that would be the fastest way for Fido to book a one way ticket to the pet cemetery. No self-respecting narcissist wants a poodle that looks like a dog. It makes one wonder if the conspiracy theorists are right, that the CIA, sensing California had become dangerously subversive in the 1970s, has put a narcotic in the water system, designed to make everybody's mind function like a bowl of ice-cream in the midday sun.

17. Calling Julia B

Does America still need the Central Intelligence Agency? It had a poor track record even before communism collapsed. If the Soviet Union hadn't committed suicide, the KGB would probably still be kicking the CIA's ass. From the time the KGB kept Americans out of Berlin for two months after the end of the Second World War, the contest was like watching a series of games between Bristol Rovers and Arsenal. Every now and then the plucky chaps from the West would score a few goals, but mostly the East End lads handed out a thrashing, led by real gems like Stalin's Cambridge boys, with Donald Maclean using his head at centre forward.

Then, as if Highbury had suddenly become home to Mansfield Town, the Soviet colossus became a third-world country with barely enough pocket change to keep the lights on. Imagine how many tears there must have been at CIA headquarters when the Berlin Wall collapsed. Along with the evil empire went entire dominions of American espionage, spilling unemployed spooks out into the Virginia countryside.

Of course, nobody actually lost their jobs. They were secretly redeployed to missions without a purpose, where they chalked up some notable triumphs, like failing to notice India and Pakistan had developed nuclear weapons. After all, these are spies, and Harvard-educated ones at that. Those that were left occupied an uncomfortable position in a land that has practised government secrecy with as much zeal as it preached public openness.

She began calling me in the summer. From train stations, street corners and shopping malls. She had something on her conscience. She says a man died because of her and now she's sorry.

'I felt I didn't have any choice,' she told me in our first conversation, her voice rising so she could be heard over a siren wailing past the call box. 'There was a lot of pressure on me to get more information. I forced my contacts to produce, even though I knew it could be dangerous for them.'

Her name is Julia B. Until two years ago she was a CIA field officer. She's scared and nervous. 'I can't call you again until after Labor Day,' she said in August. 'I think I'm being watched. Can you please destroy the letters I faxed you?'

Julia's faxes came from an anonymous copy shop in Washington called Pentagon Graphics. Hundreds of people send material from there every week. The owners don't ask for identification or keep a list of customers. It offers complete anonymity, but that's not enough for Julia. 'I am a former CIA woman case officer,' she wrote. 'I recently resigned after eleven years of service. The CIA is a deeply troubled organization, arguably at its lowest point in almost fifty years of existence.'

Julia had tracked me down through a database called Nexis which holds thousands of newspaper articles. She had seen a series of pieces I'd written about women in the CIA. 'There's a story nobody knows,' she said. 'I'll call you in the next few days, I can't give you my telephone number.'

'The prospects for the CIA look pretty bleak,' she wrote in her second fax. 'Young case officers are leaving in droves. The majority of them are not malcontents but officers at the top of their "spy" class. Left behind is only a moderately talented team, with modest skills and intellect. The haemorrhaging is so bad that the CIA Inspector General has launched an internal inquiry.'

Even a cursory look at the CIA's recent record supports Julia's anxieties. The Aldrich Ames case, where a field officer became a double-agent for Russia and behaved like a millionaire on a $50,000 government salary for three years before he became an object of suspicion, is just the most startling example of the CIA's recent bungling. An investigation is under way that suggests the agency helped accelerate America's crack epidemic as it protected 'spies' inside the Colombian drug gangs, 'spies' who turned out to be useless. There's new evidence that the CIA helped cover up the killing of an American citizen in Guatemala and the murders of six US nuns in Salvador. In London, a CIA subsidiary lost a sexual harassment case to Irishwoman Mary Fogarty, and is now struggling to avoid a victimization suit from the same woman.

'Many people in the CIA have become disgusted with the "game",' Julia said one Sunday, from a pay phone in a shopping mall. As she dissected the CIA, muzak played in the background. It was the theme from *Butch Cassidy and the Sundance Kid*, a bloke with a French accent singing 'Raindrops Keep Falling on My Head'. The muzak had an insidious quality, as if put there by a malevolent force to make me miss Julia's message. 'The agency no longer has a clear mission, now the cold war is over. The agency's job is to steal secrets, but whose? From which countries? France? Japan? Kenya? Without a mission, the line between right and wrong blurs and case officers, who master the skill of rationalizing any action, become victims of their own art.

'Working as a case officer has become a slippery slope,' she continued. 'When your job is to subvert people – to lie, cheat and steal for God and country – a deep sense of personal integrity and a belief that your work matters is the only thing separating you from the traitor across the table. Without a clear mission, it is hard to justify putting someone's life on the line.'

Sandi Lucas is a former CIA officer who retired in 1997 from her post as deputy chief of operations. Lucas says Julia's knowledge and behaviour confirms that she is an ex-CIA case officer. Lucas shares Julia's belief that the agency may be destroying itself from within. 'A case officer's killer instinct begins with recruitment,' she says. 'You have to be prepared to go for the jugular. You have to be able to look a potential asset in the eye and say, "I want you to commit treason, an illegal act, because it's the right thing to do." You can only do that if you have a mission.'

Lucas says without a clear purpose some officers lose their sense of direction and morality, with catastrophic results. 'I think that's what happened to me,' says Julia B., as she began describing how pressure from above led her to endanger an 'asset'. 'I had originally been assigned to the Soviet Union. After communism collapsed I was reassigned to drug operations in Latin America, that's where my crisis began.'

CIA insiders say many case officers have struggled with the switch from Eastern Europe, where they mixed largely in diplomatic circles, to Latin America, where the action takes place at street level with much more immediate consequences.

The CIA's strategy in Colombia and other drug manufacturing countries has come under frequent fire. The Drug Enforcement Agency once had the territory largely to itself. In the post-cold-war era, the DEA has found itself in competition for work with the CIA and the contest has often been bitter. 'It's fair to say we did things the DEA knew nothing about and would not have sanctioned,' says Julia. 'The DEA's role is to enforce drug policy at home, to keep drugs off US streets. The agency was prepared to let drugs get into the country if it helped "win the war" against the drug cartels.'

By 1995, Julia had risen in the ranks. Her promotions followed her success in recruiting 'contacts', people who were prepared to betray their associates in return for money or protection. 'The short cut to seniority is often through recruitments. We rarely worried whether the information from sources given was something the US really needed,' she wrote in one of her clandestine faxes. 'Spying is often reduced to a numbers game – how many agents can you bring on – rather than the value of the information they provide.'

'This "game" has undermined the integrity of the organization and the case officer ranks,' says Sandi Lucas. 'Especially for women. They are under extra pressure to recruit. If they don't bring in more assets than men, it's interpreted as a sign they're not up to the job.'

Julia B. felt that way and went to extreme lengths in search of new recruits. 'I was taught a trick by a senior case officer,' she says. 'He told me potential spies who would not co-operate could be blackmailed. I should tell them I had photographs of our meetings which would be sent to "the right people". I was offering them a horrible choice – spy for the CIA and have our protection, or don't and we'll let people know you're one of ours anyway.'

In December 1995 Julia says she used the blackmail stratagem on a lawyer who was working for a leading Latin American cocaine distributor. 'I thought if I could get one more significant asset that year, I'd satisfy my superiors,' she told me from a railway station telephone. Track announcements punctuated her anxious testimony. 'I even thought the lawyer's value as a source might get me my next promotion. Instead I think I got the guy killed.'

Within three weeks of the lawyer acquiescing to Julia's threat he had disappeared, a few days after she had picked up his first communications from a dead drop. His body was found in February 1996, his tongue and hands had been cut off. 'That was the last straw for me,' she says. 'I realized I'd lost my mission, just like the agency. When there was an obvious threat from communism, I could accept the agency's intrusion into my personal life, like the annual lie-detector tests where they asked me increasingly about my sex life, and their harassment of any man I dated, but without a clear sense of purpose I felt the job became something perverted, a form of state-sanctioned sadism.'

Since January 1995 all staff members of the Central Intelligence Agency have had to take a polygraph or lie-detector test at least once every year. It seems like a sensible idea in the light of Aldrich Ames, but there's a side effect which some insiders say could destroy the CIA's effectiveness more readily than a whole army of turncoats. 'The polygraph test is undermining morale throughout the agency,' says Michael Kelly, a former intelligence officer who is now an attorney specializing in employee lawsuits against the CIA. 'Good people are leaving rather than face an annual ritual of humiliation.'

The CIA has always required new recruits to take a lie-detector test as part of the entry process. Julia took one and promised she'd never have the kind of conversations she's been having with me since her mask cracked. Her test covered a wide range of issues and this pre-recruitment test is still used to weed out anybody who might be concealing a dodgy past. Once that hurdle was overcome, prior to the Ames scandal, a further lie-detector test was uncommon unless a case officer became the target of specific allegations. No longer. Lie-detector tests are now being used as a constant reminder to officers that every detail of their lives belong to the CIA. Julia says it is one of the reasons she felt herself losing control, a sensation shared by others in the agency.

'Sarah' began spying for the CIA in 1987. We can't use her real name because unauthorized contact between a CIA employee and the press is a federal offence. Sarah believed a position with the CIA was her dream job. A linguist with fluency in five languages, she left university in Virginia wanting to travel and meet interesting people. The CIA sent her to more than a dozen countries in her first five years and the people she met were far from dull.

Like all her colleagues, she took a pre-entry polygraph test.

'I was a bit surprised by the intimate nature of the questions,' she says. 'I figured it was a one-off deal and let it ride. They asked me about my sex life. Luckily I didn't really have one at the time so there was not much to say.' That changed after 1995. By the time in-service polygraph tests became routine Sarah had a boyfriend and was able to supply far more lurid details for the inquisitors at 'the farm', the CIA's headquarters in Langley, Virginia.

Like Julia, one of the few female case officers to reach a senior operational level within the Agency, Sarah says she felt her last polygraph was an exercise in abuse and intimidation. 'They kept coming back to my sex life,' she says. 'They asked how many times we have sex in a month, what kind of sex we have, what kind of positions, what I was wearing, why I "submit" to oral sex, as they put it. How can I have a normal sexual relationship now, knowing that whatever I do in bed I might be asked to describe in detail to one of my superior officers?'

The CIA's lie-detector test relies on standard polygraph equipment. The secret agents of the world's most powerful nation are accustomed to telling lies. It's part of their job description. If they start lying to their own side it may take months for senior officers to discover the deception. That's where the lie detector with its bundle of wires and rubber suckers becomes a prime weapon on the side of truth. At least that's the theory.

For their test, case officers are led into a windowless room somewhere deep inside the farm. There's a large table with chairs on one side. At the head of the table there's a solitary stool – that's where the officer sits. According to sources who have taken the test, the atmosphere is tense and formal. A technician applies a device like a blood pressure cuff to the officer's arm. The device is wired to a machine that records temperature, pulse rate and moisture on the skin's surface. The officer will also have finger pads applied to the left hand. There are more than 2000 sweat pores on each fingertip, and the pads measure perspiration and the rate of electrical current across the skin. If either the cuff or the pads indicate rates of tension above a certain level, the officer will fall under suspicion.

'So, imagine you've just been asked how many times you and your boyfriend had sex last week,' says Sarah. 'That's likely to make your heart rate rise a bit. A normal person might perspire somewhat before answering.' That's when the trouble starts. According to Sarah, the interrogators then zero in, asking repeated questions about sex and very little else.

'I don't see why officers should be asked about their sex life at all,' says Michael Kelly. 'The lie-detector tests should be far more limited. Officers should be asked if they have had unauthorized contact with foreigners and if they have passed any classified material through unauthorized channels. If an officer's answers to these show no signs of deception that should be it. Instead they insist on probing the most personal details and that has made many officers angry.'

In Julia's case it also made her feel she couldn't trust her superior officers – they had invented so many espionage worlds within worlds to replace their old adversary the KGB that now anyone was fair game, including and often especially their own staff.

Case officer 'Mary' is a good example. On assignment in Turkey she fell in love. When it came to her polygraph test, officers took her through a list of the most perverse sexual acts, asking her if she had ever practised them with her new boy friend. 'I felt there was a degree of sexual harassment involved,' she says. 'I think the interrogators got a kick out of asking the questions. My feeling was that it was no way to treat a fellow professional. With the prospect of similar tests at least every two or three years I decided to resign.'

Mary was not alone. Since the Berlin Wall came down the CIA has lost case officers at a rate of about 20% above average, compared to the last ten years. A large proportion of these defections have been young members of staff, the master spies of tomorrow. It has become hard to fill key positions, intelligence gathering has been interrupted and morale is said to be at critical levels. 'The case officers who have joined in the 1990s were hoping for a new CIA,' says Kelly. 'They hoped that senior officers would have a different attitude towards staff and a different approach to espionage. They have been largely disappointed.'

Nor are the problems associated with the CIA's lie detector confined to women. Many men are struggling to pass the new tests. 'The tests are extremely fallible,' says Dr Greig Veeder, a New York polygraph expert. 'Many states in the US, like Florida, will not permit lie-detector evidence. Liars have trouble with polygraphs, but so do people who tend to feel more guilt and those with greater doubts about their abilities.'

Michael Kelly agrees. 'People with strong religious backgrounds have huge difficulties with the lie detector,' he says. 'I always had trouble with the drug section even though I had nothing to feel guilty about.'

Kelly says he never took drugs at school or university, which left him open to mockery from many of his acquaintances. 'That memory make me sweat whenever the subject of drugs comes up, it brings back the often vicious teasing I went through. That translated in the test to my seeming to lie about drug use. I cleared it all up with the agency but it was tough.'

The CIA has been told by the US Congress to increase its recruitment of women by 30% in each of the next five years. Allegations from serving officers about the lie-detector tests are having a marked negative impact and CIA recruiters are finding it hard to meet their targets. Those difficulties have been amplified by a series of sex discrimination and harassment suits against the agency, some of which are related to the use of polygraphs. 'There's a feeling the agency is still locked into an atmosphere of espionage and deception,' says Kelly. 'Whereas in the post-cold-war era the CIA's primary function should be intelligence gathering. There are too many senior officers who still think they're in a macho fight to the finish. If the agency's recruitment difficulties persist, the quality of information gathered by the CIA will continue to diminish and that will be a problem, for the US and its allies.'

Senior case officer 'Jane' agrees. She has recently resigned from the CIA but requested a pseudonym because she is planning a discrimination law suit against the agency. 'I guess using a false name is also a habit, from all those years of spying,' she says, laughing. 'I loved the job but eventually the new obsession with lie detection gave me an unacceptable choice.'

In 1995 Jane, on a posting in Asia, met a foreigner and they fell in love. When she reported the relationship, as required by CIA regulations, she was subjected to repeated polygraphs of a most intimate nature. 'I passed every one,' she said. 'Whatever they asked, I was clean.' Then Jane decided she wanted to marry. 'The agency told me my fiancé must take a polygraph. He did, and he failed. He's not an intelligence professional and I think he was just spooked.' Jane was given a choice. Dump the man or leave the agency. She chose the man. 'I have plenty of marketable talents and I can survive without the CIA,' she says. 'The question is, can the CIA survive without me, and the hundreds of people like me who think the senior officers have made conditions intolerable because they can't risk another Aldrich Ames?'

Julia had been through all these difficulties. She had dumped a boyfriend in similar circumstances to those faced by Jane. She had been determined not to lose her place on the promotion track, but when her ambition led to her asset's death she faced another problem which on the surface seemed to be in no way the CIA's fault. Before he died the lawyer she'd forced into spying had told his wife about his CIA handler.

'I noticed I was being followed, by a woman. I had no idea who she was,' says Julia. 'I thought it was a government agent. After a week it stopped.' Unfortunately, that was not the last time Julia saw her pursuer. 'I was leaving an embassy party in March. It was dark. My car was parked in a side street. As I put the key in the door, she jumped me, with a knife. She was screaming about her husband, she wanted revenge. She vowed to kill me, whatever it took. I managed to push her away and drove off. I was shaking for days.'

Within a week Julia had obtained special leave and departed for Washington. She never went back, her resignation was tendered the moment she entered CIA headquarters in Virginia. 'I'm sure his wife is still looking for me,' Julia said during our last conversation. 'That's one reason I can never meet you, or give you my home number. Actually, right now, I don't even have a telephone at home.'

'Julia is a CIA officer, that part I'm sure of,' says Sandi Lucas. 'I don't think she's called Julia, although I believe her name does begin with "J", that would be part of her tradecraft. We are always told to chose an alias that begins with the same letter as our real name. I'm doubtful about her reasons for leaving the job. It would be highly unusual for a case officer to be successfully identified by a contact's family. Whatever the truth, I think the most important part of her story is how paranoid she sounds. Julia B. is a perfect example of the problems the agency faces. There are hundreds of talented officers like her who are being driven crazy by the job. The polygraph tests are just the most egregious example, but the most insidious cause is the CIA's lack of a mission. That's robbed this very American institution of its momentum, so now the agency's past is catching up with it and every day it has to admit more errors it made in the days when nobody dared subject espionage to too much scrutiny.'

'The agency must define a new mission,' says Julia. 'Otherwise it will become a danger to itself and the country. In Russia, against a foe that has become a mix of gangsters and shyster politicians, intelligence has degenerated into a seedy sport, but there are still plenty of casualties, only now all of them senseless. In Latin America, the ground rules make devils out of everybody, even those with the best intentions. That's what happened to me. In all conscience, I could not advise anybody to join the CIA today. For case officers, all the risks are still there but nobody has any real idea what we have to gain.'

Julia B. still calls me, still from her anonymous payphones, like the good spy she is, out there somewhere in the cold, looking over her shoulder, jumping at every shadow, afraid of any woman with a Latin face who might carry a curse in her heart, a knife in her pocket. Once she had a mission, a devotion to God and country. Now, as old-fashioned espionage plays its last few hands, all she has left is fear and an instinct for self-preservation. Without the CIA, America is at least half-blind. With it, in the current form, it is paranoid and delusional.

18. The Florida
Hit Parade

At 6 p.m. the lounge in Fort Lauderdale's Kelly Green Hotel opens for happy hour. Outside the sun is still equatorially hot and the sand is whiter than a sheet of fresh typing paper. But the lounge is dark. It was somehow designed so that the sunshine of the Sunshine State is forever banished. Through the thick tinted windows the shimmering blue sea looks like a dark smudge lined with grey. Everything about the place seems to be trapped in the 1950s.

In the middle of the room an unhappy pianist plays a Steinway grand which has been violated by the hotel management. On its sides they have attached an undignified Formica shelf. The bar's customers bring their free happy-hour snacks back to stools around the piano and perch their plates on the Formica. As they sit down, little sparks of static fly into the gloom from their pastel-coloured polyester 'pants'. Mostly retirees from New York, they recently watched in horror and excitement as a svelte young woman was arrested. She had just offered a detective posing as a hit man $4000 to kill her husband.

Behind the bar Pete is reluctantly ready to serve. 'I'd rather be anywhere else,' he said. Everything about him appears despondent, from his poorly shaven chin to his bow tie, which is so greasy it could be used to fry chips, but when asked about Al Smith, he looks livelier. 'That's where Al took her down, right there,' he said. 'She was in this amazing dress. It was leather and short. It looked like it had been sewn on to her body. They bent her over that table to get the cuffs on and man, I couldn't stop thinking about her butt for a week.'

'Pete, you're a dirty old man,' said a new arrival. It was the Al in question, Al Smith, also known as Al Sinetti, forty-five-year-old faux hit man, a detective who catches professional assassins and the people who hire them. Al stands 6′ 4″ tall and has a well-defined muscle for every inch of skin. His trousers are blue jeans cut to accommodate snakeskin cowboy boots. Beneath his jacket there's a sparkling white T-shirt and a Sig Sauer semi-automatic. Without people like Al, America would not be America.

'This is one of the best places to catch killers on the Florida coast,' said Al. The barman pours him a lite beer and offers him a bowl of pretzels. Al scans the room which does not seem to be full of murderers. He's edgy. 'I may have to leave, I have the word out to find this guy who may have hit a real-estate agent's wife last week. I really want to take him down.'

In police vernacular, the Kelly Green is a 'bait room', a place where Al entices people to come when he hears they are looking for a hit man. It's a job that brings him into contact with a wide range of human tragedies and some of the most evil people in the US. 'Sometimes, I'm watching TV, a cop show,' he said. 'I'll see something about a hit man. I suddenly realize that's my life, catching people who don't have the guts to kill somebody themselves but will pay a bad ass to do it. I have a hard time deciding who is worse, the people who pay or the hit man who will pull the trigger in cold blood on somebody they've never met before. It makes me real angry and I have to keep a hold on that or I couldn't function.'

Americans are using hit men for their problems in growing numbers. It's all part of the culture. If there's a problem, there must be a solution and a price tag to match. The FBI says in 1980 there were less than a 1000 attempts at professional hits. Last year there were more than 5000. 'The rise has been caused by tougher divorce laws which force the guilty party to fork over more money,' said the FBI's Tom Masters. 'There has also been a glut of cheap guns and an increase in violence which has cheapened the value many people put on human life.'

'There's also the book,' says Al. He's referring to *Assassin*, put out by renegade publisher Paladin Press. A do-it-yourself manual for hit men, *Assassin* has sold more than 50,000 copies and is the subject of five multi-million-dollar law suits from relatives of dead victims. 'I think that book has created quite a few hit men,' says Al. 'It gives them the idea to do it, and the means, because it shows them how. It makes it look easy to earn quick money. I'd like a few minutes in a locked room with the guy who wrote *Assassin*.'

Between $5000 and $10,000 is the going rate for assassinations in the US – about the same price as a cheap family car. Most hit men charge somewhere between those two figures. Most customers say that's the kind of money they are willing to pay and that includes husbands, sometimes wives, who are looking at losing millions in a divorce settlement if their spouse stays alive. The clientele is often middle class; many of Al Smith's targets have been suburban housewives and frequently they try to make a down payment with their credit card, delivering the balance once they have received life insurance money.

Kelly Green became a 'bait room' for Smith because it's off the beaten track. 'Nobody but the old folks have this place as their regular,' he says. 'The targets can't claim they were here because it's where they usually go for a drink. Plus, they have surveillance cameras and I'm known to the management.'

All that helped when thirty-two-year-old Sandra Pierce wanted to kill her forty-year-old husband Andrew. The Pierces had an amicable divorce, leaving Sandra with custody of their four-year-old son Brad. Then Andrew took up with a younger woman who had two boys of her own. Brad loved being with the new girl and her boys and Sandra got annoyed. 'Sometimes that's all it takes,' said Al. 'They get ticked off and it begins to fester.'

Sandra had a girlfriend who was dating a man recently released from jail. She asked the friend to see if the ex-convict might know someone who could help. The man happened to be earning money as an informant for the Dade County Sheriff's office, where Al Smith works. The detective was assigned to make contact. 'The informant was told to give Pierce the name Al Sinetti, my undercover alias, along with a beeper number,' he said. 'It is always up to the suspect to call. We don't want to be accused of entrapment. She got in touch and I asked if she wanted to meet. She suggested a motel parking lot.'

Smith agreed. He likes to meet suspects in a vehicle. It helps him put them at ease. 'I have my car wired. I won't get in their cars. I tell them it's because I'm afraid of being set up. I always insist on searching the "client" at our first meeting to make sure they aren't wired. That usually removes any of their suspicions. Then I drive away from the meeting place with them and do some standard anti-surveillance moves, like I'm shaking off a tail. Within half an hour I have them eating out of my hand.'

So it was with Pierce, and once she had relaxed, Smith suggested a drink at the Kelly Green to 'talk business'. This tactic is used because he reckons, even if a suspect is wary, the change from car to bar is reassuring. 'Most of them think we wouldn't bug two locations. It's also a public place but quiet, with lots of empty tables.'

In truth, everything the suspect says is recorded. Smith has a transmitter built into the handle of his gun and a second in the lining of his holster. 'It's the perfect place because no hit man is going to hand his weapon over to a client. They can search me all they like, but I tell them beforehand I'm armed, so don't go there, don't touch my piece.'

Sandra Pierce did not want to search Smith. She was fooled by his routines and his disguise. When catching 'customers', Smith assumes the name and clothes of Al Sinetti, an Italian-American with links to Sicilian organized crime. He dresses up to the image with a dozen pieces of gaudy gold jewellery. Thick golden chains nestle in his dark chest hair, chunky gold rings with red stones for his meaty fingers, and an inch-wide golden identity bracelet with the initials AS. He knows it makes him look like a comic book Cosa Nostra. but the clients lap it up. Despite the suffocating effects of political correctness there's nothing America likes better than a good racial stereotype.

'Pierce told me I looked "dangerous" and how much she liked that,' he said. 'Once I got her into the Kelly Green we were set. My back-ups were already in place and she got right down to it, she wanted Andrew Pierce killed at work. She was the beneficiary of his insurance policy as part of their divorce settlement and got paid double if he died on the job, almost two million dollars. The husband was a cop.'

Knowing that made the Pierce case all the more satisfying. 'She said she'd give me $4000 for the hit plus a $5000 bonus when the insurance money came in. She got nervous then, and said she wouldn't have the $4000 for a few weeks, but wanted the hit done immediately. She shuffled around a bit, then basically offered sex as a down payment.' Pierce was a 'Green Widow', like a Black Widow except unlike the spider she doesn't want the victim's body to eat, just his dollars to spend. She also revealed she had been shopping around. She said she had met with another guy who would do the job for $20,000 out of the insurance with no down payment. 'That got me real interested,' said Smith. 'I asked who the guy was, said I wanted to know my competition. She gave up the name of a well-known minor hood who worked as a bouncer at a big night club.'

Smith then asked Pierce what she was going to do with all the money and suggested a trip to Paris for a few weeks. 'Paris' was the code word for Smith's colleagues to crash the Kelly Green happy hour and that's when Pete the barman got his free table show. 'They were a bit rough with her,' says Al. 'I think because her husband was a cop and all. She did end up all over the furniture. I used to have more sympathy for these people. I'd try to find some redeeming qualities. Not any more. They're basically driven by greed and jealousy. I think those are the two most ignoble human sentiments. The clients are treating somebody's life as just an annoying obstacle to what they want to do. So to hell with them.'

It was 1989 when Al Smith first began hunting in the world of hit men. In eight years, he has put eleven assassins and thirty-nine 'customers' behind bars. Before the police force, he spent seven years in counter-intelligence as part of the US Marine Corps. He has been assigned through the International Police Association to train former KGB officers in private security techniques. His former pupils now guard businesses against infiltration by the Russian mafia. He is an expert in 'weaponless defence tactics', i.e. breaking people in half with his bare hands.

'That's a useful skill but it doesn't reassure my wife much,' he said. It was the next day and Pauline Smith had joined us for an off-duty lunch. She nodded vigorously. 'I'd like him to move out of this line of work,' she said. 'I think he likes the macho part of it, though. He'd find it hard not to work undercover now. It is hard on me. There are many nights I go to bed scared. But I knew what I was taking on. Our first date, we're in a restaurant and he has to rush off. I'm with him in the car. He and five other cops end up in a gunfight with six guys, three of whom were shot dead.'

Despite that Pauline persevered. They've been married five years. 'Sometimes when he's busy I wonder if I'm talking to Smith or Sinetti. He really gets into his role on a job and becomes hard to reach. It can make it difficult for him to focus on mundane stuff like bills or mending a bookshelf.'

'I get scared myself, I've talked to her about it,' said Al. 'I probably shouldn't, you know, I ought to just play the tough guy, but Pauline would never believe that. Undercover work can always go wrong. If somebody realizes I'm a cop, they don't have to tell me. It's not like hide and seek, so they'd suddenly say "Gotcha" and it's game over. They could make my true identity and play me along until they are ready to take me out. Except if I win, they just go to jail. If they win, I'm going to the cemetery. I guess we are playing for keeps.'

Al has never been injured on duty but Pauline has had plenty of nightmares. 'I worry he'll hook up with somebody and they'll get cold feet and want to cover their tracks so they'll try to have Al killed. Or that his cover will get blown without him knowing. It's not like he's an accountant so when he's late home I can watch *ER* without anxiety. I know it sometimes makes me emotionally distanced from Al. Even after being married to him for this long, I think I reserve parts of myself from him because I'm scared the day I give it all is the one when he ends up dead.'

Lunch was almost finished when Al's mobile phone rings. The other hit man Sandra Pierce had talked to was in a bar called Florio's two miles away, a place that's owned by a mob associate. We're off at high speed, saying rapid farewells to a resigned Pauline. A hundred yards from the target Smith has to go solo. From the surveillance car he can be heard in the bar's car park. 'Check one, Squad 82. Check two, Squad 83.' Then it's showtime.

Except it isn't. The guy has already left. Al is not happy. He smacks his fists against his steering wheel, which looks like it might break in half. Then he gives a despatcher at police HQ a dozen curse words to mull over whilst criticizing the speed with which they put out the call. 'At one level, hit men are kind of a joke. They make funny movies about them, but these guys are killers. Really vicious killers. I hate it when we miss one. I should give all this up soon. I know. It's getting to me.

All the time I'm working these cases, the problem is just getting bigger. I think we are increasingly desensitized to other people's suffering. Murder used to be the ultimate taboo. Now people think: "Screw them, they want my money. They deserve to die." '

An hour later, Al had developed a new strategy. He gets word to the owner of Florio's through a mobster who's also a police informant. Al, now playing a cuckolded husband, wants his wife killed and wants the Pierce's bouncer to do the job. A meeting is arranged for that night and Smith is calm again, ready to go back through his favourite cases.

'There was this guy who wanted me to drive to Maryland and kill his wife's ex-husband. He wanted a photograph of the corpse before he would hand over any money,' said Al. 'We like to get some cash in hand before we bust. It's the most crucial type of evidence. So I took the intended victim into some woods and fired three bullets into his shirt, after he'd taken it off, of course. I splashed tomato sauce all over to look like blood. Then the victim puts the shirt back on and lays motionless on the ground where I take his picture.' When the faked evidence was passed over to the client, he smiled until Smith slapped on handcuffs. He is now serving a twenty-year prison sentence which may soon be extended by another fifteen. Not having learnt his lesson, the client tried to have Smith killed from jail. Another inmate testified that he was approached to find somebody on the outside to do the job.

Smith is surprised at how normal most customers appear to be. One of the most vicious worked for a local municipal authority. 'He was a computer nerd, slender, glasses, neat briefcase, a real bookworm type,' Smith recalled. 'He told me he'd just tried to make amends with his wife, but she had said she didn't want to get back with him. He wanted me to blind her, deafen her and rip her voicebox out, but not to kill her because he wanted her to know everything that was going on. He then wanted me to kill his wife's young daughter and his wife's new boyfriend.' This client's way of settling his bill was unusual. 'To pay me to do this he wanted to stage an accident in a shopping mall in which I would have punctured his left eye with a screwdriver. He would then have sued the mall for half a million dollars and would have given me 10%.' The man was jailed for twelve years.

Al says there are some rare occasions where he sympathizes with the client more than the intended victim. In one case a twenty-two-year-old woman wanted him to kill her husband, a man with a long record of abusing the women in his life. 'This is Florida, but he wouldn't let her wear bathing suits; she couldn't associate with any other men. He monitored her comings and goings, he even checked the mileage on her car.' The woman told Smith she could not afford the $5000 he quoted as a price for the 'hit' and instead wrote him a cheque for $100, to pay for a gun. She was jailed for two years.

Many people shopping for a hit don't care how their hired guns do the business, they just want a corpse. Others, however, want murder with panache. 'One guy who wanted me to kill his wife told me to say: "Consider this a divorce," just before she died,' said Smith. 'Some of them want me to tell them who ordered the hit.'

One killer by proxy wanted Smith to tie up and videotape his wife. 'Just before I shot her he wanted me to say I was going to kill her children next. He wanted to see her reaction when I told her,' said Smith. 'I said he should just come along, hide in the closet. Surprisingly, he agreed. We put a camera and handcuffs in a motel room and had him come over to inspect the set-up. He was so cold-blooded, changing the camera angles and telling us to make the handcuffs tight. He was a mortgage broker, seemed an all right guy on the surface but he was full of anger. His wife had had an affair with one of his colleagues and I guess he became unhinged, still that's no excuse. When the wife found out what he'd planned, she had an uncle working in the prisons spread the word the guy was a child molester. He was sexually assaulted in the showers by a biker gang. I would have liked to have felt sorry for him but

I've seen women where the husband hires a real hit man and believe me it's ugly. A professional killer doesn't mind if he causes a lot of pain first. For them it's whatever the customer wants, so long as he has the money. I have trouble believing in God, but when I think about some of these guys I have no trouble believing in the devil.'

One constant surprise is how most people are skinflints when it comes to hired killers. They offer prices that are peanuts and get predictable results. 'Most of these people are middle class, so they don't know many criminal types. They end up talking to me or a fool or somebody who is not going to keep his mouth shut after a murder for just a thousand bucks. You can't buy a murder and the killer's loyalty with pocket change. A real professional, a guy the mob might use, he gets paid at least $100,000 a job.'

There are those who take being cheap to extremes. In November, Al arrested a man with more than a million dollars in the bank. He had offered a small-time crook $500 to kill twin brothers, one of whom had been the man's lover. The potential assassin knew he could get more than that from Florida's Metro-Dade police department for informing on the client. When asked why he had offered so little, the millionaire said he didn't think the two men's lives were 'worth any more than that'.

Some people, like Sandra Pierce, have no money to pay upfront. 'A man had taken out a personal ad in a newspaper saying: "Forty-six-year-old white male wants relationship with white female of similar age." This woman writes back and says: "I'd like to have a relationship with you, but first I've got to kill my husband." Then she mails the letter to the man's post office box number, which happens to be shared with a friend. The friend opens it by accident and brings it to the police department. The friend posed as the guy who took out the ad and I posed as a hit man. I told the woman my usual fee was $3000. She said she didn't have that kind of money, so she wrote a cheque for $500. The joke was that it was a joint account, so her husband would have been paying for his own murder.'

The biggest surprise Al ever gave a husband looking to kill an ex-wife was in 1996. 'The guy hires me for $5000. He says he's going to pay with the proceeds of a drug deal in Miami. That's also his alibi. He's going to be with his mistress in the Hilton. The ex was a friend of our Chief of Detectives and got some special treatment. At the time the husband thinks we are offing his old lady, the hotel room door comes crashing down and six cops crash in. Once the room is secure, the ex-wife is allowed through to "identify" her husband with me by his side. The guy soiled his pants.'

It was time to go and get Pierce's alternative hit man. With remarkable calm, Smith changed into a light-coloured business suit. The meeting was taking place in a McDonald's and the detective could not be wired or armed in the usual way. On these occasions, he uses a secret form of listening device that he does not want publicized for obvious reasons. 'The technique is to make the target feel comfortable,' Smith said. 'I have to appear nervous and edgy. I keep changing my mind, saying maybe I shouldn't do it. Once the guy agrees to do the job, I give him a deposit, a thousand bucks. That's normally enough for an arrest.'

It was sufficient that night. Joe Vantona seemed in a hurry to make a deal and it was all over in ten minutes, the hapless hit man handcuffed and on the way to jail. It's not always that easy. 'A lot of these guys, hit men for cut-price jobs, they come from Hell's Angels gangs. They're dangerous, real volatile, and usually heavily armed wherever they go.'

Last summer Smith had just such a case. The 'good' twin sister of a woman in Fort Lauderdale had married a baptist preacher in Tennessee. The 'bad' twin worked hard to win her sister back to Florida and a life of vice. A classic battle between the different ends of American values. 'Bad twin won,' said Smith. 'The preacher divorces his wife and gets custody of the kids. One of the twins – we're not sure which yet – goes back to Tennessee with George Alexis, a biker. He put on a suit and posed as a lawyer, talks his way into the house and blows off the preacher's head. Boom, with a Medusa 547, a real killer's gun – it will fire any kind of 9mm and .38 ammunition.'

The Florida police were told Alexis had come back to Lauderdale. Tennessee warned Smith they didn't have enough evidence to confidently prosecute the killer, they wanted the hit man hunter to get more. 'I got word to Alexis I was looking to kill my boyfriend. It was kind of psychology, a Hell's Angel would think no cop would want to pose as a gay guy. I didn't give a damn. I said I'd meet him in this gay S and M club, or not at all. I said I had $10,000 as a down payment.'

Smith and Alexis adjourned to a rest room that had been wired. The hit man frisked Smith thoroughly, an event recorded on a video recorder hidden in a towel dispenser. 'Then he put a knife to my chest,' said Smith. 'Told me I'd be castrated and turned into a girl in jail if I let myself get arrested and implicated him. The guy had some balls. He was a foot shorter than me.' Alexis insisted Smith find $15,000 for the down payment, then offered to throw in optional extras like cutting the victim a little first. 'I pretended to be real interested in that. I asked him what kind of things he might do, who he'd done that stuff to before. We got enough to put the guy on death row.'

When Al plays the hit man he has one cardinal rule. He never lets the potential victim know what might be in store for them. 'I avoid contacting the target. They might turn violent themselves. They might change their behavioural patterns, which will make the client suspicious. When the perpetrator has been arrested we tell the victim. Most are in complete shock. With lovers where the relationship has gone sour, most say something like, "I knew things hadn't been going so well but I never dreamt..." then they gaze off into the distance with a faraway look. I guess some are imagining themselves dead.'

At night along the main strip of Fort Lauderdale, raucous

clubs for the twenty- and thirty-something crowd are full from early evening. The dance floors smell of sexual tension as men and women in scanty outfits dance through the heat. Sweat and spilt drinks flow along the floors in shallow rivers. As the clock chases the dawn people get a little desperate. Relationships are formed here that have no rational basis. Later some of them will become part of Al Smith's caseload.

'This is a holiday town,' he said. 'People come here from everywhere, give up their roots, meet people with whom they have little in common. Fall into bed full of booze and hormones and decide to stay, get married. It's a poor basis for marriage but real common around here. Then some get desperate for a way out. That's why we have the country's biggest market for hired assassins. A really proficient hit man could live a fine life in Florida. Fortunately, none I've ever met were that good.'

Back at the Kelly Green, Al is relaxing with another lite beer. Pete is clearing chicken bones from the Steinway. A few OAPs are asleep, their heads resting on the piano's grotesque skirt. 'Pete came from Ohio,' says Al. 'Got married to a girl from Seattle. They split, she wanted all his money, he had a little computer business. He tried to hire me to kill her. I talked him out of it, he had no record, seems like a nice guy. When his business failed I set him up with this job. Now he wants to become one of my informants. Says he heard one of the pensioners talking about getting his wife killed to marry some younger woman.' Smith laughs and takes a deep pull on his beer. 'Maybe Pete could be a hit man hunter. After all, he knows the territory. He's been there.'

19. Don't Burn the Sand

It's five o'clock in the early evening and I'm naked in the desert, along with four others, two of whom are women who have more tattoos each than all us men put together. I have no intention of staying out of my kit, but there was kind of this dare and there was money involved, but now nobody seems to know who won.

There must be ten thousand people just over the hill behind us, howling and drumming, drinking and dancing, setting off fireworks, shooting guns in the air. People screaming: 'Fuck shit up,' 'Burn shit down!' A futuristic-looking dune buggy rumbles past down below, welded together from rusty sawblades. A naked woman in a cowboy hat swills from a petrol can and spews out flames, incinerating a cardboard statue of comedian Jim Carrey and hollering about Texas as it burns.

To the south, pyrotechnicians, who are high on multiple narcotic substances, are setting off explosions, rolling red fireballs which billow and flare against a sunset that looks dull by comparison. There is a genuinely wild, anarchic energy surging across what was a lake a million or so years ago, a feeling that anything could happen, a riot or an orgy, or some new and unimagined form of mayhem – a visit from space aliens, an asteroid filled with bugs, a delegation of honest politicians.

We are thirty miles from the remote hamlet of Gerlach, Nevada, on a 400-square-mile dry lake bed in the Black Rock Desert. There are a few dozen cops around, but they are out-numbered and outgunned and, consequently, polite, tolerant and well behaved. In fact, all but one of them is drunk. Most of the festival-goers are unarmed, but there are at least a hundred and fifty hard-drinking gun freaks – rednecks, bikers, anarchists, punks, Vietnam vets – armed to their gnarly, broken teeth with assault rifles, shotguns, semi-automatic pistols, and revolvers. Firearms are supposed to be kept unloaded on the lake bed, but the gun goons have been shooting live ammunition all weekend. The trick is not to be near them when they get upset. I think taking our clothes off was all about keeping Van happy. She's one of the two women and she insisted on keeping her ankle holster on whilst disrobing. There had been an argument earlier between her and Cham-Cham, one of the young men beside me, who is demonstrating along with myself that men are generally better at getting naked in the dark.

There's an astonishing sound nearby, like an elephant head-butting a moving train. A reveller in a jeep with a .50 calibre machine-gun on the roof is raising hell with the Portaloos, lassoing them with a rope and dragging them around with the hapless occupants still inside. Two sheriff's deputies watch and do nothing, just lean against their truck with their arms folded, resigned to having lost control. Their inertia is being fed by a bottle of ice-cold Jack Daniels in a bucket at their feet. One of the Portaloos splits open and a man spills out covered in chemically treated excrement.

At the north end of the lake bed, the 'playa', as they call it, an artist named Steve Heck has built an open-roofed structure out of eighty-eight pianos, which he trucked out here from Oakland, California, 300 miles away. It took him two days to bolt them together and install a bar, where people have been drinking and pounding on the piano wires with pieces of scrap metal. Now he douses his creation with petrol and flicks a match. As it burns, the wires warp and snap, making strange, anguished music. The destructive act is typical. These people live in a country with far too many possessions, both owned and coveted. Nobody wants to leave Gerlach with anything but all their limbs and a stinking good hangover.

Needless to say there used to be a big contingent of Navajos here, the place where the bored sons and daughters of corporate America get their pre-employment dose of anarchy. If the original Americans truly left an insanity curse, this is where it bites and real hard. Charlie Horse wouldn't come with me to Gerlach. He said the Navajo demons will be hunting for scalps, and by the look of the crowd they will be spoilt for choice.

The people are white San Franciscans for the most part. Men and women are represented in about equal proportions, and, if so inclined, you could subdivide them into various urban tribes: slackers, hackers, hipsters, ravers, deadheads, artists, drag queens, techno-hippies, neo-pagans, plus the aforementioned gun freaks, and some slumming professionals who saw it advertised on the Internet and liked the idea of all those naked chicks. Or you could lump them all together as alienated from mainstream American culture; resentful of authority and jaded with mass consumerism. These are the people who have watched one too many episodes of *Melrose Place* and the *Jerry Springer Show*. It has either made them rebellious or screwed them up so far all they want to do is 'fuck stuff up', probably the latter as rebellion requires a consciousness of a wider set of needs than is appreciated by most Americans.

Over the last four days, the Gerlach mob have created a city on this treeless, waterless, perfectly flat lake bed, a surreal shanty town of tents, shacks, art installations, Portaloos and electricity generators. It has eight pirate radio stations, a daily newspaper and cellular modem links to the World Wide Web, so Gerlachistus can smugly let the world know what they're missing back in suburbia, where you don't 'fuck stuff up' because, in all probability, it's still to be paid for on credit cards. They call the encampment Black Rock City, and at its centre is a 40-foot-high sculpture of a man, made out of wood and blue neon, soaked with petrol and stuffed with fireworks. In an hour or two, the organizers will set it on fire and the thirteenth Burning Man Festival will reach its climax.

The founder of the Burning Man, an elegantly ravaged San Franciscan artist and landscape gardener named Larry Harvey, can discourse for hours on the meaning of the festival. Sitting cross-legged in a dark suit and stetson hat, smoking cigarette after cigarette, he spins and weaves his theories, explaining the Burning Man in terms of post-Freudian identity crises, the demise of primitive mythocentric religions, and the sterility of the corporate-controlled consumerism which passes for culture in America these days. 'These are post-modern times,' he says at one point. 'Everything that's ever happened before is happening now, in one form or another, but none of it really compels us, and transforms us. We can access unimaginable quantities of information and images through the Internet, we can communicate with everyone in the world, but so what? The Burning Man Festival celebrates technology as a potential tool for freedom, but it also reverts back to something prehistoric. Throughout our evolution, in all corners of the planet, human beings have come together and gathered around fire, and this ritual still invokes a very basic, primal response.'

In other words, Larry Harvey watched way too much *Melrose Place* as a young man. The first Burning Man Festival was held in 1986 and was a lot less meaningful. Larry Harvey and twenty friends burnt down an 8-foot wooden man on Baker Beach, California. Why? To exorcise a failed love affair, honour the summer solstice, and for the hell of it. It became an annual event, with taller effigies and bigger crowds each year. In 1990, the San Francisco police clamped down and, at the suggestion of a local anarchist group, the event was relocated to the Black Rock Desert, and shifted in time to the Labor Day weekend at the end of August. A hundred people made the first trek out into the desert, and attendance has more or less doubled every year since.

You pay $70, to defray the costs of staging the festival, and you are expected to bring everything else you might need to survive for four days in this harsh desert environment: food, shelter, enough water to keep you hydrated through the long, 107° days, enough alcohol and/or drugs to fuel the nights. There is one coffee shop, one juice stand, one burger shack, and an ice truck that comes once a day – if the driver does not get scared off by the gunfire. Apart from that, there is almost nowhere to spend money, none of the concession stands, souvenir vendors, corporate advertising, ringing cash registers and whirring credit-card machines that normally attend any large-scale gathering of Americans. There are plenty of drugs around but no drug-dealers, and the artists create their work in order to smash it to pieces. The guiding principle of the festival is 'no spectators, only participants'. Most people respond by decorating their camp sites – plastic palm trees, Astroturf, pink flamingos and white picket fences are especially popular – or by dressing up in weird costumes, or, indeed, by going naked, just like me and my new friends. In fact, once we'd dumped the clothes, I felt strangely conformist because so many others had suddenly done the same thing. If I wanted to be original, a Savile Row suit would have been the thing, but might have been against the spirit of the event.

With the sun gone, the feel of anarchy and destruction in the air, everything has changed. The playa is cloaked in a gauzy mist of fine grey dust (the pulverized, wind-whipped surface of the lake bed), which coats the palate, clogs the eyes, and turns nasal secretions into something like freshly poured concrete. The dust cloud is haphazardly lit by fires, explosions, car headlights, and as I walk through it to escape Van and Cham-Cham, things loom up suddenly and fade away. A 6′ 5″ male skinhead in a pink cocktail dress. A shark car with 15-foot fins. The Aesthetic Meat Foundation: young German performance artists making industrial noises and carving up dead animals. I expect to see the Teletubbies with the Pamela Anderson/Tommy Lee porn video playing on their internal TVs whilst Laa-Laa rolls a round of joints.

Victoria appears. She is wearing cut-offs and a bra, which is around her head, not her breasts. There's a half-gallon jug of rum hanging from her belt and a loaded shotgun in her hand. Her boyfriend, who is as drunk as she is, grabs the gun and fires both barrels across an empty stretch of the playa. He reloads and hands it back to her. I realize I'm out of Van's pan and into Victoria's line of fire. She pulls the trigger and the recoil knocks the gun out of her hands. 'Hey, watch out,' calls a cyclist, who could have been me if Victoria had stumbled one more time before firing, 'you almost hit me!' 'Watch where you're fuckin' goin'!' she yells back.

The aimless Victoria tends bar in San Francisco and designs outfits for strippers. 'I got a three-year-old kid in the city and this is my vacation. It's my second Burning Man and I fuckin' love it. You can get fucked up, naked and crazy, shoot your guns, fuck under the stars, and if the cops give you any shit, they've got a war on their hands.'

From the dark emerges Earl Fisher. He wears jeans, cowboy boots and a feed-store cap. This is not an ironic fashion statement. Earl is about thirty-eight and works on a ranch over in the next county – 'Ah'm jes' an ole-fashioned redneck checkin' things out,' he says. When the Burning Man first landed in Pershing County, Nevada, the locals were convinced it was a Satan-worshipping festival. Over the years, they have accepted that it is – but they no longer mind. Now Burning Man attracts a good turnout from the locality. Miners and ranchers come to gawp at the big city freaks, and challenge them to a shooting contest. Earl tells me all about it while we observe a fashion show and a formal cocktail party. A transsexual accordion player on 8-foot stilts walks by. A man in a black leather codpiece and mask starts whipping a dreadlocked teenage girl on the buttocks. She looks Earl straight in the eye and whines, 'Oooh, daddy, c'mon! Ride this big horse called love with me.' Earl averts his eyes and slurps his beer. 'Yup, sure is different around here.'

About 9 p.m., everyone starts to congregate around the Man. The complaint is voiced again: why doesn't he have any genitals? I asked Larry Harvey about this and got an absurdly politically correct answer – we don't want the Burning Man to be exclusionary, or to be perceived as sexist. So think of it more as a Burning Person.

I am now clothed again, thanks to an emergency supply of shorts and T-shirts stashed inside my truck's glove compartment. I am in the crowd with my campsite neighbours, Kelli and Nicole, wild women from San Francisco in a band called Underpants. Around us in the milling throng is a man wearing nothing but a glow-in-the-dark cock ring, a fully clothed Irishman with a gallon of whiskey, and a local ranch family: grandma, father and mother, and eight-year-old son. Father takes a belt of the Irishman's whiskey and wipes his mouth. 'Here, Gran'maw, take a slug of this here firewater.' 'Don't mind if I do.' Nearby a woman called Crimson Rose has just instigated a game of 'fire badminton' – a contest played with rackets, net and flaming tampons.

The death of Burning Man begins with the torching of hay bales and some neo-pagan dancing and processions. The crowd gets impatient, rowdy, obscene. 'Burn, you dickless wonder!' yell Kelli and Nicole. 'Burn, motherfucker!' yells Cock Ring. 'Burn 'at bad boy down!' yell the ranch family. Finally, the Man is blazing, and everyone is screaming, howling, yelping like coyotes. Bullets and fireworks whistle overhead. Bangers explode from the Man's back and he starts to twist and thrash from side to side. People grab his mooring ropes and jerk him further off-balance. After a two-minute struggle, the flaming giant is brought to the ground, and we all charge forward, a mad, trampling, scalded mob. Nicole and Kelli have become like dogs who ate too many doped Bonios. 'Fuck shit up!' is their cry, as they tear around the playa, kicking in the side of a shack, ripping a toy rabbit out of someone's hands and throwing it into the fire. Nicole is wearing a lacy slip, combat boots and a cowboy hat, screaming to the crowd, 'Burn your fuckin' underwear,' cackling and hooting when they comply, throwing flaming tampons at anybody who doesn't.

The festival rumbles and rages on until dawn, then the dusty, brain-baked revellers head for home. A week from now, every trace of it will be gone. A team of clean-up volunteers will restore the playa to its pristine emptiness, to a place where the Navajo once linked arms and fought to the death for their freedom.

20. Bobby Collins and Rachel

In the autumn of 1997, Bobby Collins was arrested for criminal recklessness after he fired six bullets into his $900 Sony Television set because his forty-one-channel cable TV service provided him with 'nothing to watch'. He told police, 'I don't see why a man can't shoot his own TV if he wants to.' Bobby says his anger began mounting two years ago. 'That's when I met the aliens, in the desert,' he claims. 'They came down and inspected my body.'

Rather than pay his fine, Bobby ran away to Rachel. That's not a woman but a town. Travel north on Route 93 from Las Vegas and the countryside shifts from verdant to barren in the space of a tank of gas. At Crystal Spring there is a four-way junction. East takes the traveller to Mormon country, with multiple wives and minimal booze. North heads into ski country and the wood lodges of the glittering few; next stop: Robert Redford's house. South takes you back to Vegas, but that crazy city is relatively sane compared to what awaits if you turn west on Route 375, America's Alien and Extraterrestial

Highway, which has had more UFO sightings than any road in the US.

Roughly at the mid-point of 375 is Rachel. 'There are UFO sightings all the time around here,' says Sally Clayton, the manageress of the town's Little A'Le'Inn hotel and restaurant. 'I have often seen lights and things that can't be explained. They don't fly like a plane or like anything from our world.' Rachel sits on the east side of Area 51, the infamous top-secret USAF base. Despite the strange lights over the area every night, the federal government denies there is a facility in the area, even though you can buy maps of the place in Rachel, where just about everybody believes in UFOs. That's the thing about the West, with its great expanses of empty land and sky. Out here, everything is bigger and there are strange things which change people.

Driving on Route 375, the top down, the sky a piece of polished coal, the radio beats in time with the desert's mysteries. Tune to 530AM at midnight and there are the creepy crawlies on medium wave. 'Welcome to Dreamland, a programme dedicated to an examination of areas of the human experience not easily or neatly put in a box, things seen at the edge of vision, awakening a part of the mind as yet not mapped.' So bellows Art Bell, the Wolfman Jack on Rachel's waterfall of fantasies.

'Dreamland' is also the name used by military pilots for Area 51. Whatever the Pentagon says, it is where pilots get to fly experimental craft they fantsized about in primary school. Bell was on his way home from Vegas one summer night when he had his own close encounter. Just before midnight, Art and his wife Ramona were about a mile from Pahrump, on the opposite side of Area 51 from Rachel, when Ramona blurted, 'What the hell is that?'

Art cut the engine, and the two of them looked behind the car and up. Hovering over the road was an enormous triangular craft, each side about 150-feet long, with two bright lights at each point of the triangle. After a while, the craft floated directly over the Bells. The thing was barely moving. And, Bell says, 'It was silent. Dead silent. It did not appear to have an engine.' After a few moments, the craft floated across the valley and out of sight. Bell calls this his 'UFO experience', and says flatly: 'It really doesn't matter that much if anyone believes me. Thousands of people seeing the same thing cannot all be wrong.'

Dreamland ends at 3 a.m. Pacific time, and Bell steps out into the cool desert air. He stares up at the mountains, walks around, then slips inside the grey concrete building he has just erected behind his trailer. It looks like a truncated barn; inside, it is a racquetball court and steam room. It is where he goes for a return to earthly reality. 'There is a difference in what people are willing to consider, daytime versus night-time,' Bell says. 'It's dark and you don't know what's out there. And the way things are now, there may be something.'

Just like there was earlier, a call came in on the Area 51 Caller Line. Art Bell answered on the air, unscreened, as always. A panicked, hysterical man says he was just let go from a top-secret government compound deep in the Nevada desert. The man cannot divulge his location. He is in a hurry. 'They'll triangulate on this position really soon.'

'Give us something, quick,' Bell urges.

Through the miracle of satellite technology, the talk-show host transmits the disturbing call to more than 400 radio stations across the nation – more than any other radio show except hate-radio hosts like Rush Limbaugh and Laura Schlessinger. Bell broadcasts from a beige easy chair, sitting alone in a tiny bedroom of his double-wide trailer deep in the desert, with Area 51 in plain view.

'What we're thinking of as aliens, Art, they're extra-dimensional beings that an earlier precursor of the space programme made contact with,' the paranoid caller blurts out. 'They have infiltrated a lot of aspects of the military establishment, particularly Area 51. The disasters that are coming, they – the government – knows about them... They want those major population centres wiped out, so the few who are left will be more easily controllable. I say we g—'The man is weeping now, and suddenly there is only silence. One, two, three, four, five seconds of dead air – a radio eternity. *Dreamland* has vanished into the ether. And then Bell's theme music swells, and the host's calm, resonant voice returns: 'Weird, weird, weird stuff. In all my life... My uplink transmitter was dead as a doornail.' For the first time in all his years of broadcasting, Bell had lost his connection to the transmitter. Smack in the middle of that call. Later that night, Bell offers listeners his take on the event: 'That's beyond coincidence. It was done to you.'

The desert, it is said, does strange things to the eye. It is true: that man with a straw hat, quivering in the remote distance, turns out to be a clump of cactus. That cloud, on closer inspection, is a mountain. That fog is faraway ice. Bell's Pahrump sits in the midst of this natural hallucinogen, an ancient Indian settlement poised for development as the next gambling paradise. Not far from the town's main attractions – legal brothels called Sheri's Ranch and the Chicken Ranch – Bell's trailer commands a plot of sand and rock, surrounded by satellite dishes and a chain-link fence.

By day, it's nothing special, the hideout of just one more American who found his piece of paradise and straightaway nailed up a 'No Trespassing' sign. But at night, when the crystal-black sky explodes with stars and the mountains offer a scarf of purple, this trailer is transformed into a transmitter of freakish fear and the sweetest of hopes. Kept company by a fistful of phone lines, a trio of computers, an atomically synchronized clock and a framed, bare-breasted photo of the actress Shannen Doherty, a fifty-two-year-old man who hasn't had a good night's sleep in nine years offers an insomniac nation a host of extravagant, extraordinary, even extraterrestrial possibilities, and millions tune in. Bell is in sync with the nation's mind-set, a swirling tornado of fantasies that threatens to suck America's sanity into its vortex.

While the other big names of radio traffic in standard-issue news, politics and family concerns, Bell's midnight talkfest concentrates on conspiracies and cover-ups of the gravest order: alien abductions and crop circles, cloning and bird flu, El Niño and pfiesteria, cattle mutilations and anthrax scares. In Bell's world, visitors from other dimensions win equal time with Clinton and Lewinsky. Callers who use remote viewing to look ahead in time are taken as seriously as Washington pundits who claim to peer into the presidential future.

Yet it was Bell who led me to the real secret of Area 51, and it had little to do with aliens. The demonic power behind the base's sensors and chain-link fences walks on two legs and can wear an average-size hat.

In the Hollywood version of Area 51 in *Independence Day*, the base is the scene of humanity's last stand against the aliens. The Hollywood-scripted inhabitants of Area 51 are at fault for keeping secret a visit by the aliens fifty years previously, but all is redeemed when the UFO they had kept hidden since 1946 is used to conquer the space monsters. It is a sanitized version of the base. Area 51 may one day save the human race, but so far it has been a pestilence on the land and the cause of horrible death for dozens of men.

In the dim light of her tidy trailer fifty miles from Rachel, a widow dabs at her eyes and presents proof that the man she loved for more than four decades – 'my Wally' – existed. Proof that he was born, worked, sacrificed, lived and died. His name was Walter S. Kasza, and Stella Kasza wants you to know that, damn it, he existed. He was her man. She displays his army papers: he landed in Europe in 1944, fought in the Ardennes, earned three bronze stars. On the panelled wall hangs their wedding portrait – St Norbert's Church in Detroit, 1950 – and pictures of their children. 'You're together that long, you eat together, you sleep together,' Stella says, her voice dissipating to a sigh. More tears, another tissue.

From the pantry she retrieves a brown paper bag full of empty pill vials. For years the doctors couldn't figure out why Wally was coughing so much, why his skin cracked and bled, turning their bedsheets red. They prescribed unguents, antibiotics, decongestants, painkillers. His guts ached for years, too, and when they finally found the kidney cancer, even morphine didn't help the pain. He died in April 1995, a wraith, seventy-three years old.

'Memories,' she says bitterly, tossing the vials into the bag. 'Nobody gives a damn. Nobody.'

Stella Kasza, silver-haired, strong-willed, blames the men in Washington who built Area 51 for what happened to her Wally, and one big shot in particular. 'If Clinton was here right now I'd look at him and say, "You know what you did to my man? You took my life away. You −".' She spits out several curses. Bill Clinton certainly did not kill Wally Kasza, but he has been forced to deal with his angry widow. The administration maintains an abiding interest in the lawsuit Stella Kasza has brought against the federal government. Under a 'presidential determination' that he must renew annually, Clinton has decreed that potential evidence related to Kasza's death is classified, top-secret, a matter of national security − and that 'it is in the paramount interest of the United States' that none of it be disclosed. Officially, Stella's husband does not exist.

Why should Wally Kasza matter? He was a sheet-metal worker. For seven years he put up buildings and installed cooling systems for a defence contractor that built Area 51. In the imagination of Art Bell's listeners, Area 51 is where the government harbours space aliens and conducts experiments on recovered interstellar craft.

What's really being covered up there, according to lawsuits filed by Kasza's widow, another worker's widow and five former Area 51 employees, are brazen environmental crimes. For several years, the workers say, they laboured in thick, choking clouds of poisonous smoke as hazardous wastes were burned in huge open trenches on the base. Military officers armed with M-16s stood guard as truckloads of resins, paints and solvents − materials used to make the Stealth bomber and other classified aircraft − were doused with jet fuel and set ablaze with road flares.

Another sheet-metal worker at Area 51, Robert Frost, died aged fifty-seven, allegedly from exposure to hazardous wastes. Biopsies showed that his tissues were filled with industrial toxins rarely seen in humans. Men who worked there from the late 1970s into the early 1990s say that inhaling the smoke resulted in persistent respiratory distress, cancers and strange rashes. 'Fish scales', the workers call these hard membranes. Some use sandpaper to remove the embarrassing growths from their hands, feet, legs and arms, but they keep coming back. They slather themselves with Crisco to stop their skin from blistering and cracking.

What is the government's response to these horror stories? The government says...nothing. The policy is that nothing illegal can have occurred at Area 51 because, officially, nothing occurs at Area 51. It is one of an increasing number of black holes in American politics, designed to keep an increasingly sceptical and suspicious public out of the government's business.

Employees at 51 cannot talk about the work they do. Everything and everyone connected to the base is classified – part of the US military's multi-billion-dollar 'black budget' operations. 'Specific activities...both past and present... cannot be discussed,' the Air Force says in a statement.

That position infuriates Stella Kasza because it makes her husband disposable, a nonentity. She sees it this way: if, officially, Wally Kasza didn't work at Area 51 for seven years, then, officially, his death had nothing to do with his job. He didn't wake up with bloody pyjamas from the fish scales, didn't hack his lungs out in the middle of the night kneeling next to the bed. Didn't get cancer. Didn't suffer so horribly that his son wanted to smother him with a pillow to end it all.

Stella Kasza staunches her tears, points to a table in the living room and says, 'There is something he made.' It's a miniature, felt-topped craps table, perfectly detailed; Wally was quite the handyman. Now it holds Stella's legal papers, medical reports, clippings, letters. Thick envelopes full of evidence that she hopes will be enough to prove in federal court that Wally worked and died for the United States government. Officially.

'Someday I hope to visit Stella and not make her cry,' says Stella's attorney Jonathan Turley, driving away from his client's triple-wide trailer in the Desert Inn Mobile Estates. It's a sun-blasted retirement community near a blue-collar casino, whose billboard advertises: 'Cash your paycheck – win up to $250,000!' These money-pits are where most of the gambling industry's profits are made. They wear their devotion to exploitation openly, happy to rip off the elderly and offer them suicide counselling should all their pension go down the drain.

Turley is a law professor at George Washington University – he directs its non-profit Environmental Law Advocacy Center, funded in part by Hollywood do-gooder Barbra Streisand. He flies here every few months to meet with the clients he is representing in a lawsuit against the government – Area 51 workers past and present and their families. He represented Wally Kasza before he died. The brash young lawyer would meet the sick old man in secret, in cars and garages, fearful of detection by military investigators. If Turley seems paranoid – he avoids using hotel phones, travels under phony names, swears he is being tailed – he has his reasons.

His campus office remains sealed by federal court order – students and others are not allowed to enter because the government says Turley's files hold documents that are classified. A sign posted on his door warns them away. In effect, Turley's own office is now a state secret. In a letter, a Justice Department attorney helpfully called Turley's attention to the specific statute that, 'as you know, prohibits unauthorized possession of national security information' and provides a mandatory ten years in prison for violators. Turley has appealed the order that classified his office six times. The Area 51 workers he represents also face ten years in the slammer if they are caught disclosing anything about their jobs. In court papers, they are identified only as 'John Doe'. Their affidavits express fear of 'retaliation, harassment and injury' if their civilian employers or the military finds out who they are.

'These are deeply patriotic guys,' Turley says of his clients, many of whom have military backgrounds. 'They are trained to go with the programme and trust the line of command. It took a great deal for them to even talk to an attorney.'

Turley represents more than twenty-five workers at no charge. He filed the case three years ago against the Environmental Protection Agency (EPA) and the Department of Defense. The plaintiffs aren't asking for money; they want information on the chemicals they might have been exposed to so they can get appropriate medical treatment. They also want the military to admit that burning barrels of toxic wastes – allegedly twice a week for more than a decade – was wrong. And they want an apology. 'Let them admit the truth,' one worker says.

They'll probably get none of the above. So far, the government's arguments for absolute secrecy have largely been upheld in the US district court here. Unless they win on appeal, the Area 51 workers will face the same fate as the nuclear test site workers, uranium miners and the hapless citizens of Nevada and Utah who were exposed to radiation during the heyday of atomic bomb testing: many got sick and died, and the courts held no one liable.

'I don't like to be discouraging, but I fought these lawsuits for fifteen years and we failed, we failed in all three cases,' says lawyer Stewart L. Udall, who was US Secretary of the Interior during the Kennedy and Johnson administrations. 'You have to ask which is more important: grave damage to this vague concept of "national security" or grave damage to American democracy?'

Turley had hoped that, when confronted with credible testimony about environmental crimes and evidence of the workers' illnesses, the Pentagon might cover their medical bills, or allow them to be treated for free by military doctors with the proper security clearances. He asked the Justice Department to give his clients immunity and launch a criminal investigation. Instead, the Justice Department, the EPA, the Air Force and the White House erected a stony wall of secrecy – not denying the charges, but not confirming them, either.

A few months after Turley sued, EPA officials conducted their first ever inspection of Area 51. It was a victory, but a hollow one. Backed by Clinton, the Air Force refuses to disclose the results of the inspection – meaning the workers can't know what hazardous wastes might have been incinerated there. 'President Clinton's decision protects the environment and national security,' the Justice Department intones.

The US Air Force boasts about its 'strong environmental record', but spokesmen refuse to address any questions about Area 51. 'Most people understand that there is some information the government has to keep secret... to protect national security and the military personnel who keep us all safe,' the statement says.

The Wally Kasza litigation puts the government in the Orwellian position of trying to keep secret a 40,000-acre complex where airplanes and buses full of workers arrive every day. (Hundreds of them commute from Las Vegas's main airport on 737 jets bearing no external identification numbers.) Not only have Russian satellites photographed the base, but it can be observed from a nearby mountain. Locals also call 51 the 'Test Site' – a name that dates from the fifties, when you could frequently sip 'atomic cocktails' in Vegas while watching mushroom clouds rise over the desert.

'There is no name for the operating location near Groom Lake,' an Air Force attorney named Richard Sarver insisted to federal judge Philip Pro in 1995, during one of the few public proceedings in the Area 51 lawsuits. 'Please ignore references to Area 51 in previous cases and in 300 pages of job-related and government documents obtained by Turley,' Sarver said. 'Your honour, there is no name.'

The weathered metal sign at the border of Area 51 identifies it in large red letters as a 'Restricted Area'. It warns that anyone who trespasses comes under the jurisdiction of military law. You may be buzzed by a helicopter or an F-16. You may be shot. 'Use of Deadly Force Authorized,' the sign on the fence says, citing, in smaller print, the 'Internal Security Act of 1950'. In many ways the place is an anachronism, a vestige of the days when unquestioned military authority seemed necessary to keep the world free. At Area 51, a rigid cold-war mentality still prevails: America's enemies are everywhere. Workers tell of an intimidating security apparatus within the base, of wiretaps and gunpoint interrogations.

Established by the CIA in the mid-fifties, the base sprawls over a dry lake bed that once served as a landing strip for the U2 spy plane. The reasons for calling it Area 51 are obscure, but declassified manuals cite an equally mysterious Area 27 and Area 12 in the vast, federally owned desert.

Solar-powered robotic video cameras observe anyone who approaches Area 51's perimeter; parabolic microphones pick up conversations. There are motion sensors beneath the dusty soil. 'They're watching you now,' Jonathan Turley says, hiking up a ridge about 13 miles from Area 51. He focuses his binoculars on the spindly robot, and scans the ridge for evidence of jeep-driving security men, known locally as 'cammo dudes'. None is visible. 'They're being shy today,' he says.

Trying to prove a point, Turley has brought us to the base's one public border that can be reached by paved road. When a white-and-silver bus with blackened windows barrels by in a cloud of dust, he is ecstatic. 'Did you get a photo?' he shouts.

Typically, those bus riders would be union labourers – the Wally Kaszas of Area 51 – who rise at 3 a.m. for the haul up from Vegas. The bus is evidence that people work at Area 51, of course. But Turley also regularly photographs the buses and planes to document what he calls 'activity consistent with hazardous waste storage'. If there are vehicles, there must be batteries and fuel on the base, he argues.

The Air Force refused to admit even that much in its legal briefs. The government's lawyers say that acknowledging the existence of innocuous and essential items would place the nation at grave risk. The 'mosaic theory', the Air Force calls it. If, say, the Iraqis or North Koreans were to learn about any materials or chemicals used at the Groom Lake base, the argument goes, they could puzzle out how we make secret weapons and radar-defeating planes. CIA officials raise the prospect of spies skulking behind saguaro cactuses, sniffing for smoke, combing the desert around Area 51 for clues. 'Collection of information regarding the air, water and soil is a classic foreign intelligence practice', the agency states in a 1995 affidavit, 'because analysis of these samples can result in the identification of military operations and capabilities.'

The workers say that under the mosaic theory, nothing could leave the base, and that's why everything was burned, from old computers to entire articulated lorries. Some men had to scramble into the pits after the ashes cooled to ensure complete incineration – increasing their exposure to toxins, according to the lawsuits.

Environmental crimes are particularly insidious because, as Turley points out, the victims often don't know they are victims. The burnings alleged by the workers are punishable by up to fifteen years in prison. From their perspective, the evidence has been suppressed by the most powerful man in America. Federal environmental law requires public disclosure of the results of the EPA's inspection of Area 51. To prevent this, President Clinton invoked the military and state secrets privilege, specifically exempting the base from disclosing any pollution reports.

'Clinton doesn't want these crimes made public,' says Turley, building up to a full-fledged rant: 'When we finally prevail in this case and the truth comes out, I think the public is going to want to burn the Justice Department to the ground – followed quickly thereafter by the White House.' Prone to hyperbole and something of a media hound, Turley is the grandson of a former United Mine Workers official who contracted black lung. He likes to quote his grandmother's recollections of how mules were deemed more valuable than people by the coal companies.

Turley sees delicious hypocrisies in the Area 51 case. It allows him to target a president who's often touted his environmental record. And who claims to have empathy for working-class citizens wronged by government experiments. In October 1995, Clinton publicly apologized to victims of secret radiation tests in New Mexico. A few days before that speech, Clinton signed the first order exempting Area 51 from disclosing its pollution records.

Sitting in a seedy motel room near the Vegas Strip, his back to the window, the man offers a handshake and introduces himself. 'John Doe,' he says in a phlegmy voice. He proceeds with his story of how 55-gallon drums of classified chemicals were trucked in from a California aircraft facility and routinely set ablaze at Area 51. 'The barrels would blow up and vaporize, like a huge smoke grenade. The smoke was dark, greyish white – it was as thick as London fog.' He hacks, wheezes and clears his throat. 'When I went up there I was in good health – healthy as an ox,' the man says. He's never smoked, he says, and coughs again. 'I'd like to know if there's a remedy to reestablish my breathing – or will I be like this the rest of my life? Has my life expectancy been shortened?'

As a condition of conducting the interview, Turley says we can't describe the man or his work in any way. The lawyer believes the Air Force's Office of Special Investigations (OSI) is trying to photograph or otherwise hunt down the 'John Does', to bring charges against them for breaching national security.

Turley paces nervously, drawing aside the curtains on the room's only window, checking the peephole at the door. He turns up the television – a precaution, he says, against electronic eavesdropping. 'I'm sure the room's clean but that window bothers me,' he says. Laser microphones can pick up conversations from vibrations on glass, even from the ice in a drink. Turley keeps up on spook technology. He once did a stint in the general counsel's office of the National Security Agency.

He instructs John Doe to take a seat further from the window. The man goes on: how workers were denied breathing masks; how he was told to quit if he didn't like it. But the money was good – at least $15,000 above the annual wages in Vegas. You just had to get used to a climate of fear. If you were ordered not to look up at some crazy new plane overhead, you kept your eyes on the dirt. 'It was very understood that when you left there, you never talked about this. You can't divulge anything, not even its existence. How can a guy go and make a claim for compensation if the investigator can't investigate what it was?'

Suddenly, Turley is pushing aside the curtains. Trouble. 'A van just pulled up next to the window,' he announces. 'Three guys, clean-cut, are getting out.' He terminates the interview. 'We stayed too long.'

The van's passengers have put its hood up. To Turley that's a classic sign of surveillance: the old car-trouble ruse. The lawyer picked this motel because guests must park in a central courtyard. The room's window faces a rarely used road. What is that van doing there? One of Turley's assistants drives around the side of the building to case the van. The men are gone. It's a dark blue Dodge, a bit beaten up. Its licence plate reads . . . 'US Air Force. For Official Use Only'.

It was all a coincidence, an Air Force spokesman at the Pentagon says later. Yes, the Office of Special Investigations routinely probes national security leaks, but that wasn't an OSI detachment, he assures us. The Air Force traced the licence number of the blue van. It turns out that the men came from a C-141 transport plane and were overnighting in Las Vegas because of a bunk shortage at nearby Nellis Air Force Base.

Can we have the van's maintenance records, to see if it really had a breakdown? Sorry, the spokesman says, that information is confidential.

Another hotel room, another John Doe. This one is weeping at the memory of his co-workers. 'I'm sorry I get so emotional,' he says. 'It's hell to watch someone die.' He may be next. Ugly, crusty scales cover part of his body. How easily the tears come in this arid place. But how quickly they dry – as if they never existed.

All of this started because of $300. About ten years ago, Robert Frost, who was foreman of the sheet-metal workers at Area 51, became so ill that he missed a week of work. By then his face and body were scarred by scales and red welts. He would drape himself in a blanket to shield his skin from the sun. His legs buckled when he tried to walk. Frost filed a claim for lost wages; his employer, Reynolds Electrical and Engineering Co., fought it. By the time a hearing was held in 1990, Frost was dead of a liver disease that doctors associated with exposure to smoke containing dioxin and dibenzofurans, chemicals found in plastics and solvents. But the compensation claim was denied after a company superintendent testified that no burning ever occurred at Area 51. Frost's widow, Helen, got a belt-buckle in the mail – 'in appreciation of Robert's ten years of continuous service with REE Co,' the accompanying letter said. 'We deeply regret that the award cannot be presented to him.'

Furious, she wanted to file a wrongful death claim, but the lawyers in Las Vegas told her there was nothing to be done – the military and its contractors were too powerful. Eventually Helen Frost found a Washington watchdog group, the Project on Government Oversight, that was willing to investigate. She knew of several other widows and workers. One of them was her husband's good friend Wally Kasza – a guy so tough, he worked up at Area 51 until he was sixty-nine, when he became too sick to go on.

Wally and 'Frostie', as friends knew him, were union brothers in Local 88. Now their widows are united in their scorn for the federal government, lending their names to the lawsuits Frost v. Perry (against the former Secretary of Defense) and Kasza v. Browner (against the EPA administrator). Turley, who took over the case from the oversight group, is like a son to them. When he comes to call, they have cookies and pies waiting, and the latest proud stories about their grandchildren. They would be the most American of Americans were it not for their hatred of their government

They are a lot alike, Stella and Helen. They grew up in ethnic 'rust belt' towns that defined the US mid-west until the 1980s, met and married their men as teenagers – they never thought they'd lose them. Their men had fought wars, come home to tell about it. How could the government they fought for betray them, put them in mortal danger without fair warning? How could everyone right up to the president deny it? Keeping secrets is one thing, the black-budget widows say. But people still ought to count for something. The truth ought to count. Stella Kasza points to the wall. A studio portrait taken several years ago captures her loving gaze as she poses next to a still-handsome old devil with wavy grey hair, the guy whose big grin and blue eyes first made her swoon when she was fifteen, when he lived down the block.

A sappy country song is playing on the radio. Stella turns it up, up, up – as loud as she can stand it. Something about having one last night together on the town. She sways across the room, alone, trying not to cry again.

'Those crazies in Rachel, who say Area 51 is covering up UFOs. That's bull, Wally never saw a UFO. The government is covering up something there but it ain't little green men.'

Art Bell has followed the Kasza case carefully. He has talked about it often on the *Dreamland* show, adding government conspiracies to the alien fantasies which fill the jet-streaked air around Area 51. He has come to a conclusion. 'Kasza is a government set-up. It is designed to draw attention away from the real mission of Area 51.' Which is? 'The reverse engineering of space craft that have crashed on earth,' he says, without hesitation. 'There can be no other explanation for the secrecy and what I and others have seen.'

The parable of the little boy who cried wolf states that, by alarming his village too often about the threat of wolverine monsters, they failed to listen when a real beast came by. In the period since 1945, the US government has lied to its people without hesitation about almost every aspect of its operations. It has created a collective political insanity where many people no longer believe a word they hear from Washington. In that truth vacuum the fantasies which naturally occur in America's open spaces have multiplied.

Mary Ford peers over the steering wheel of her VW bus and points a manicured fingernail towards the soft golden sky. To the west, halfway below the horizon, the sun looks like the entrance to a tunnel of fire. 'Perfect weather to pick up saucers,' she says.

On many a cold lonely evening the forty-five-year-old former Las Vegas blackjack dealer and beauty school graduate has pointed her video camera hopefully at the desert sky and taken pictures of what look like nothing – only to have the film reveal dark landscapes punctuated by odd squiggles of light or ghostly blobs. She agrees with Art Bell, the Kaszas are a put-up job. Ford is one of the 56% of Americans who believe in UFOs and one of the 32% who think they have already visited the US. She knows the Kasza story is a ruse because Bobby Collins told her and he's had real conversations with aliens.

After Bobby shot up his TV and moved to Rachel he met Mary, and they now live together on the outskirts of Rachel in a double-wide trailer that Bobby picked up cheap in Florida after it was storm-damaged. The trailer lacks a back end, which they have covered in a blue tarpaulin Bobby has decorated with symbols from the language of the planet B'hartyse. Inside, Art Bell is on the radio. Bobby doesn't have a TV in his new home. The people of B'hartyse were the ones who made Bobby TV-shooting mad, but they came to him again a few months ago and this time he's just fine about it. 'They said I shouldn't listen to stories about Kasza, it's bull,' he says. He sucks down half a bottle of Rolling Rock. 'They said they lost one of their craft in Area 51 and they want me to go get it back. They also said Clinton is an enemy alien and one day soon they are going to take him out.' He paused. 'They want my help for that too.'

On the road back to Vegas, I had Art Bell on the radio, talking with a guy who said he'd flown his F-16 into a squadron of UFOs over Vietnam. The night sky was full of swirling clouds and faraway stars. At an intersection there was a sign for Flagstaff, where Charlie Horse had escaped from the FBI. Charlie knows about the dreams that fill the heads of people around here. He says his people put them there.

21. The Survivors' Club

Rita Quam still remembers the rock, its jagged edges dripping with her own blood. It wasn't the first weapon hit man Arthur Smith used when he tried to kill her. He'd already fired at Quam with a silenced semi-automatic hand-gun which jammed before he could hit his target. Then there was the knife which broke when it hit her collar bone.

'He was determined to kill me,' says Quam, a petite fifty-five-year-old estate agent. 'He just wasn't very good at his job.' Smith was allegedly hired by fifty-nine-year-old Howard Quam, Rita's multi-millionaire husband. After an eighteen-year marriage and a good life as wealthy pillars of the Denver community, the couple became mired in an acrimonious divorce with more than $5 million at stake. According to Rita, husband Quam decided to cut his losses the easy way.

'Howard hired Smith, an ex-policeman, to organize security at the company. He would often drive me places when my husband was out of town,' says Rita Quam. 'I had no reason to suspect him until the attack.' Which is a shame, because in his private life Arthur Smith was broke, drinking hard and fighting his wife for custody of two children. He was in desperate need of fast cash when Howard Quam allegedly began making discreet inquiries about hiring a hit man. Smith, who had ties with organized crime in Chicago, supposedly offered himself.

Smith's planning began well. He shipped a selection of black-market hand-guns from Chicago to Denver using a private courier. The cache included a silencer and lethal hollow-point bullets. He then put Rita under surveillance, something he'd done before when trying to get evidence to help Howard Quam with his divorce. He also bought a disguise.

After a week of spying, he decided to follow Rita on a chilly Sunday morning. A talented amateur landscaper, Quam was heading for a quiet mountain pass to collect special red-coloured rocks for her garden. Within thirty minutes she found a recent rock fall and pulled over. Smith drove past and parked around a bend to put on a wig and a fake moustache. He then walked back towards his target, hiding behind trees.

Rita filled a sack with rocks then stopped work to smoke and admire the view. Savouring the last puff, she was about to stub out her cigarette when a bullet flew past her ear. Stunned, Quam turned to see Smith in a crouched shooting position. He fired another shot which also missed. 'I was frozen in place,' says Quam, her voice quivering. 'I saw Arthur, in this stupid disguise. He raised the gun again and I know I began praying.' Rita heard a click, followed by another which was accompanied by a loud curse. Smith tossed the gun, drew a small knife from inside his coat and advanced towards her. Screaming, Quam began to run around her car, trying to get inside. Smith caught her on the second circuit.

'I felt a sharp pain in my chest, I thought he'd stabbed me in the heart. I fell down,' she says. In fact Smith had hit her collar bone with such force that the blade shattered. The hapless hit man then picked up a rock from Rita's reject pile and began pummelling his target's skull. Quam went into shock. 'It was kind of a dreamlike state,' she says. 'I could see the rock with my blood dripping from it. I'd stopped feeling fear, it had been replaced by a bizarre sort of curiosity. I knew I was going to die. I wondered what it would be like.'

Quam lost consciousness but before Smith could finish her off the wet rock slipped out of his hand. He began strangling the helpless woman instead – just as a police car on routine patrol screeched to a halt alongside. For Smith, overweight, stressed out and pumped full of adrenaline, the shock of seeing police officers was too much for him. He had a heart attack, dying with his hands still around his victim's neck. Rita Quam regained consciousness in time to catch a last glimpse of Smith as he was zipped inside a body bag.

The police quickly focused their suspicions on Rita's property-developer husband. He had just been forced into a divorce settlement with his ex-wife that obliged him to pay $400,000 a year in alimony. The man clearly had motive and opportunity, but without evidence from the assassin it has been hard to put Howard Quam permanently behind bars.

'Most of these cases are solved because the assassin gets cold feet and snitches to us,' says Detective George Forsyth, a Maryland detective who has foiled more than a dozen contract killings, sometimes by posing as a hit man himself. 'Nine times out of ten, even people with brains and money hire losers and pay no more than $10,000. That's not enough to keep a guy's mouth shut. It's crazy. When you want somebody dead, that's not the moment to start shopping for a bargain.'

Smith would probably have told the police who had hired him. Most hit men, when caught, can't wait to incriminate their employer, but with the world's worst assassin dead, Rita Quam could only point the finger of blame. For the police, left with just circumstantial evidence linking Howard Quam and Smith, that wasn't enough.

'They released Howard from jail two months after his arrest,' says Rita. 'For the first year after the attack I lived in fear.' That included vivid dreams of death. In the worst one, which recurred about every five days, a man dressed in luminous green overalls crawled out from beneath her bed and stabbed her through the heart with an ice pick. 'I woke up in terrible pain and anguish, with the wound in my shoulder throbbing. I could never get to sleep again until it was light.'

Then Rita heard about Jerrie Heston, a young teacher from South Carolina. Married to a navy officer who had left the service under a cloud, Heston was targeted for death after she tried to leave her husband for another man. 'I read about her case in a newspaper on an airplane,' says Quam. 'It was an accident that I knew about her at all. I already knew I wasn't the only woman to be on a hit man's list, but here was another victim with a name and a face. I decided to call her and see if we had anything we could share.'

Heston's husband had decided to kill Jerrie rather than let her go. The man he hired turned out to be an undercover police officer. 'Kevin Heston was very specific about how the death should be arranged,' says Detective Paul Fraser from Virginia, where Heston tried to place the contract. 'He wanted her shot in the chest three times and before she died he wanted me to say: "And now I'm going to go and kill your kids", then he wanted me to shoot her in the head.'

Fraser met with Jerrie Heston and the two went to a firing range. There, Fraser tape-recorded a fake hit, including sounds of gunfire, Jerrie Heston crying for mercy and then her screams as she was shot.

In a dingy bar back in South Carolina, Fraser played the recording, with another tape machine hidden, getting everything the murderous husband said on a tiny microphone. 'You got her!' he screeches on the audio tape played at his trial. 'The bitch is dead!' Heston was arrested and charged with murder.

Jerrie went into shock for more than three weeks after Heston was taken into custody, and needed psychiatric care. Like Rita Quam, she had terrible dreams of men with guns or knives suddenly confronting her. 'I found it so hard to cope with the feeling Kevin wanted me dead, that another human being would rejoice at the sight of my corpse.' Jerrie says eventually she also felt a strange new sense of purpose. 'Around 200 American women a year die after their husbands put a contract on their lives. I began wondering if I could do something to stop these needless deaths. That's when Rita called me.'

The two women met and instantly became friends. They were both survivors and that gave their relationship an immediate intimacy. 'Survival always makes the survivor feel guilty,' says Quam. 'I wondered, "why me" when so many people die before their time.' Quam and Heston began gathering statistics on hits, and soon had a list of women who had not survived. So many of them shared the same backgrounds, women enjoying comfortable lives with professional husbands, until they found themselves in divorce courts.

'We tried to find a pattern,' says Heston. 'We wanted to identify what kind of man decides to pay for a contract killing. We hired a former FBI expert from the bureau's behavioural science unit, made famous in *Silence of the Lambs*. He built a profile of the typical hit-man-hiring husband.' That is a man with money in the bank who tends to be frugal, has a short temper, a poor relationship with his parents, no children or just one child and finds it difficult to relate to women outside sex. They also tend to drive fast cars, like violent movies and work in professions that require quick decisions under stress.

'What amazes me is that the idea of hiring a killer is something now considered by so many people,' says Dan Archer, a University of California professor who consulted with Rita Quam. 'There's a moral threshold that doesn't seem to exist any more. Middle-class people have begun to see the availability of this. With all the violence out there, it's not much of a stretch to think you can get away with finding someone to solve your problems.'

Whilst Quam and Heston conducted research, they began hearing from other women. Jane Roper from Indiana, whose husband wanted her blinded before her death. Dione McGann from Virginia; her husband wanted her drowned. Magaret Kogan from Chicago, a survivor of a bomb attack by a hit man paid $50,000 by her lawyer husband. Suddenly, Rita and Jerrie felt they had started something. 'We began calling ourselves "The Survivors' Club" and we mentioned this to other women. They loved it. Now we are officially taking the name into business. We have an official Survivors' Club membership, a toll-free number for women who feel threatened and we will advertise in women's magazines.'

With typical American marketing flair, the Survivors' Club intends to focus on up-market publications where they can catch the eye of middle-class women. 'They are most at risk,' says Rita. 'Women from poorer backgrounds do get targeted, but those hits rarely happen because their husbands can't afford more than a few hundred dollars. When the contract is worth at least $10,000, there's a strong chance a wife is going to get killed.'

People who call the Survivors' Club toll-free hotline will be offered counselling from Rita or one of her group. They can also get a booklet that lists the danger signals. These include a spouse with a history of violent behaviour, one who has any access to the criminal world or who is a hand-gun enthusiast. The club also urges women to monitor their husband's bank account with great care. Any large withdrawals of cash are a red flag. Quam also says if a relationship has been sour for some time and the husband starts being excessively pleasant, wives should treat the turnaround with great suspicion.

'The niceness is usually caused by guilt and a desire to avoid being blamed,' says Quam. 'If a man you are divorcing suddenly switches from venom to charm, it's a sure sign he has a hit man on your tail. Be careful.' Heston says women should also monitor their husband's telephone calls, if they can. If he begins calling unfamiliar numbers, these should be investigated. 'A woman should never be afraid to hire personal protection or point a finger at their husbands,' says Quam.

'Don't be embarrassed to make accusations, even if it means seeming paranoid. It's better to be wrong than dead.'

Detective George Forsythe agrees. 'Many hits never happen because somebody gets cold feet,' he says. 'If a husband thinks he's under suspicion he will call it off. I've posed as a hit man to more than fifty husbands and only two dozen wanted to go ahead with the killing. The others got scared about being found out.'

The Survivors' Club is a peculiarly *fin de siècle* phenomenon, one that suits a culture addicted to easy solutions and pervasive violence. It's also part of a growing American thirst for revenge. The club plans to offer members expert legal advice so they can ensure guilty spouses stay in jail for a long time. That won't be necessary in Rita Quam's case. Her husband died of bone cancer eighteen months after Rita was attacked. 'I don't feel sorry for him,' she says. 'In fact, he still terrifies me. I'm scared he'll try one last time to have me killed, from the grave, so I can't spend all his money, which I inherited under Colorado law.' To Rita that would be a terrible irony. To have set up the Survivors' Club only to die from one final act of hatred. 'Let's just say I'm going to be really careful,' she says. 'I'm going to hire a bodyguard who, unlike Arthur Smith, actually knows how to shoot.'

22. The Saddest Song

Charlie's people rode wild horses across the plains for centuries. There's a reason he's called 'Horse'. Tribal elders say Charlie could get inside the head of a mare or stallion within seconds and give it the dreams required for smooth riding. As a four-year-old he got on his first pony and rode all night, but now most of his people would fall off anything more frisky than a donkey, and the animals that were once their soul mates run wild across land now owned by the federal government but leased back to industrial farmers. Although it is illegal on federal lands, these beef barons will hunt wild horses from helicopters, blinding them with bright lights and rotor-borne dust before shooting them with high-powered rifles. The farmers say the cull is necessary because the horses eat grass they need for their cattle, the raw material of a billion McDonald's that have turned the American roadside from a chromium diner explosion of diverse imagination to the sickly yellow conformity of Golden Arches, the biggest visual curse ever to hit a country's landscape.

William Frederick Cody, better known as Buffalo Bill, loved horses almost as much as the Navajo. He invented the horse rodeo to celebrate their spirit when he thought up that uniquely American extravaganza called the Wild West Show, which featured plenty of faux Indians, for Bill was nothing if not politically incorrect. In 1882, Cody organized a fourth of July blowout for his hometown (North Platte, Nebraska) that awarded prizes for roping, shooting, riding and bronco breaking. By the time he established his showbusiness imitation of what Charlie's Navajo ancestors had done naturally all their life, the Navajo tribe had already been exiled from its native lands. To add insult, Cody had a comedy turn where Native Americans allowed themselves to pose as horse-riding incompetents whilst dressed as a cross between Geronimo and Coco the Clown. Bill may have loved horses, but with people he was a dead loss, a contradiction Charlie just cannot understand.

Frontier Days in Prescott, Arizona, held annually since 1888, calls itself the world's oldest rodeo, and it would have made Buffalo Bill proud. Held in July, this year the five-day celebration included a carnival, a golf tournament, the Happy Hearts Rodeo for Exceptional Children, a parade, the Sons of the American Revolution Ice Cream Social, and over 2,000 taking part in 'street dancing' to country music bands inside a tent.

In the rodeo, life is measured in unpredictable increments of just a few seconds, the time it takes to rope a steer or ride a bareback bronc, and you just never know who'll get thrown, who'll get hurt, who'll get the money today. But the structure of a rodeo is one of remarkable uniformity. Across the country during the month of August, 142 rodeos recognized by the Professional Rodeo Cowboys' Association are held, and every one follows the same format. After the Grand Entry parade introduces the rodeo royalty, stock contractors, announcers, judges, clowns and other notables of the rodeo arena, the seven standard events will follow in almost invariable order: bareback bronco riding, steer wrestling, team roping, saddle bronco riding, calf roping, barrel racing and bull riding. Interspersed are exhibitions by trick riders and draught horses and bull fighters – not matadors, but cowboys, these madmen provoke bulls to get competition points – and a lot of predictably lame rodeo humour.

In the 1950s, the golden age of rodeo, the only way to distinguish contestants from fans was the number pinned on the cowboy's shirt. Folks in the audience were dressed just like the riders in the arena, in boots, jeans and cowboy hats. There is still the cowgirl with big hair, tight jeans, red-heeled boots and a sequined vest patterned like the American flag. But most people seemed to be wearing baseball caps, $200 gym shoes and big T-shirts advertising a product or point of view.

Rodeo is one of the fastest-growing sports in America, complete with big prize money, corporate sponsorship and politically incorrect aspects. But its practitioners are a breed apart. The best cowboys, those who finish in the top fifteen for an event and earn an invitation to the National Finals Rodeo, will travel to as many as 125 rodeos a year, covering over 100,000 miles, and must pay not only their travel expenses but entry fees for every event they compete in. Perhaps two dozen make more than $100,000 in a year. The rest are fanatics, forever addicted to the smell of straw and saddle soap, the romance of the old West, the roar of the crowd as each rider is catapulted through the gate.

Though bull riding is the glamour event because it is so dangerous, it is saddle bronc riding, invariably introduced as rodeo's 'classic event', that epitomizes both sport and myth. The image of a rider on a bucking horse appears everywhere – on jewellery, Western wear, all items produced by the Professional Rodeo Cowboys' Association, even the licence plates of the state of Wyoming. The symbol outside the Prorodeo Hall of Fame in Colorado Springs is 'The Champ', a 20-foot bronze statue of Casey Tibbs, the nine-time world champion, riding the legendary saddle bronc Necktie.

Sit behind the chutes during the saddle bronc event, and the passion the sport generates can be felt everywhere, a real physical presence. While the preceding event is going on, the saddle bronc riders climb the side of the chute containing the broncs they've been assigned in a random draw. At a nod from the chute boss, the ground crew slowly tighten the two cinches on the saddle of the first rider and then the fleece-lined flank strap. The horse rolls her eyes, madness building to perfect pitch, 300lb of animal anger set to detonate along hard strings of taut muscle. The cowboy straddles the chute and eases himself down like a man about to sit on a mean-tempered rattlesnake, dropping until he's crouched in the air right over the saddle, ignoring the fate of the contestant in the arena before him. The tension in both horse and rider is palpable, but fear is usually only felt by the one wearing chaps.

When the chute boss nods again, it's time to go. The cowboy hangs on to the top of the chute with one hand as he gets into the saddle, putting his ass on the snake. He grips the 6-foot braided rein in his other hand, and eases his feet into the stirrups, a means of binding himself more closely to a force that wants to hurt him real bad. There is a moment of perfect stillness. The horse, a pro getting set in her own right, gathers herself, knowing full well she's the boss. Then the cowboy takes a breath and nods, the chute gate swings open sideways, and the bronc comes out like she's running from the devil, surging and lunging, twisting in the air, landing in stiff, juddering hops and bucking again. The rider is required to begin the ride with his feet over the bronc's shoulders, but with the next lunge his knees bend and his boots strike the cantle on the back of the saddle.

He looks like a rag doll, legs kicking, free arm flailing, daylight between his arched body and the horse's. His free hand may not touch the horse, the rigging, nor any part of himself, or he will be disqualified. The bronco plunges her nose between her forefeet and curls her hind legs under her belly, before shooting her heels towards the sun; for an instant she is almost vertical. The rider's head snaps back and he lies back till he appears to be standing straight up, before she sunfishes away, leaping and twisting and bucking until the horn or buzzer or gunshot signals that eight seconds have expired, and the pickup riders close in to ease the rider from her back.

To the spectator it is inconceivable that there is any element of control in this situation, but in the first second out of the chute, the cowboy is looking for the rhythm of the ride. There is no conquest of the animal involved, more a seeking for balance, mid-air communion, a very brief union of man and beast. Sometimes he finds it. Sometimes he's dumped. Occasionally he breaks something, but in most falls he just gets the wind knocked out of him, and not even his pride is injured. The audiences know he'll most likely be going home with nothing but the memory of their cheers, so they try to make it worth the trip. Even if he stays aboard for the full ride, there's no guarantee he'll be in the prize money, especially if the bronc gave him an easy ride. The horse and rider are judged equally, each performance worth 50 points. At good rodeos it may take at least 80 points to be in the running for the money.

The top three rodeo association events in North America, in terms of prize purses, are the National Western Rodeo in Denver (January), the Southwestern Exposition and Livestock Show in Fort Worth (January–February) and the San Antonio Stock Show (February), but one of the most famous pays hardly any cash and gives some improbable riders the chance to get killed or be a temporary star. It is held once a year at the Louisiana State Penitentiary, otherwise known as Angola Prison, the place where prison guards invented the phrase 'Dead Man Walking' – it is what the senior officer shouts when a Death Row inmate begins his military-style march to the execution chamber flanked by six other guards.

Nick Nicholson dreamed of being a cowboy when he was a child in Walkill, NY. He had to kill a man in Louisiana to see that dream come true. On his first day at America's only prison rodeo, the wild bull Nick drew even smelt mean, a trembling 2,000lb mass of muscle, hooves and horns. But as he eases himself carefully on to its spine, there is no fear that he will lose his life. Life, to a man sentenced to for ever, is pretty much lost already. Nick will never be a dead man walking but he will never be free either. All he lives for all year is the glory of that moment as the gate swings open, as the bull twists like a Texas cyclone, as 6,000 people in the tightly packed grandstand gasp, clap and roar for a man who can never buy a pack of cigarettes from a regular store again. A former all-around champion of the Angola Prison Rodeo, Nick has served sixteen years. His sentence was life without the possibility of parole. He is thirty-three.

'I beg for a bull,' he said.

The Angola rodeo began in 1964, an annual event that may be as close to the Roman coliseums as is available in the twentieth century. Like gladiators, the inmates – some of whom have never been on a horse in their lives, let alone a bucking bull – are thrown, stomped, gored, pawed, kicked and bitten. Before the injuries begin they sign a legal release saying that they take part in the rodeo of their own free will, and absolve the prison and state of Louisiana of all culpability.

The prize money for the events – bull riding is one of the safest – is usually $50, which is a lot of money to a man who makes four cents an hour picking cotton on the prison farm. An inmate who won $300 for picking a poker chip off a bull's forehead as the animal tried to skewer him with horns 4-feet across – the horns were painted bright red, for effect – was taking away three and a half years' worth of cotton-field wages.

But Nick Nicholson and most of the other inmates say they do not do it for the money, but for the joy of it. The years drag so slowly. A few seconds on a bull's back is the only escape in the vast, dull flatness, where the inmates are expected to work in the giant fields and the Mississippi River is the only thing in sight that can make it around the next bend without being shot.

'I always wanted to ride when I was a kid, but there weren't horses at home,' said Nicholson, a handsome man with sun-streaked hair and a big blond moustache. He looks just like Robert Redford in *Butch Cassidy and the Sundance Kid*, except that a collision with the ground has scoured a square inch of skin from his nose. 'This prison is a bad place to find it,' he said of his childhood dream. 'But I found it.' The Angola rodeo is unique for a dozen reasons. The bull and bronc riding are traditional rodeo events, but some of events are modified, to compensate for the lack of skill and experience of its competitors and to increase the chance that somebody might get killed, a feature the deep-south audience seems to relish more than they should. In bull dogging, the Angola cowboys do not jump from a horse and wrestle the running steer to the ground. Here, they stand almost face to face with the thing, just a few feet from the chute, and hurl themselves at it as it comes charging out. It's doubtful anyone would do this unless they already had a death wish.

Other events are pure Angola inventions, like Guts and Glory, where all the inmates in the competition enter the arena and a wild bull is turned loose among them. Then there is Convict Poker. Four men sit at a card table painted brilliant red, on red chairs, as a wild bull is given a jolt with a cattle prod and let loose on them. The winner is the last one to get up and run, or the last one tossed or hurled from the table. Seating is determined by lottery. The man who loses sits with his back to the gate and only knows the bull is coming by listening to the pounding of its hooves, or the fear in the eyes of the man across from him.

The rodeo is a show. People pay $8 a head to see it, four Sundays in October. It draws more than the grandstand can hold, and people pour into the prison from Tunica, Solitude, Hardwood, St Francisville and other small, quiet places, to eat cotton candy and watch men try to master beasts or, at least, survive the encounter. Most days an inmate has to be carried off on a stretcher, like a man whose forehead collided with the whipping head of a bull, but in thirty-two years, no one has died. Getting hurt is expected, the inmates said.

'It takes four things to run a good prison: good playing, good praying, good food and good medicine. This is good playing,' said Burl Cain, the warden at Angola. 'They're king for a day.' The broncs burst wild-eyed out of the stalls, hurling the riders from their backs in a few seconds, sometimes landing almost on top of them with slashing hooves. The massive bulls may be more frightening, the cowboys say, but a bad horse will kill you. 'A bull won't stomp on you,' said Nicholson, who as a prison trusty, breaks horses at the Angola farm. His bronc does the unexpected. Instead of leaping around the centre of the arena, it races, bucking, towards the rodeo ring perimeter made of steel poles and thick ropes of wire, and hurls Nicholson over its neck, head-first into the unyielding fence. People in the front jerk back instinctively. He gets up and limps back to the gate. The crowd cheers. 'When you ride,' he said, 'everything blacks out around you.' For a few seconds, he forgets the fence outside the fence, the one that keeps men in their place.

One of the cowboys has dreadlocks. One is wearing a pair of Nikes. One, a skinny, long-legged black man of many incarcerated winters, rides like an expert but wears a brown cloth cap that would be more in place in a Detroit pool hall. Angola has 5,000 inmates; 85% of them are here because they murdered or tried to murder, raped, or robbed with violence. The cowboys, one after another, refuse to talk about their crimes. Not today. The stands are full of pretty girls, children and grey-haired old women who could be their mothers, if their mothers still came to see them.

It is a big crowd; prison officials had to turn people away. For a few inmates, it will be a chance to see their wives and children, if only from the stands, if only for a glance or a wave. Others, like Nicholson and a young man from Baton Rouge named Dale Langlois, perform for strangers. 'I just want to feel it, feel free for just a little while,' said Langlois, his head bound in a blazing orange headband, his arms and body crossed with jailhouse tattoos. 'Maybe it'll take my mind off this fifty years I got.' He is thirty-five. 'Maybe people think it's crazy,' he said, a few hours before he would climb on his first bull — and rapidly come flying off. 'I think it's something positive.'

Major Shirley Coody, an officer at the prison, was the first woman to traverse 'The Walk' through the prison's main inmate population. She never forgets that the men inside committed serious criminal acts, but also that they are still men, with dignity. 'The inmates were kinder to me when I first started than the free people,' said Major Coody. One inmate told her why. 'If you can pull a twelve-hour shift,' he told me, 'and make it home, then the people on the outside will know we're not the animals that people think we are.'

The Convict Poker event has drawn a bull with a split personality. He comes out of the gate a little unsure if he is mad or not at first, and then decides, as he spots the card table with the four inmates, that he is. He takes a few running steps and rams one horn into the inmate with his back to the gate, up high, across his shoulders, just below his neck. The inmate's face twists in pain, and the impact of his body against the table almost crumples it. The inmate who is hit runs away, and so does Langlois. Two other inmates refuse to leave their seats, and the bull seems to have lost interest. He snorts around a little, and ignores them. The judges decide, since the bull has turned timid, to call it a draw. 'Them fellows ain't brave,' said a trusty in the press box. 'They just be stupid.'

There are ambulances standing by and professional rodeo cowboys in the ring to draw the bulls and bad horses away from fallen men. 'We don't want anyone to get hurt,' Mr Cain said, but there are risks, as in any rodeo. Claude Roberson, a convicted murderer from Baton Rouge, said he is doing it for Christmas gifts. 'If I win something, I can send my son a present, maybe even get something for my momma. She's sixty,' he said. He is thirty-four, and he is doing life.

The bull riders are flung one by one by one, until the

question is not if, but how high. Only one rider stays on the six seconds it takes to qualify, so the judging is easy, and only one is carried off in a neck brace, injured but not seriously. 'He's talking, and that's a good sign,' the announcer says. 'I know he can hear you,' and he exhorts the crowd to show their appreciation for his valour. The inmate is carried off to cheers from behind the tall secondary fence that separates the prisoners from spectators and guards. A young woman with a little girl stands beside it, and scans the rows of inmates, searching. She finally gives up.

Even with the fence and some visible instruments of incarceration, the atmosphere is like a county fair. Inmates peddle beautiful leather crafts and gleaming cedar chests, along with paintings of women the inmates have never seen and landscapes they will never see again. With so many people milling around, it would seem that escape would be inevitable. A few years ago one inmate stowed away on a horse trailer, but was recaptured. But most inmates don't want to take the risk, for fear they'd be banned from future rodeos.

There was a time when men would have drowned themselves in the river rather than spend one more night in Angola, one of the most infamous prisons in the nation. Men were whipped for coming up light in their cotton sacks. That era is past. It is still a place where inmates grow much of their food and work money crops and cattle, where guards keep watch from horseback, but Warden Cain is determined to keep modern-day problems, like gangs, out of the prison. 'You have a gang, you make the gang leader a toilet orderly. That way no one wants to follow him.'

The rodeo heroes are highly regarded as tough men, men not to be messed with. It is a way to show that you are no one's punk.

Guts and Glory is the last event of the day. The contestants file slowly into the arena, and for a second or two you almost expect the announcer to blare: 'Those of you who are about to die, we salute you.' Then the bull charges in, and with every slash of those wide, red horns, the crowd gasps more than it cheers. Then a man in a red bandanna weaves in and, with a flash of his hand, manages to knock the crazed animal into the dirt. He raises the bandanna high in his hand. Inside the fences, where a convict makes four cents an hour, Angola has a new rich man.

Inside the rodeo pit at the Tucson Fairgrounds on a Saturday night, a 1000 miles away, Paul Dufrene's black mare bucked out of the chute and he was disqualified from the bareback competition by judge A. C. Campbell. 'A. C. Campbell can kiss my butt,' Dufrene spit as he ripped his gloves off.

That's cowboy life.

Outside the ring, Randy Hubel buried his face in his cowboy hat, shaking a little, starting to cry. Preachers Ted Pressley and Rick Barnard laid their hands on him, shaking and praying. Hubel got saved right there on the spot.

That's cowboy church.

Just call it a tale of two worlds colliding; the Lord working in mysterious ways. In the rough and tumbleweed world of professional rodeo, the Cowboys for Christ are bull doggin' the devil and lassoing lost souls.

In the rodeo life of tough luck and hard love, there's more to redemption than AM radio preacher salvation. There's the Cowboys for Christ, a brimstone y'all come caravan of cowboys, trainers and ranchers riding the range with Jesus on their side. Rick Barnard joined when he was at Angola. Now he's one of the rare inmates to make it out whilst he can still chew with his own teeth, the result of his conviction being overturned.

'It's just a fellowship with other believers who have a common interest,' he says. He's now a professional horse trainer and president of the south Mississippi chapter of the CFC. 'It's just cowboys preachin', lovin' the Lord and doing a sport we love.'

Cowboys for Christ, based in Fort Worth, Texas, boasts a membership of about 68,000 worldwide, with 300 rodeo preachers wandering through some twenty countries, but few had their lives saved by the rodeo before their souls were rescued by Christ. 'Those ten years I was in Angola, from the age of nineteen, I lived for the rodeo. It kept me going, I told myself rodeo stories every hour of every day.'

CFC was founded by Ted Pressley, a former world-class bull-dogger, back in about 1970. To the converted, he became 'The Rodeo Preacher', to the unwashed he was 'Crazy Ted', and he has, over the past twenty-five years, become a fixture at livestock and rodeo shows across America. In 1995 he was allowed into Angola for the first time and Rick Barnard was his third convert.

Cowboys for Christ now publishes a newspaper – *The Christian Ranchman* (a recent story was headlined: 'Are There Horses In Heaven?') – and sells concessions on the road, including a dinner-plate-sized belt-buckle with the group's logo on it. Barnard wears his with pride. 'It's not so much the God stuff. I do believe in it, kind of, but CFC gave me something to do, when I got free of Angola. Stopped me getting bitter inside.'

And so at Covington, as the sun set, cowboy convict for Christ Barnard held himself poised above his bronco. The screams in the crowd echoed back over a hundred years to when this land was new and Buffalo Bill rode the rattlesnake across the hot sand. A smile crossed Barnard's face and he took a deep breath. He was tasting freedom, sucking it down into his lungs as only those who have once been behind bars can do. Within seconds his mouth was full of dirt and a big bronco bruise was forming where a hoof had hit his cheek, but the smile was still there.

He came back to the pen and sat down, fiddling with his boots. 'You know, we'd sing cowboy songs, in Angola. After all the crowds had gone. All the favourites. We'd always get to "Home on the Range". To hear a man who will never be free sing those lines, "where the deer and the antelope roam, where never is heard a discouraging word and the skies are not cloudy all day", it's about the saddest song I ever heard.'

Barnard shuffled off to get ready for his bull-dogging event, and in his walk was a heaviness, a thousand memories of nights in a cell for something he knew he hadn't done. There's barely a man in jail who won't claim he's innocent, but at the Angola Rodeo they all are — for a few seconds of gut-busting exhilarating fear, even the worst murderers amongst them — innocent as babies as they cling on for dear life. That's what makes the Angola Rodeo both a release and a cruel punishment — each rider probably knows they are tasting a kind of freedom they can never hold on to for long.

23. Palm Springs Perpetuals

Palm Springs is a contradiction. It sits in the midst of the desert but there are green lawns everywhere. Nothing of substance is made in the town, but all the residents seem to be swimming in wealth. To somebody like Charlie Horse, Palm Springs must seem like a mirage.

Under the black desert sky Palm Springs exists as a place for people to spend money on themselves. It was erected within a drunken drive from Hollywood and many of the early stars chucked themselves into a convertible Cadillac with a bottle of Jack Daniels, keeping their foot pressed down hard until they zippped inside the Palm Springs city limits, in the days before every freeway in Los Angeles became coagulated with cheap Japanese cars and their Detroit-born knock-offs.

Now Palm Springs is still far too full of the self-importantly celebrated, but booze is much less part of the ethic. Palm Springs has become more spa than bar as the royal families of celluloid flood there for rejuvenation after a few taxing weeks on a movie set which leaves them so exhausted you'd think they had real jobs.

There is a certain type of Californian found only in the state's wealthiest corners and Palm Springs is their favourite destination. Tanned and fit, they ooze wealth and confidence. Most people find their self-important arrogance obnoxious. They are so concerned with improving themselves they appear to care little for anybody else. These narcissi seem to think they should be allowed to live for ever as perpetual teenagers, and a team of doctors has made their horrifying fantasy of eternal youth a reality. For a steep price the lotus-eaters of California are using a heady and controversial cocktail of hormones to turn back their biological clocks.

Astonishingly, in a significant number of cases it is working. Seventy-year-old pensioners are bounding around on mountain bikes like twenty-year-olds, claiming to have the sex lives of adolescent rabbits and the stamina of elephants. It all makes me want to crawl under the covers with a cheese sandwich and a bottle of beer.

The Mecca for these modern day Dorian Grays is Palm Springs, home to the Life Extension Institute. The institute was founded by Edmund Chein. He operates from a simple theory. As human beings age our hormone levels drop. By the time we reach our three score years and ten, hormone depletion has left us with a spreading middle, thin or sagging skin, a depleted sex drive, diminished mental capacity and poor eyesight.

There are many hormones that desert the body as we age. Testosterone is one, along with DHEA (Dehydroepi-androsterone) and melatonin but the biggest thief of youthfulness is human growth hormone, which we produce in rapidly decreasing quantities from the day we are born. That's good in one way, because otherwise we'd all be 50′ tall. It is bad in others because once the body's secretion of growth hormone is below the optimum level, reached in the early twenties, our body begins to fall apart, like a Savile Row suit made in Bangkok.

Using a solution that some experts dismiss as dangerous, Dr Chein employs hormone supplements to drive the patient's hormone levels back to those of a twenty-one-year-old. A key component is injections of human growth hormone. The patient starts old with an old body and an old person's hormone levels. Then they get a young person's hormone levels and before long, hey presto, a young person's body, and they are not old any more.

At least that's the theory. The sun was high in a perfect blue sky as Bob Jones strolled into the rose garden of a Palm Spring's spa, fresh from a morning climbing mountains. He's a patient of Dr Chein. He acts as a guide to people planning to take Chein's elixir of youth. The spa costs $300 a night and is recommended as a good place to begin hormone anti-ageing therapy. Clint Eastwood and Arnold Schwarzenegger are regular customers. The theory may be the spa relaxes clients ready for their hormone tests. It is more likely the spa's bill is a preparation for the crippling costs of being young again.

Whilst waiting for Jones, I overheard conversations from nearby tables. One was dominated by the less famous Kevin in the fine movie *The Usual Suspects*. Kev was whining like a poodle who had been forced to take a Doberman for a lover. His agent was not doing enough to get him the roles he needed for 'his talent', he wailed. I'd been warned about guests like Kev by Rose Navlar, the charming vampire who owns Givenchy. She said the new stars often lacked the manners of the old, that many of them had money but did not know how to spend it without being offensive. She complained that her staff were often upset by such people and she had begun a black list.

I hope Kevboy is on it. He was now speaking so loudly about the pitfalls associated with his good fortune that it became impossible to ignore him, which was presumably what the big baby wanted. I was hoping he'd get so offensive that the man now sipping camomile tea at my table might decide to use his considerable muscles to play Doberman to Kev's poodle.

Bob Jones pays a $1000 a month for his hormone supplements and says it is worth every penny. In some people's eyes he is right. At sixty-six he looks like a tennis club professional, one of those tanned, good-looking types who seem to have been blessed with a life of leisure. His skin looks taut but slightly unnatural, as if it has been made of high-quality plastic. His face looks like a freshly pressed shirt. It is no surprise to learn the former marketing executive has had cosmetic surgery in his desperate fight against ageing, but he says it is hormones not the knife which finally made him feel he was winning.

Five years ago Jones says he felt he was ready for a trade-in. He felt tired all the time and could no longer keep to the rigorous fitness regime he began in his thirties. Like any wealthy Californian raised chanting the holy creed of self-improvement, Jones reacted to ageing with a temper tantrum. Like a kid shouting, 'I won't', Jones stamped his foot and yelled for somebody to help him get young again. That's when he met Dr Chein, who said all Jones needed was an oil change.

It sounded too good by far, but Chein produced an impressive study of 200 Life Extension patients which made Jones sign up immediately. After 180 days taking injections of growth hormone four days a week, 88% of Chein's patients reported improved muscle strength, 70% body fat loss, 51% wrinkle disappearance, 55% healing of old injuries, 63% improved memory, 75% enhanced sexual potency and 29% had grown extra prehensile limbs. Actually I made that last one up, but seeing the fervour in Bob Jones's eyes, it wouldn't surprise me if it were amongst his claims. Jones warns that the first step to a second childhood is a tough one. Patients have to take a biological age test. Most of us know our exact chronological age but we are less practised at dating how worn out we are. That's our biological age. Does a person function as a sixteen-year-old, or a forty- or an eighty-year-old? Most Life Extension patients find their biological age is a higher number than their chronological age.

In the interests of science, I was in Palm Springs to take the test. There are many mornings when I feel older than my tender years, and I was afraid I'd discover that I really was more ancient, biologically speaking at least. Jones told me if I did, it would be a liberating experience because I could then start therapy, so long as I was prepared to sell my first-born as a down payment on the cost.

Therapy is to the Bob Jones style of Californian what tea is to the rest of us. It's something they have to get every few hours or else they just don't feel right. It must be the outstanding beauty of places like Palm Springs which induces so much guilt. After a while, residents fear they aren't worthy of the natural splendour. It also causes anxiety, because they fear it could all suddenly be taken away by an earthquake or a bank-balance-shattering stock market collapse. Jones liked finding out he was biologically fifteen years older than his chronological age. He says it gave him something tangible to worry about, and as a nurse drained a blood sample from my arm he said I'd soon feel the same way. This was less comforting to me than it might have been. Partly because Jones began explaining that a key part of Chein's youth therapy is to smear testosterone all over the face on a daily basis, which explains why Monica Lewinsky had such a good complexion when she was working in the White House. At least thinking about using the male sex hormone as a substitute for Pond's face cream took my mind off the blood sampling.

The blood test looks for current levels of human growth hormone, DHEA, testosterone, pregnenolone (a steroid that is involved in breaking down bad cholesterol) and a few others. Once the results are in, which takes two weeks, patients get a prescription for hormone capsules and a routine of growth-hormone injections. Chein's philosophy is that old age is a disease not an inevitability. It can be treated and then the patient can live easily until the age of 140 with most body functions intact.

Since Jones took the test, he has gulped a fistful of capsules containing melatonin, thyroid and others each day. These help, but the key is the twice-daily shots of human growth hormone, administered in the same way as a diabetic takes insulin. There is evidence growth hormone can cause heart disease, carpal tunnel syndrome and possibly cancer, but this research is inconclusive and does not seem to bother Bob Jones.

When he describes the effects of his therapy his eyes begin to glow like a fundamentalist preacher who believes God comes to his house for breakfast every morning. Jones says it was a revelation. His mind whipped back into sharp action, his skin went from drooping like an old curtain to snapping taut as a snare drum. He became the kind of sexual athlete he wished he had been as a fumbling adolescent. I could have sworn he was on drugs, which of course he is.

Jones is so devoted to Chein's theories he would be prepared to die an early death for them. As a spa waiter brought more herb tea stripped of all taste and stimulants, Jones considered if he would stop the hormone therapy if research proved it shortened life expectancy, as some believe. His expression became so earnest I thought I'd age another ten biological years trying not to laugh, but Jones's type take their own mortality very seriously. 'I would accept the loss of years,' he said finally. 'I could not bear going back to the old man I was. Each year of my new life is worth five of my old.'

Chein's theories are gaining greater acceptance in America, with 10,000 patients now following the regime, despite his controversial past. The forty-seven-year-old doctor wears gold-rimmed glasses and white cowboy boots, which give him the look of a poker player from Craps City, Wyoming. He grabbed headlines in 1992 as the doctor who examined police-beating victim Rodney King in Los Angeles. In trial testimony, Chein described himself as an orthopaedic surgeon and a graduate of Cornell Medical College. In fact, he is a graduate of the American University of the Caribbean Medical College, which is slightly less prestigious and he's not an orthopaedic surgeon.

In 1995, the California Medical Board placed Chein on three years' probation for ethical violations, for false advertising, for failing to share insurance payments with other doctors who provided care to his patients, and for claiming to be a doctor-lawyer. He has a law degree but is not qualified to practise. In June 1996, Dr Chein's clinic was raided by Federal Drug Administration agents. They took copies of patient files, computers and a large stock of growth hormone.

Chein says the ethical violations resulted from a 'misunderstanding' and he says the FDA have said they are taking no further action against the institute. He is pressing ahead with a book called *Age Reversal*. Within three years the drug companies which sell human growth hormone will lose their patents and the youth elixir will be available to many more, at just $40 per month. Then Chein will begin a mission across America backed by his current patients, most of whom are intelligent professional men like Bob Jones.

The prospect fills Omid Khorram with horror. A professor at the University of Wisconsin, where the original human growth hormone research was done, Khorram says the research on the substance by Chein is 'seriously flawed'. Khorram warns that if millions took growth hormone there would be an epidemic of diabetes and other serious side effects, but it is unlikely anyone will listen. Californians aren't the only ones desperate to live for ever as teenagers. Americans now spend more than $8 billion a year on hormones like DHEA which slow down the ageing process. The potential sales of a hormone that reverses ageing are incalculable.

Jones says he can't wait for America to get on growth hormone. He becomes earnest again as he describes a country full of 140-year-olds. He says people will not retire at sixty-five, they will have two or three careers and approach life less rigidly. Of course, he really means men. More than 60% of those who take growth hormone are males and it does not seem to work so well for women.

The morning my test results arrived was a bit like getting

A level results. Would I be judged too old for my years? Tearing open the envelope, I found my biological age and my chronological age were the same, but I was advised to spend a great deal of money to keep it that way. I'm tempted, but do I really want to live until I'm 140? It would mean being old for sixty years. Even with a hormone-generated sex life, that seems like an awfully long time.

Back in New York I was horrified to find Dorian Gray syndrome had spread from the always daft west coast to the much grittier north-east, in the body of Dr Adrienne Denese. She is a trim blonde with skin that is smooth but oddly hard to the touch. A series of injections of human growth hormone, or hGH, at her clinic, she maintains, gives patients glowing skin, increased muscle mass, elevated sex drive, a lighter mood, sharper mental acuity and the whizz-bang metabolism of an eighteen-year-old. It is not just Disney that's taking over New York, it's California as well.

Denese says human growth hormone is just one therapy deployed by a growing field of medical practitioners who call themselves anti-ageing specialists. Their practices are rooted in plastic surgery, but go far beyond it – to hormone replacement therapy, vitamin supplementation, dermatology, physical therapy and other procedures, both internal and cosmetic. Call it one-stop shopping for greying boomers, the youth-obsessed generation that has resolved not to go gentle into its Geritol years. With one American turning fifty every 7.6 seconds, industries that promise to cushion the indignity of ageing have become depressingly ubiquitous, from retirement-oriented investment funds to face-saving plastic surgery. Bookstore shelves are crowded with volumes like *Reversing Human Ageing* and *Stopping the Clock*.

The American Academy of Anti-Aging Medicine, which was founded by twelve doctors in 1993, currently boasts a membership of more than 4,300 United States doctors, who specialize in the all-encompassing approach to youth preservation. 'We're not about growing old gracefully,' said Dr Ronald

Klatz, forty-three, the group's president, who practises in Chicago. 'We're about never growing old.'

Cary Cimino, thirty-seven, a private investor in Manhattan who has been taking growth hormone for one year, said, 'My health and my quality of life are major issues for me.' Me, Me, Me – I suddenly hear Kevboy's whining in my ear, haunting me from Palm Springs. I hope he isn't in hGH, I'm wondering if there is an anti-hGH which will make some people grow old more rapidly.

Cimino told me his views whilst speaking by cellular phone during a workout at the Reebok Sports Club on the Upper West Side, an establishment that charges so much for annual fees that a family of five in Appalachia could live off the dues for three years. 'I used to be the hedonistic yuppie of the 1980s who was only concerned with his Mercedes-Benz,' says Cimino in a voice that sounds like Kevboy – on hGH! 'Now, I'm the hedonistic yuppie of the nineties who is only concerned about his health and well-being. And who will do anything for it.'

The good thing about New York before Super John Wayne Cop-Mayor Rudy Giuliani and the dramatic fall in the crime rate was that muggers could be relied upon to venture from the ghettos and take down a few Cary Ciminos every year, a kind of Malthusian self-regulation mechanism. I knew a stockbroker in the 1980s who kept a helicopter under the 34th Street FDR overpass, in case the brothers rioted and occupied the bridges and tunnels which are the only escape routes from the city by car. Now that Giuliani arrests any vaguely threatening person from Harlem who ventures into Manhattan on trumped-up offences like jaywalking, the broker has sold the chopper and probably takes hGH instead. Before long, the city will be overrun by Cary Ciminos in their nineties, rollerblading with the aid of Zimmer frames. It's not what Sinatra had in mind when he sang 'New York, New York'. I miss Old Blue Eyes and wish he had taken hGH, if only so I could hear him sing, 'I want to wake up/in a city/where no one dies' – although if that applied to Kevboy also, I'd rather be eaten by small flies with razor-sharp teeth.

'My hGH patients who used to take anti-depressants don't take them any more,' said Dr Denese, whose practice includes models, bankers and the occasional faded rock star (Deborah Harry of Blondie is a client – still 'Hanging on the Telephone'). 'They take hGH and it makes their mood lighter. Even I take it, and I'm more animated, I feel good and I don't take Prozac any more.' And I say God help us all.

Chris Stein, another Blondie member and patient of Dr Denese's, said hGH had increased his energy level. 'People say my skin looks smoother, too,' he said. 'Although after I get the injections, I'm a little jittery, like I've had too much coffee.' Dr Denese has passed the certifying exam invented by the American Academy of Anti-Aging Medicine, although the academy itself is not recognized by the American Board of Medical Specialities, the federal arm that regulates groups professing medical expertise.

Dr Bruce J. Nadler, a plastic surgeon who started to incorporate hGH therapy into his practice after hearing about it from the anti-ageing academy and who prescribes it to about fifty patients in Manhattan, acknowledged that when used in higher than recommended doses, disastrous effects can occur. 'Have you seen the covers of those body-building magazines?' Dr Nadler asked. 'Do you notice how the body builders have spaces between their front teeth? That's because they're taking too much hGH and their skulls have grown, causing their teeth to spread apart.' I ran to take a look at a photograph of famed hGH-user Arnold Schwarzenegger. Those interested in a little cheap humour should do the same.

Despite the potentially dangerous and freakish side effects, the mystique of hormones as a quick-fix seems to be growing. One of Dr Denese's patients, a fashion publicity agent, has referred at least three friends for hGH shots. 'There are probably about twenty doctors, in Beverly Hills and Hollywood, who between them have hundreds of clients,' says Dr Lawrence, an

LA doctor who prescribes some hormones to fight ageing, but not hGH, which he considers too risky. He compared the movie colony's interest in hormones to the plot of *Death Becomes Her*, a film in which Goldie Hawn and Meryl Streep drink a potion that will render them not only immortal but also firm of thigh for ever.

'But no one will talk because people in the movie industry are close-mouthed about their medical histories,' Dr Lawrence said. 'Everyone's very concerned about hiring an actor for a movie and hearing people say: "He's on what? What's he taking that for? Is he sick?"'

The actor Nick Nolte, for one, was spotted at the last convention of the American Academy of Anti-Aging Medicine, held in Las Vegas, Nevada, in December. Mr Nolte went from booth to booth, collecting literature. Dr Eric Braverman of New York said that Mr Nolte is a patient of his and a devotee of hGH. Another physician, Murray Susser, based in West Los Angeles, says he treats about fifty members of Hollywood's élite, from movie stars to studio heads, and has even treated the ailing labrador retriever of one of his clients. 'The guy sent his private jet for the hormone, and the first day the dog got up from his bed,' Dr Susser said.

In Las Vegas, Dr Alan P. Mintz, a former professor of medicine at the University of Chicago, oversees the hormonal futures of more than sixty patients from across the country. At his clinic, the Cenegenics Anti-Aging Center, patients undergo a day-long physical examination and blood tests that look at hormone levels; Dr Mintz and his staff then prescribe a daily dose of hormones, enzymes and vitamins. The cost: $1,300 for the physical, and up to $1,600 a month for the supplement package. (That's $19,200 a year. Dr Mintz recommends the package for life; it is not covered by health insurance.)

'Our goal is to bring the endocrine system back to where it was at age thirty,' said Dr Mintz, who himself takes scores of vitamins, hormones and enzymes on a daily basis, which he injects under the skin, inserts under the tongue, rubs into his skin and ingests in pills, capsules and powders. 'I've been taking hGH for three and a half years, and I've never felt better or stronger,' he said.

In his offices on what might be called Plastic Surgery Mile on Manhattan's Park Avenue, Dr Bruce J. Nadler performs the standard symphony of plastic surgery procedures and is popular with the youth-elixir crowd. He says he has more than fifty patients on hGH; he and his wife also take it. A competitive body builder by hobby, Dr Nadler, sixty-three, likes to show visitors to his New York office a picture of him clad only in a bikini-brief bathing suit, posing next to his silver BMW Z-3 convertible.

So the truth is out. The baby boomer generation, that group of self-centered Americans who wore flowers in their hair and believed the world owed them the best of everything, this slice of the US population that thinks it's better than anything before or since, the people who have stopped eating almost everything so they are immune from the ancient Native American curse – they plan to live for ever and be vigorous whilst doing so. There is only one solution. We will have to declare war against the elderly, shooting them on sight whenever they emerge from a doctor's office where they prescribe hGH. It's a tough decision but somebody has to do it. It's either that or rounding them all up and shipping them to an immortals' reservation in the Arizona desert.

24. Last Orders

What do you eat when you are never going to eat again? President Mitterand chose the illegal ortolan songbird preceded by foie gras and three dozen oysters. Then he fasted for seven days until his heart stopped. That's a bit of an exception, though. Few of us know what our last meal will be, but a Louisiana restaurant-owner has taken the trouble to make a study of last meals, at least amongst America's ever-growing population on death row.

For those about to die in Texas, king of the death states, burgers top the entrees. Twenty-two men chose double cheeseburgers, fifteen opted for single cheeseburgers, nine for hamburgers. Next most popular were steaks, typically T-bones, with twenty-seven requests, and eggs (ten requests, most for scrambled). Most desired overall is a side of French fries (fifty-six requests). Ice cream is the most popular dessert (twenty-one requests), Coca-Cola the most popular beverage (thirteen, just edging out twelve requests for iced tea). And twenty-four inmates declined any last meal at all.

The final meal is typically the last formal request that condemned inmates are granted before being strapped to the lethal-injection gurney. Of course, their requests amount to statements in themselves, and while many men just seem to want a last few bites of comfort food, others offer different messages.

Take James Smith who, just before being put to death in June 1990 for a robbery-murder in Houston, asked for a last meal of dirt, apparently for a voodoo ritual. Dirt not being on the prison system's list of approved foods, Mr Smith settled for yoghurt. Still others order elaborate meals, only to refuse them altogether. But the condemned typically consume a good part, if not all, of what they've ordered, according to prison officials – including the steaks they have to saw through with plastic knives. God knows where they find the appetite, but then the condemned to die are different from us, they no longer care about calories or money.

Jonas Parsons, owner of The Last Resort restaurant in New Orleans, is the man behind this collection of final requests, which all came from Gainesville Prison, Texas, and the Angola Penitentiary, Louisiana. He has them pinned to the walls of his saloon and in the dining room the menu has a special insert with over twenty death-row menus listed, all of which can be ordered and will be served on prison chinaware Parsons bought from a jail that closed in Phoenix. The choices suggest murderers largely want comfort foot before they pass 'Go' for the last time.

Calvin Baines, executed 23 July 1996: Last meal request: T-bone steak (medium to well-done), french fries and ketchup, whole kernel corn, sweet peas, lettuce and tomato salad with egg and French dressing, iced tea, sweetener, saltines, Boston Cream Pie and rolls. (Nobody in the prison kitchen knew how to make Boston Cream Pie. A recipe was faxed from a pastry shop in New York that belonged to a brother of another death-row inmate.)

Raymond Hernandez, executed 30 January 1987: Last meal request: Beef tacos, beef enchiladas, jalapeño peppers, salad onion, hot sauce, shredded cheese and coffee.

Mikel Derrick, executed 18 July 1990: Last meal request: Rib-eye steak, tossed green salad with blue cheese dressing, baked potato with sour cream. (Refused last meal because his steak was not done medium-rare and the prison governor said he did not have the budget to provide a replacement.)

Lawrence Buxton, executed 22 February 1991: Last meal request: Steak (filet mignon), pineapple upside-down cake, tea, punch and coffee. (Buxton's execution took place twenty minutes late because he had to go to the lavatory twice on the way to the death chamber.)

Ignacio Cuevas, executed 23 May 1991: Last meal request: Chicken dumplings, steamed rice, black-eyed peas, sliced bread and iced tea. (The Chinese food was brought in from a local take-out. Cuevas even had a fortune cookie. The message inside said: 'You will live long and prosper.')

James Demouchette, executed 22 September 1992: Last meal request: Grilled steak, baked potato, any vegetable except squash or okra, any dessert and anything to drink except punch or milk.

Ruben Cantu, executed 24 August 1993: Last meal request: Barbecue chicken, refried beans, brown rice, sweet tea and bubble gum. (Bubble gum is not permitted under Texas prison regulations. The governor was not prepared to make an exception for Cantu who then tried, unsuccessfully, to blow bubbles with his beans.)

Anthony Cook, executed 10 November 1993: Last meal request: Double-meat bacon cheeseburger and a strawberry shake. (Cook specified fresh strawberries which were provided by the governor's wife from her own garden. Cook pronounced them delicious and thanked the green-fingered benefactor from the gurney as part of his last words.)

Harold Barnard, executed 2 February 1994: Last meal request: Steak, French fries and wine. (Water was substituted. Barnard complained and described the switch as 'cruel and unusual punishment'. The governor refused in part because Barnard had killed his mistress with a broken wine bottle after they participated in a drunken binge. The couple had begun their evening at a steak house that Barnard frequented because of their high-quality French fries.)

Robert Drew, executed 2 August 1994: Last meal request: Steak (cooked rare), ham, two hamburgers, two pieces of fish and a chocolate milk shake. (Drew took just one bite from each item but drank all the milk shake.)

Denton Crank, executed 14 June 1994: Last meal request: Cheeseburger (double meat, double cheese), with lettuce, pickles, tomato, onions and mayonnaise, onion rings and two chocolate shakes. (Crank specified that the onions must be fresh not canned or dried. He also asked for a packet of Tums which Americans take by the truckload for indigestion.)

Noble Mays, executed 6 May 1995: Last meal request: four or five fried eggs (sunny side up), three sausage links, three biscuits and coffee. (Mays was given six eggs, five sausages and four biscuits but only ate the number he had requested. Halfway through the meal he asked for maple syrup but didn't use any when it was provided.)

Richard Brimage, executed 10 February 1997: Last meal request: Pepperoni pizza (medium) and a Dr Pepper soda. (Brimage was condemned to death for a double shooting at a

Pizza Hut which he was trying to rob. The prison gave him Diet Dr Pepper, which Brimage rejected. He accepted Coca-Cola as a substitute.)

Charlie Livingston, executed 21 November 1997: Last meal request: Ribs smothered in onions and gravy, rice with butter, ice water and Dr Pepper.

Larry Wayne White, executed 22 May 1997: Last meal request: Liver and onions, cottage cheese, red tomatoes and a single cigarette. (The cigarette was denied under prison policy which in Texas and Louisiana now bans smoking in all state prisons, even for men in the last few hours of life.)

Vernon Sattiewhite, executed 15 August 1995: Last meal request: Six scrambled eggs with cheese, seven pieces of buttered white toast, fifteen pieces of bacon, three hash browns, a bowl of grits with butter, jelly and orange juice.

Kenneth Gentry, executed 16 April 1997: Last meal request: A bowl of butter beans, mashed potatoes, onions, tomatoes, biscuits, chocolate cake and Dr Pepper with ice.

Richard Beavers, executed 4 April 1994: Last meal request: Six pieces of French toast with syrup, jelly, butter, six barbecued spare ribs, six pieces of well-burned bacon, four scrambled eggs, five well-cooked sausage patties, French fries with ketchup, three slices of cheese, two pieces of yellow cake with chocolate fudge icing, and four cartons of milk. (Beavers ate every morsel, proclaimed his innocence all the way to the death chamber and burped frequently on the execution gurney before breathing his last.)

Some death-row denizens took a much more minimal approach than Beavers. James Russell, executed 9 September 1991, asked for a single apple. Johnny Garrett, executed 11

February 1992, requested fudge-flavoured ice cream. Stephen Morin, executed 13 March 1985, asked for and received unleavened bread. Jeffery Barney, executed 16 April 1986, treated the event like a kid's breakfast. He wanted two boxes of Frosted Flakes and a pint of milk. These were the exceptions. According to Jonas Parsons, most want a blow-out, like John Kelly, executed in 1997 for killing his hunting partner. Kelly asked for wild game and cold lemonade. He was served a cheeseburger and French fries, but he declined the meal, after all a burger is not the same as venison.

Jonas is from Dallas originally and chose New Orleans for The Last Resort because the city contains the most obese people in the United States, an honour that takes real work to win but comes as no surprise to locals. 'When we heard that, we were like, well, "Duh",' said Siona Carpenter, a waitress in the Spiced Shrimp restaurant. 'People in Louisiana name their dogs "Boudin Noir".'

Eating poorly is a mortal sin in Louisiana and good food simmers in both $100-a-plate restaurants and in the most humble shotgun houses. It would be taken as a disaster if New Orleans were not the top of the Stuffing Yourself Silly list. New Orleans people even name themselves after food. Miss Carpenter, doing a recent computer search on sandwich shops, turned up an obituary for Leonard (Po-boy) Charles, who died last year. In Lousiana, like Texas, po-boys are French bread sandwiches, but the New Orleans' versions tend to be stuffed with fried oysters, lettuce, tomato and tartar sauce, among other things.

Of the nation's thirty-three largest cities, New Orleans has the highest percentage of obese people at 37.55%, according to the study by the National Center for Health Statistics. People are considered obese, more or less, if their weight is more than 20% higher than ideal weights as listed in standard charts on the subject. This means that more than one in three residents of the New Orleans area has absolutely no business being in those long queues at the drive-through of Popeye's

Fried Chicken (which was, of course, founded here).

New Orleans leads the porky list purely because 'of its quality, and quantity, of great food', said Jim Hooter, an antiques dealer on Magazine Street in the section of the city known as the Irish Channel. Mr Hooter described a nearby restaurant, the Pie in the Sky, which serves a fantastic roast turkey po-boy, on home-baked bread, with sweet purple onions. 'But they could put cat food in there and it wouldn't matter,' he said, 'the bread's so good. It's not just something to eat, it's a pleasure to eat, and there's a thousand of those places all over the city.'

His mind drifted down a river of red beans and rice, through rapids of gumbo. 'Roast beef po-boys, with gravy and mayonnaise,' he said. 'When you eat it, it just runs down your arm. And when you go home to eat, you got the same stuff, only it's better.' In the nearby St Thomas housing project, he said, stoves would be smoking with red beans and rice and macaroni and cheese. You do not have to have a lot of money, he said, to eat well here. But there is no excuse, none, said Mr Hooter and others, for eating badly. At Guy's Po-Boys, on Magazine, the special was pork chop po-boys.

New Orleans was followed by Norfolk, Virginia (33.94% obesity, attributed to grits, biscuits and fried chicken) and San Antonio, Texas (32.96%: enchiladas and chicken fried steak) and Kansas City, Montana (31.66%: ribs). New York came in roughly in the middle of the field at no. 18 (27.05%: good Chinese, but many health clubs). Denver (22.10% obesity: bean sprouts) barely edged Minneapolis (22.63%: fish caught through holes in the ice) as the least obese city in the country.

The health experts who conducted the study were careful to point out that the country as a whole is getting more obese, because Americans are eating more fat and exercising less, but no other city could hold a spatula to New Orleans (bread pudding, pralines, beignets, cream sauces, smoked sausage, shrimp and cheese pies, fried chicken, fried fish, fried oysters, fried soft-shell crab, fried crawfish tails, onion rings and, perhaps the greatest indulgence of them all, a 'potato po-boy', stuffed with French fries, turkey, gravy and mayonnaise).

Anthony Uglesich, who owns Uglesich's, one of the city's best restaurants for traditional New Orleans food, said his chefs were conscious of cutting fat where they could – they used low-fat oils and egg substitutes like Egg Beaters – but he conceded that it was hard to cook great food, New Orleans style, with diet in mind. 'Fried grits and shrimp,' Mr Uglesich said. 'Fried green tomatoes topped with shrimp and remoulade sauce.' He was only quoting from the menu, but he made his point.

Now and then, chefs in the fancier restaurants talk of 'low-cal' New Orleans food, but those pretensions are usually blown away by the waiter's query of, 'And will you be having the bread pudding soufflé, tonight?' 'People come here to indulge,' Mr Uglesich said of visitors to New Orleans. It would be unfair, and unreasonable, to expect residents to abstain. Food is life, in New Orleans, or an echo of death if you are at Jonas Parsons' Last Resort.

'Maybe I kinda wanted to remind people that a meal can precede death for people other than prison inmates,' he says. 'I thought we needed a timely reminder to watch what we eat, but mostly people just love to eat with all these pictures of death-row criminals around them. It makes them feel happy to be so much more fortunate.'

This has been a theme of Parsons. I first came across him in Dallas, he was driving an open-top Lincoln Continental. We glided slowly by Dealey Plaza to the sound of cheers and wild applause. Suddenly, as we approached the now notorious grassy knoll, rifle fire cut the air. The limousine stopped, then sped off to Parkland Hospital with sirens wailing. Thirty-three years after President John Kennedy was assassinated in Dallas on 22 November 1963, Parsons was running a macabre tour recreating his final moments in gruesome detail. The package was drawing tourists who wanted to get closer to one of the world's most famous murders than a museum exhibit. Parsons was in business with Paul Crute, a former Dallas salesman who was just a baby when Kennedy was murdered. Their JFK Presidential Limousine Tour uses a 1964 Lincoln Continental, remodelled to match the one that took Kennedy on his fateful journey, and the haunting sounds of that day are replayed to tourists over the car's stereo system. For $25, visitors get a one-hour tour that retraces the route taken by the president and the almost equally famous Jackie Kennedy, from Love Field Airport into the city centre and past the Texas School Book Depository, where authorities say Lee Harvey Oswald fired on the couple from a sixth-floor window.

Demand for the tour picked up sharply in advance of the thirty-fifth anniversary of the assassination that changed the course of history and inspired scores of dark conspiracy theories. As the replica limousine enters Dealey Plaza, its stereo blasts out the sounds of cheering crowds and radio reports from 1963. Then shots ring out and a voice cries: 'My God, they are going to kill us all' – the voice of John Connally, who was Texas governor at the time and was wounded in the attack. When the limousine arrives at Parkland Hospital after a mad dash along a major highway, a sombre radio announcer's voice from 1963 is played, describing the scenes of chaos and giving the tragic news: 'President Kennedy has been assassinated... It's official now. The president is dead.'

The tour has been lambasted by critics as a tasteless scam that exploits Kennedy's memory to make a quick buck. Parsons and Crute seem genuinely surprised that anyone would take offence, and insist that every one of his passengers has said the tour helped them understand what happened here.

'It allows you to relive a pivotal event in history,' said Crute, adding that he uncovered other details of Kennedy's assassination that would have made the tour even more dramatic but did not use them because it would have been in 'poor taste'.

Tacky or not, most customers said the tour was effective. 'It gave me goosebumps, knowing we were on the same route that he (Kennedy) took. It really brings it home,' said Elizabeth

Jackson, a middle-aged housewife from Wisconsin, who took the tour with her husband, who was crying by the time they reached Parkland hospital. Gary Mack, an expert on the assassination and archivist at the Dallas County Historical Foundation, said the most important thing is that Kennedy is remembered. 'While researchers personally may really despise the tour and some of the more bizarre (conspiracy) theories that come out, they realize that you have to keep up the attention. And this stuff does that,' Mack said.

But many Dallas vistors say they found the idea of the limousine tour distasteful. 'No, I don't think I'd want to go on that. It cheapens his memory, turns it into a circus,' said Maggie Peterson, a New Yorker who was in college when Kennedy was assassinated and has visited the site of his death several times. Experts say the tour's mere existence illustrates that the Kennedy assassination has become less painful to Americans than it was just a few years ago. 'Something like that would never have happened ten to fifteen years ago because there would have been such an outcry in the community. It just wouldn't have been allowed,' said James Pennebaker, a psychologist at Southern Methodist University who has studied the impact of the murder on Dallas residents.

Jonas Parsons says he thinks death has become the single most important focus of the American consciousness since Kennedy's assassination, hence the Dallas tour and his New Orleans restaurant. 'I think there is something Oedipal about it, as if Americans hold themselves responsible for killing the nation's father figure, in Kennedy,' he says. 'I think our reaction to Jackie Kennedy when she married Onassis proves that. We wanted her for ourselves when her husband was killed and then she just goes off with some other guy. And another thing – obesity has been rising since Kennedy died. I think we are still on a guilt binge, eating ourselves to death.'

Yes. That is what he said. America is eating itself to death – and maybe going a little crazy along the way?